The Fashion ❋ Director

What She Does & How to Be One

31   Read Chapters 3 & 4

of Director responsibilities:

1. Image of store through merdse – research
   direction – buying – presentation. training

2. Image – through promotion – special events
   P.R. Charities

Research Market
   Manufactures
   Resident Buying offices
   Designers
   Textile Mfg
   Reading Trade Publications
   Magazines

The Fashion * Director

What She Does & How to Be One

* ELAINE JABENIS

JOHN WILEY & SONS, INC.

New York   London   Sydney   Toronto

Counseling office Thursday 10:30 - 11:30

Copyright © 1972, by John Wiley & Sons, Inc.

All rights reserved. Published simultaneously in Canada.

No part of this book may be reproduced by any means, nor transmitted, nor translated into a machine language without the written permission of the publisher.

Library of Congress Cataloging in Publication Data

Jabenis, Elaine.
  The fashion director.

  Bibliography: p. 395–396
  1. Fashion as a profession.   I. Title.
TT507.J29   391'.0023   72–768
ISBN 0–471–43125–7
ISBN 0–471–43126–5 (pbk.)

Printed in the United States of America

10 9 8 7 6 5

This book is lovingly dedicated to

My husband, *Mace*

Son, *Jon Lance*

Daughter, *Karen M'Lee*
Who helped me become a Woman

My Management and Associates at *J. L. Brandeis,*
Who helped me become a Fashion Director

Kay Corinth,
Who helped me become an Author

❀ *Foreword*

In *The Fashion Director,* Elaine Jabenis has brought together for the first time a wealth of information concerning an extremely important profession. Every aspect of fashion coordination, changing styles of dress, and retailing has been described in vivid, easy to read language.

I found the history of this vast subject fascinating. Mrs. Jabenis takes us back to the first women of Virginia who landed in this country in 1619, wearing the dress of the Englishwoman in the last years of the reign of James I, and to the first women of New England who brought with them a combination of English-Dutch dress styles, simple, devoid of any trimmings, but made of sturdy fabrics in somber colors. Their styles are a far cry from today's colorful, often avant garde, even bizarre fashions worn by both men and women.

But one thing remains constant in American fashion: fashion designers looked then and continue to look for trends from abroad. The style capitals of the world, such as Rome, Florence, Paris, London, Zurich, Vienna, and Copenhagen all play their part in determining what the fashionable young lady or best dressed man of the year will wear. Mrs. Jabenis has been to all of these fashion centers and speaks and writes from firsthand experience. In sharing her experience with us, she makes her subject come to life, sparkling with wit and humor.

The Fashion Director is a "how to do it" book for both beginners and experts in this growing field. Actually, the text was written because Mrs. Jabenis, as corporate fashion director for J. L. Brandeis stores and author of a weekly fashion column as well as the writer for a TV show, is besieged with hopeful young men and women who ask, "how do I become a fashion director?" What then, does a fashion director do? Specifically, she surveys the market prior to the buyers to determine trends and coordinate fashion direction, works with the fashion magazines on tie-in promotions and editorial credits, works with the fibre and fabric manufacturers on promotions for the current and coming seasons, uncovers new resources, and arranges and stages fashion shows. This is but a sampling of the work involved in this behind-the-scenes everyday life of the ever-active fashion executive. No wonder so many starry-eyed youngsters knock at Mrs. Jabenis' door!

Mrs. Jabenis further tells you how to work with management, where to get sources of advanced fashion information, and how to use the advertising media to best advantage in exploiting your product. Being realistic, Mrs. Jabenis presents both the advantages and disadvantages inherent in participating in this multi-million dollar profession.

For anyone who is interested in the field of fashion, for those who want to know more about how fashions and styles develop and who manipulates them, and, above all, for the young high school or college graduate intrigued with the world of fashion and eager to break into the field, *The Fashion Director* will be essential.

Mrs. Jabenis has done an outstanding job, and her writing is a joy to read. I know no other book in the field comparable to this one.

BENJAMIN FINE, PH.D., ED.D.
Education Editor, North American Newspaper Alliance
"New York Times" Pulitzer Prize winner

✻ *Preface*

Perhaps because of fashion's mysterious ways, it was felt for too long a time that the field of fashion directing and its relationship to merchandising could not be systematically taught. In fact, until recent years, too few schools were available for comprehensive courses in this area.

Through extensive interviews with students, educators, merchandisers, and other professionals connected with the fashion world, there appeared to be a tremendous lament that a text book, dealing exclusively with the field of fashion coordination and the career of the fashion director, did not exist. To my knowledge, this is the first text of its kind, written by an active fashion director, that totally zeros in on the career of the fashion director. The book not only spells out who she is and what she does, but it also provides practical guidance on how to arrive well prepared for employment in this area.

In this age of specialization and greater competition, a thorough study of the requirements, demands and responsibilities is most essential. With a more affluent and better educated consumer to serve, those responsible for the merchandising of fashion need strong professional know-how. Through the speed of communications and extensive travel, today's well informed customer is less in need of being told what to do about her fashion, but rather to be supplied, quickly and effectively, with those things she wants.

Fashion institutions are growing larger. Areas of responsibilities are becoming more specialized, and even those organizations which never utilized the services of a fashion director before are now recognizing the great value of this kind of fashion specialist. More comprehensive training, therefore, is very much in order to turn out well-equipped prospects to fill this need. Those of us who are deeply involved with the fashion industry and who are extremely proud of its contributions are most anxious to attract good people into the fold. Practical tools are necessary to mold such new blood. This text is designed to serve as one of those tools.

The book is written from the vantage point of retailing, a field that has been long-recognized as an excellent training ground for all careers pertaining to fashion direction or coordination. Later in the text (Chapter 14), when the student is ready to evaluate the information, the text includes all the other relative areas in which fashion coordination jobs outside of retailing are available. These areas are often overlooked by beginners because they are not aware that they exist. In this text the student has a chance, under one cover, to explore all the different possibilities of this field and to decide which way to go.

So that the student may study the subject with less mystery, and also in order to assist the instructor in presenting an all-encompassing picture at the outset, the first chapter embraces most of the pertinent facts, divided and studied in detail later.

Chapter 2 provides an important look backward into American fashion history and a look at how this special fashion career came into being. All this helps the reader achieve the sound foundation and greater sense of adventure that are essential in fashion.

The number of things for which a fashion director is responsible are many. To give the student a clear-cut picture of what those areas are, and to provide the instructor with a workable basis for assignments, each responsibility area has been carefully separated and spotlighted in a specific chapter—3 through 13. The text has been designed to show exactly how a fashion director works. I have tried very hard to give both the teacher and the student what they really need, that is, less of the "should do," and more of the "how to."

The last chapter is extremely important; it testifies to the sincere effort to provide a honest evaluation of this profession, pointing out both the advantages and disadvantages, presented in this book. It makes no effort to glorify or skirt any issue; it makes no bones about what to expect or what to look for.

The opportunity for innovation in classroom procedure or technique, certainly for the instructor and ultimately for the student, is enormous.

While writing the book I envisioned less use of lecture procedure and more student involvement. Throughout the text I have tried not only to describe the fashion director's responsibilities, but also to give actual examples of how those responsibilities are executed.

The technique of role playing would be highly desirable in a course of this kind. I would love to see the teacher turn the classroom into a fashion office, directing the students in interpreting the various roles of the fashion office staff. The student could assume one role and the responsibilities connected with that role, then exchange roles with others, until all assignments are covered. Through the playing of roles, the student would not only learn how each area of the fashion office works, but also experience the relationship of inter-play with other members of the fashion office while assuming a specific duty. Before the semester ends, each student would have had a chance to make a fashion presentation; write and produce a fashion show; merchandise a fashion ad; coordinate a TV commercial, a promotion, and a window; report on a market trip—everything.

Because of the tempo, drama, and creative texture of this profession, the application of dramatic involvement helps the student acquire a more realistic foundation before entering the world of fashion, a place where drama is a way of life.

Omaha, Nebraska   *Elaine Jabenis*

✱ *Acknowledgements*

In addition to the many fashion leaders mentioned elsewhere in this text, I gratefully acknowledge the valuable assistance of the following notable fashion executives:

Lester K. Marcus, Vice President and General Merchandise Manager, J. L. Brandeis, Omaha, Nebraska

Professor Helen Faith Keane, Institute of Retail Management, New York University, New York

Letitia Baldrige, Director of Consumer Affairs, Burlington Industries, Inc., New York

Marjorie Deane, Chairman of the Board, Tobé Associates, New York

Lenore Benson, Merchandising Editor, *Mademoiselle Magazine*

Grover Higdon, Vice President and General Merchandise Manager, Associated Merchandising Corporation, New York

Florence Lentz, Fashion Promotion Director, Burlington Industries, New York

Nancy Hawes, Executive Vice President, Corinth-Hawes Marketing Associates, New York

Rosemary Sheehan, Fashion Coordinator, Galey & Lord, New York

Eleanor McMillan, Fashion Group, Inc., New York

Don Arje, Display Director, Bonwit Teller, New York

Alice Ginther, Regional Coordinator, Celanese.

June Mohler, Fashion Coordinator, Fieldcrest, Inc.

Walter Hazeltine

Rita Perna, Assistant Vice President and National Fashion Coordinator, Montgomery Ward

✻ *Contents*

Contents

The Fashion ✳ Director

What She Does & How to Be One

❋ *Chapter 1*

❋ *Fashion Coordination in Retailing*

Which Way to the Fashion Office?

Nearly every day in most large department stores throughout the country, some young woman steps off the escalator or elevator and asks:

"Which way to the fashion office?"

It would be difficult to remember how many girls or young women have approached me since I have entered the fashion field, but the moment I see one across my desk, I know who she is and why she is there. I recognize that unmistakable look, and when I see it, I know what is coming. In fact, the speech she is about to make is so typical, I can almost mouth it with her, word for word:

"Could you give me some advice? I have always liked fashion . . . would love to work around clothes . . . I took a modeling course last summer . . . and, well, I kind of thought I'd like to work in this field. So, I wondered if you could tell me . . . how do I get into fashion?"

To begin with, the question itself has always amused me. Over sixty percent of the how-do-I-get-into-fashion inquiries are made much like the above quoted speech, a vague statement with a not-so-vague revelation that the inquirer is not too sure about what she is asking.

1

About the only rapport some girls have with fashion is that they wear clothes. If they turn to this field with no more qualification than their sex and a hand-shaking experience gleaned from shopping for their own wardrobe, it is obviously not enough. So, naturally, if an honest answer is to be given, a process of elimination must come first, or at least a setting straight of the record.

The ensuing interview between the fashion aspirant and me usually goes something like this:

"How do you get into fashion? Well, I would need to know what aspect of fashion interests you before I could advise you."

"Oh, I . . . don't know. I'm not exactly sure."

"Well, you said you would like to work around clothes. You could do that by being a salesgirl . . ."

"Oh, no. I don't want to sell."

"You mentioned modeling. Would you like to pursue that? If the answer is yes, we consider her qualifications, advise her about the opportunities and problems on both a local and national level, and the interview is over. If the answer is no, modeling is fun as a sometimes thing, but she prefers something more challenging or substantial in fashion (not so much a job, but perhaps a career), the interview takes a different direction. If she indicates a strong interest and aptitude towards fashion illustration, we send her to the advertising department. Display? We send her to the display department. If she has brought with her a presentation of her own fashion designs, we recommend good schools (if she needs further study and instruction) or suggest how she should go about applying for a job in that area.

"What about merchandising?" I usually ask next. "Could you envision yourself a buyer?"

If interest is indicated, we tell her about our training squad program for training young executives, and if she is still interested we direct her to talk with our personnel department or a divisional merchandise manager. If we hear instead: "Oh, no. I have had a course in merchandising, and I don't feel I am right for it."

"What then?" I ask.

"Well . . ."

"Well . . . what?"

And then it comes. "I'd like to do what you do."

"Be a fashion director?"

We have hit a responsive nerve. "Yes! Oh, yes! I'd be willing to start at anything if I could work with you in the fashion office . . . anything."

It soon becomes apparent that the reason so many young women come to the fashion director about getting into "fashion" is because it seems to be the most glamorous job in the fashion business. Ninety percent of the applicants will admit this is true, and they will also admit that they come without really having too much of an idea about what a fashion director does.

Therefore, young lady, it is time to set you down and give you the facts of a fashion director's life, share an experience, offer workable directions to show you the best way to the fashion office, and find out if a nice girl like you belongs in a place like this.

What's a Fashion Director?

Good question. I wish there were a good, simple answer. However, the very fact that the answer is not simple is an immediate clue to the complex nature of the job. Complex, true, but it is challenging and exciting as well.

Naturally, there is an important basic need a fashion director fills and, therefore, basic responsibilities she must execute to fulfill that need, but here is the rub—of all the thousands of women (and some men) working under the title of "fashion director" (often called "fashion coordinator," "fashion consultant," and sometimes "stylist"), there are hardly two in all the world who work exactly alike. That is, hardly two have the same assignments.

No need to be a shy little violet in the face of this bewildering truth. In fact, this truth is an immediate promise of a career that is amazingly elastic, never static, ever changing. Getting in a rut is not very likely in the field of fashion coordination. There are many plausible reasons for the variant duties of the fashion specialists, whatever their title, but three are most conspicuous and seem to show up in almost all cases.

1. The kind of responsibility awarded the fashion office (usually influenced by the firm's personality, management structure, and responsibility breakdown on the rest of their executive level)
2. The amount of true fashion authority and direction taken from the fashion director by her firm

3. The amount of talent, creativity, originality, strength, and vision of the fashion director

What's in a Name?

Not only do the fashion specialist's assignments and responsibilities differ from store to store, but so does her title. A general merchandise manager, for all practical purposes, is always called a general merchandise manager. So it is with a divisional merchandise manager; and a buyer is always a buyer. But in all these merchandising careers the responsibilities are usually completely defined and relatively the same. The fashion executive's responsibilities are almost never the same. Sometimes the title is clearly indicative of the fashion specialist's position on the store's executive list; sometimes it is deceiving. Assuming that the title is a reflection of her function, the following definitions should hold true.

1. *Fashion Administrator.* The fashion administrator, a comparatively new title in the field of fashion, is at the top of the ladder of accomplishment. To date, it is the label attached to high-level responsibility and can carry with it the title of vice president. Such is the case of the fashion administrator and vice president of Macy's New York, the number one volume store in the nation.

2. *Fashion Director.* In recent years the title of fashion director has appeared as an award to the corporate or over-all head of a fashion office. It is certainly more efficient in an office that has other fashion coordinators to distinguish the head or overseer of the office from subordinates. According to many presidents and general merchandise managers of leading retail firms, the title of vice president is a possibility for an outstanding fashion director.

3. *Fashion Consultant.* This is a title more often associated with consulting firms to which retailers subscribe for additional fashion guidance, but sometimes a retailer will have a fashion consultant on staff (in lieu of a fashion coordinator) who concentrates on the merchandising of fashion almost exclusively.

4. *Fashion Coordinator.* There are more people working under this title in the fashion office than any other. It is the one most frequently used for both *members* of a fashion office and for the *head* of a fashion office. It is the updated version that became popular somewhere in the thirties

when the title of "stylist" was eliminated from general use in retail stores. Most stores have been locked in with it ever since.

5. *Stylist.* Even though the first fashion coordinators were called "stylists," the title seldom is used today in the retail area. It is, however, still very prevalent in other areas related to retailing. All the same, it is a fashion coordinating career and, therefore, is included later in this text.

The above titles were in no way arranged in "order of importance." A fashion "director" may head up a large office or a small one. A fashion "coordinator" may be a subordinate in one office or the head of the largest type operation in another. For example, the fashion expert with Montgomery Ward is called a national fashion coordinator.

If the fashion director sounds like a woman of mystery, it is unavoidable. She is. The mystery exists because of the inconsistencies found in everything from her title to her responsibilities. It all contributes to her somewhat elusive image. What is a fashion director? It depends on who you ask.

The Public View. If you ask those who have no direct association with her (those on the outside looking in), she is something special and awesome. She is the retail glamor girl . . . the head-turning fashion plate who has so much fun doing all those lovely fashion shows . . . the woman who gets to work around all those beautiful clothes . . . the one who knows all the inside secrets about what's going on in the fashion world. She is the woman quoted by the press, radio, and television on her opinions of fashion trends . . . the awe-inspiring fashion authority who makes impressive personal appearances at benefits, civic, social, or cultural events and is always so handsomely dressed. She captures the spotlight as a panel member, lecturer, beauty contest judge, commentator, advisor. This lucky woman is always dashing off for exciting trips to New York, California, Dallas, Miami. She gets to travel to all the fashion capitals of the world— Paris, London, Florence, Rome, Copenhagen, Spain, Israel, Hawaii, Canada, Mexico. She knows such interesting people—all those glamorous, currently-in-the-news celebrities, fashion designers, fashion magazine editors, stars of stage, screen, and television. What a woman! *Would absolutely love to have a job like hers!*

Her Co-workers' Views. If you ask those with whom she works (those associates whose work-a-day world she affects), she is the fashion-know-it-all, a tyrant, an opinionated rock, and a steamroller of fashion information. They find her sometimes lovable, sometimes fearsome. They might regard her as a reliable source of valuable fashion guidance and forecasting today . . . an impractical dreamer tomorrow. Associates confess they often lean heavily on her to do all the advanced leg work, to uncover fashion trends of a coming season; they need her to project, ballyhoo, glamorize, and stir up excitement about their merchandise—to stimulate appetites for whatever the store has for sale. They also find themselves admitting that they don't know where she gets her energy. They truly wonder how she covers all the bases she covers. Her pace is so fast and varied they don't know how she does it. *Wouldn't have her job for the world!*

The Fashion Director's View. If you put the question directly to a fashion director (ask her what a fashion director is), her answer may have little or no resemblance to the two images just described.

Again, it depends on who you ask. One fashion director might tell you her duties are far from glamorous. Just reams of directives, magazines, bulletins, and releases to read constantly; a lifetime of revolving doors, elevators, and hard chairs in designers' showrooms; volumes of note-taking and a fortune in expendable shoe leather. Another might wear so many hats (handling market research, special events, public relations, youth activities, etc.) she may describe herself as "vice president in charge of headaches." Others regrettably admit, "I really don't know who I am . . . and I don't think my management does either."

Many a fashion director laments the image she has with her company. If her job as fashion director is the newest addition to the company's executive list (and this is true of many retail or fashion firms), she is often regarded with reservation, sometimes with resistance and not altogether with the clear-cut understanding of her function which is enjoyed by other executives or associates in her firm. On the other hand, in a great many organizations, and certainly among the giant retailers, the fashion director is awarded great power and has top-of-the-heap responsibilities for the fashion growth of her company.

Fashion Coordination Outside Retailing

Retail stores are not the only employers of fashion directors or coordinators. Not by a long shot. The field is extensive and varied and constantly growing. To name a few:

Advertising agencies
Public relations firms
Photographers
Cosmetic companies
Fragrance companies
Pattern companies
Home furnishings
Linens and domestics
Fashion manufacturers
   Women's ready-to-wear
   Men's ready-to-wear
   Children's ready-to-wear
   Intimate apparel
   Fur industry
   Shoe industry
   Hosiery industry
   Accessory firms (handbags,
   gloves, belts, jewelry,
   millinery)

Fiber producers (such as)
   DuPont
   Celanese
   Monsanto
   Hystron
   Dow Badische
   Allied Chemical
   Eastman Fibers
Fabric Mills (such as)
   Burlington Mills
   Milliken
   J. P. Stevens
   Indian Head
   United Merchants
Trade Associations (such as)
   Wool Bureau
   National Cotton Council
   Corduroy Council
   Irish Linen Guild
   Fur Fashion Information Council
   Millinery Institute
   American Wig Association
   National Shoe Retailers Association

The Buying Offices. In addition to the above list is another great consumer of fashion coordinating talent. This is the resident buying office, which services independent retail stores or groups (chain stores have their own buying offices) with complete departments of fashion coordinators who cover specific markets and report back to a fashion director.

Fashion Consultant Firms. The fashion staff of consultant firms work in a similar manner to that of the resident buying offices. The main functions of coordinators working with consultants are researching the market and reporting their findings. The fashion consultant services the retailer by supplying professional evaluation of market research, advice and guidance on coming trends, and direction toward applicable resources for the individual store's needs.

Transportation Industry. Careers directing fashion trends are available in the automobile industry and the airlines. A car must have fashionable upholstery and appealing fashion colors. A woman doesn't live who bought a car because of what she saw under the hood. The airlines have experienced more than a brush with the glamor of fashion, whether it was a high-fashion color for the exterior of the plane, or the fashion-right uniforms of the stewardesses. In fact, the choice of designer and his creation, selected for the stewardesses of every notable airline has always been important fashion news.

And so, on and on it goes. Everything is fashion. Fashion has invaded every aspect of living—what we wear, what we live with, the music we hear, the food we eat. Fashion is big business, and fashion is big news. We have witnessed its ability to capture headlines, become an international conversation piece, stimulate discussions on every talk show on the air, provoke heated debates among officials of school, church, and business and, as always, the mirror of our times.

Retailing—The Great Training Ground.   A fashion career in retailing is advantageous from two directions: (1) as an important training ground in working with and servicing the public, and (2) as a stepping stone to other fields that look favorably on applicants with retail background.

If everything is fashion, then it is understandable that fashion direction must be available, in one form or another, in all areas relative to the production and consumption of most consumer products. Retailing has long been regarded as the excellent training ground for fashion careers elsewhere, primarily in those organizations related to retailing or those strongly involved in servicing the retailer.

Gordon Morford, former publisher of both *Mademoiselle Magazine* and *Harper's Bazaar*, said, "Retail background is very desirable, particularly in the merchandising division of a magazine, which is devoted to the servicing of the retailer. We believe the retailer is a showcase for the magazine. People with retail background are valuable in their know-how of playing back the editorial product to the store, who will present it to their customer and our reader."

Don W. Gay, manager of the Knitwear Division of the Textile Fibers Department of E. I. du Pont de Nemours & Company, related that in the 1960's Du Pont began to take a more sophisticated approach to its marketing services organization, which was set up by Du Pont in 1955, to call on cutters and retailers to "pull our fibers through the distribution chain on to the consumer. In the 1960's we began to specialize more—to break up our marketing organization into smaller groups of specialists. For example, a specialist for hand knitting yarns, a specialist for 'over-the-counter' piece goods, a specialist for men's wear, etc. As we increased our specialization, we began to look more to the retailing community for some of our new marketing personnel. To date, about five percent of our marketing organization personnel have had retail backgrounds before joining du Pont. I would expect this to grow with time to perhaps ten percent."

George McGuire, vice president and management supervisor of Grey Advertising Agency, indicated that "an advertising agency that services textile and retail accounts would certainly benefit from having people who either have merchandising background or are merchandise oriented. Understanding the retailer's needs and his point of view is a must."

Why Coordination is Needed

Fashion is the mirror of our life styles. It reveals and reflects everything that is happening everywhere, and it does it with mind-expanding speed. Now, in the seventies, more than any other time in fashion history, due to our immediate and extensive coverage in communications, the buying public is not only better informed about everything, but more quickly.

It is extremely important, therefore, that the selection and presentation of fashion be handled in a most professional manner to better serve a more knowledgeable consumer. Hence the coordination of fashion becomes, when done with the utmost of speed and accuracy, the very lifeblood of fashion in retailing.

Seeing is Believing.   Imagine, if you will, stepping inside the door of a major department store.

Look around.

It is only February first, but if you had any doubts that spring is just around the corner, or had forgotten that Valentine's Day is February fourteenth, the timely displays and fresh, new merchandise effortlessly remind you. In fact, the bank of windows outside had already told you that a vibrant new shade of "loving red" was available in coats, suits, dresses, sportswear, and accessories, as well as in gift ideas that otherwise might not have occurred to you. A ride up the escalator reveals on all sides that the valentine and spring story is consistent everywhere. Every mannequin, every display area, and all fashion departments underline the importance of the coming event and the coming season.

On one floor is a special "Shop for Lovers," a charming little boutique (that wasn't there the last time you were in, by the way) designed and decorated especially for February fourteenth fans. It has everything from music boxes to heart jewelry, from romantic record albums to devastating lingerie. Once inside, you hear the latest romantic hit music gently emanating from the four walls. You are surrounded with the theme, the mood, the idea.

Up on the furniture fashion floor, you might have expected to be completely out of that world of red valentines and the promise of spring, but, here again, the theme is expressed. You wander through a group of new model rooms which have new spring fabrics, new spring colors, and (especially created to tie in with the store's total look) a sample "pad for Young Marrieds" with red shag carpeting, sleek chrome and white leather furniture, and red pillows (one even heart-shaped) tossed generously on everything for that "easy-to-live-with" look.

If you are especially perceptive, you notice that the continuity does not stop here. In this morning's newspaper was a color ad, inviting you to come see the store with the "loving red" heart. The signing in the windows, in every fashion department, beneath each interior display, and on every applicable counter repeated the same terminology. Tonight on television, the store's Valentine's Day commercial, in living color, will be aglow with "loving red."

To go one step further, you may become aware that the salespeople who help you know exactly what to advise regarding the newest accessory color to go with your selection of a red costume. They know whether a sheer or an opaque leg is best, which scarf you need, and how to wear it. A most refreshing experience. It is all clearly spelled out and appetizingly presented.

In addition to all this, a customer would also soon discover that among all the new spring arrivals, to coordinate with the new ready-to-wear— every component part, from intimate apparel to shoes to hats, was already available. The customer would have no difficulty in pulling her entire ensemble together, head to toe.

The Fashion Storyteller.   When you see continuity of a promotion, easily understood and clearly presented in newspaper ads, windows, interior displays, signing, radio, and television, you can be sure that a very alert fashion director has done a great deal of leg work and in-store coordination to bring you the up-to-the-minute fashion story, well told. The store's sales personnel, too, credit their fashion knowledge to the fashion director, who instructed them in fashion clinics on the newest trends and how to sell them.

Such a fashion story, with everything moving in the same direction, is a joy to behold. The customer may not be analytical about why she enjoys the store, but she will very likely look forward to the next inspired promotion, and the next, and the next. This, she decides, is an exciting store. She grows to love it and, what's more, to depend upon it. Here is a store that has everything and has it first.

The continuity in all areas didn't just happen, of course. When a promotion is decided upon (Valentine's Day is used here because it is a simple, annual example) the system of "creative teamwork" begins. All who have a responsibility in getting the show on the road—the store's sales-promotion manager, fashion director, advertising director, and display director (often referred to as the creative team)—meet to discuss and decide what the direction will be.

Without total continuity, the effectiveness of the campaign is watered down or totally lost. For example, if the advertising director decided to call the new color "lipstick red," the display director decided it was more of a "flaming red," and the copy writer for the television commercial called it "romance red," the customer might come in looking for three or four different colors, when, in truth, they were all the same. Or, if the junior department decided they had such great looking yellow pieces they would display yellow that week, and the sportswear department hadn't been informed at all about the red promotion and didn't have any red merchandise to tie in, much is lost. It is very necessary, therefore, that the co-ordinator makes sure that everyone knows what is going on. It is even better, if possible, that everyone agrees. A promotion of any kind works much better if everyone involved believes in it and backs it up with that belief.

At any rate, communication on what is expected must be set up early enough so everyone is protected and then followed through with all details (scheduling of windows, interiors, ads, television, etc.) to run within a reasonable time segment. This must be all geared, of course, to the arrival of the merchandise the store is promoting.

More than ever before in the history of merchandising, fashion trends come in and out as fast as a spin through a revolving door. The speeding up of the life cycles of fashion has made it more difficult to coordinate what should be included, what should be omitted, what to play up big, or what deserves only moderate attention. It takes careful analysis. It takes planning. It takes coordination.

Three's a Charm.   Three magic words, that must constantly be a part of a fashion director's vocabulary, are continuity, timing, and flexibility.

1. *Continuity.* A promotion or fashion projection must be carried out in all areas to give the customer the story from all vantage points.

2. *Timing.* Make plans for a promotion or fashion projection far enough in advance, with schedules and releases set so all store personnel involved will be "on cue."

There is one more important factor, which requires the careful attention of the fashion director. Occasionally, a fashion trend looks good at the outset, but does not develop as expected. It takes quick thinking and quick decisions to pull out of a fashion plan and then quickly replace it with something else. Also, very often a trend will be a "sleeper," but signs begin to indicate that it's the beginning of something big. A good example of this was the short skirts that forced the panty hose business into the spotlight in the mid-sixties. Many stores who were not watching closely enough were far behind in adding this innovation to their hosiery departments in the strength it deserved.

Therefore, the third important word must be:

3. *Flexibility.* Keep a fashionable ear to the ground to sound out changes in time to incorporate them.

Fashion Director's Responsibilities

As indicated earlier, one fashion director seldom works the same as another. Even if her duties are somewhat the same, her system of executing those duties may differ considerably, either by her own choice or that of her management. In spite of the variety of assignments and the differences of execution, there still exists a fundamental framework into which the responsibilities of almost all fashion directors fall.

1. The projection of the fashion image of the firm through promotional and public relations activities.
2. The projection of the fashion image of the firm through the presentation and selection of merchandise. That is, to be responsible for getting the right fashion story to the consumer (presentation of merchandise) and to make sure the store has the right merchandise to back it up (selection of merchandise).

The first is promotional in nature; the second is merchandise oriented. The first is mostly concerned with the store's efforts with displays, fashion shows, special events, and promotions. The second is highly involved in market research, merchandising objectives, and personnel training. Even within these two areas a fashion director's responsibilities reach out into many other areas. Therefore, the ideal breakdown of responsibilities required by the masterminds of most major retail operations follow this outline rather closely.

Merchandising Responsibilities: Before Market

1. Research. (a) Visiting and consulting with fiber companies, fabric houses, and the leather industry on colors, textures, and trends. Because fashion most often begins at the fabric level, many a clue is to be found in this area.

Example: Prior to one spring season, the fabric house of J. P. Stevens announced that a new look and updated use of denim was evolving (influenced by Europe and seen at St. Tropez). The demand from all fashion areas was so great, they said, that the supply might not meet the demand. Careful note of this fact would lead the perceptive fashion director to be on the look out for denim and how it was being manipulated in the ready-to-wear market.

(b) Working with leading designers and reviewing collections of important resources in New York, California, Dallas, Miami, Canada, and Europe.

Example: Along with other trends, denim seemed to be showing up very strong, with enough different choices in color, texture, and silhouette to indicate a very dominant trend. What's more, it was everywhere, manufacturers were cutting it in all classifications—play clothes and dress clothes, children's, men's and women's. A further check of the accessory market showed it was being highly utilized in bags, belts, hats, and boots.

(c) Gathering information from the leading fashion magazines and learning what they will be covering editorially in advanced issues.

Example: Along with all the other important fashion news showing up, the fashion magazines were very excited about denim. One magazine was showing it "educated and elegant" in embroidered denim, printed denim, quilted denim. Another magazine was planning on doing an entire section on the young looks of denim, the country girl and country boy of the seventies. There wasn't a fashion magazine around that hadn't included denim in their plans.

(d) Attending seasonal or predictive meetings at the store's resident or national buying office.

Example: Everything discovered so far was substantiated. Denim was underlined as number one.

(e) Attending New York Fashion Group shows, an international organization of women executives in fashion, bringing together the best of the American collections, for example, for the coming season.

Example: This was an excellent place to see that almost every designer represented used denim in one way or other.

2. Evaluation. In addition to what she has found, she evaluates what others have found. An alert fashion director daily reads the trade publications and leading newspapers—especially *The New York Times*, the Fairchild publications, *Women's Wear Daily*, *Home Furnishings Daily*, the *Daily News Record* for men's wear, and *The California Apparel News* (a weekly about the California market). She also reads carefully and religiously the up-to-the-minute evaluation forecasts coming across her desk from the store's associated buying office and from fashion consultants.

She can't do too much to uncover the facts, verify them, and reverify them. Then, and only then, is she ready to evaluate. The process of evaluation goes something like this:

1. List all trends in order of importance.
   (a) leading silhouettes
   (b) leading fabrics
   (c) leading colors and patterns
   (d) newly projected combinations of colors, patterns, and fabrics
   (e) newest accessory treatments
2. List all the above that are promotable.
   (a) store-wide
   (b) departmental

Next, the fashion director must take a hard, honest look at the entire list and decide which are suitable for her particular store and which are not. In some stores all leading trends are promotable and salable. In other stores the same items would die. Also, budgets must be considered. How many promotions and trends can the store successfully handle? It is wise to consider the possibility, if necessary, to do a few things well, rather than many things badly but without sacrificing leadership.

It is at this point that the process of evaluation becomes a process of elimination. The fashion director will now probably decide to list the trend prominently showing up far above the others as the leading promotional one, and then list all the others below, in the order of importance, according to their potential in her store. Through this system, it is easy and time-saving for her management to select those from the top which they feel best apply to their needs.

3. Interpretation.   After the fashion director has made her evaluation of all the trends for the coming season, she does not simply submit a typed or written list, per se, to her management. It is the all-important "translation" of all the facts, presented orally along with printed material and an illustrated presentation, that makes all the difference (see Chapter 5). The strength of her enthusiasm about what she has found, how she can see the store's own interpretation of the trend, how strongly she believes in what she is presenting, and the extent of her conviction (awarded only to those things she knows the store must not pass up), all combine to give her management confidence as to which way to go.

Obviously, the words "denim is going to be big" would tell her management nothing. But, if she dramatizes the availability of extensive, well-done, beautifully executed, extremely salable, priced-right merchandise in denim, and if she points out exactly what areas are most important, which resources look best, how it can be tied together through all departments, and what promotional handles are possible in order to stimulate the customer to "dig denim," then everyone in her organization will be moved to strongly consider her recommendation that "denim is number one for promotion next spring."

A great deal is riding on her recommendations. No room for a head in the clouds. No place for just "hunches." That is, hunches are fine as long as they are backed up with good, sound research.

Merchandising Responsibilities: During Market

Shop the resources with buyers and merchandisers:

1. To help guide for good fashion selection and avoid duplications
2. To help guide for good coverage of trends planned for promotion
3. To buy for windows, displays, and fashion shows
4. To introduce buyers and merchandisers to new resources

With a good basic plan in mind of what the fashion campaigns will be in all areas for the coming season, the direction of fashion choice is fairly well spelled out. However in many cases of shopping resources good and important things show up that must not be eliminated simply because they do not fit into the master plan. There must be flexibility for additions or subtractions, and decisions very often must be made while in the market. Therefore, the necessity of teamwork is emphasized again. Everyone should be considered, everyone heard, and then a decision most suitable to all will come to the fore.

Merchandising Responsibilities: After Market

Coordinate with management to schedule:

1. Store-wide promotions
2. Departmental promotions
3. Fashion advertising
   (a) Newspaper
   (b) Radio
   (c) Television

4. Display changes
   (a) Windows
   (b) Interiors
   (c) Shops
5. Fashion shows and fashion events

At this point all changes have been made as to exactly what the fashion campaigns for the coming season will be, and, with the exception of an item or new development, the plan is firmed up. Copies of what the projection will be are sent to all department heads and all personnel affected. The decisions are made. The die is cast. Now the action begins, putting all the effort behind the campaigns to make them work.

Fashion Training of Personnel

A most vital part of the "action" put behind fashion campaigns to make them work is the training of personnel. It is very important that all the store's people, on all levels, have a uniform understanding of what the fashion direction will be and how to use it. Therefore, comprehensive training clinics should be set up and scheduled prior to the arrival of merchandise in the following manner:

1. Executive level
   (a) General merchandise managers (supervisors of merchandising staffs, see Chapter 4)
   (b) Divisional merchandise managers (supervisors of buyers, see Chapter 4)
   (c) Buyers
   (d) Assistants to all the above
   (e) Sales-promotion director (supervisor of publicity and advertising, see Chapter 4)
2. Advertising staff
   (a) Advertising director
   (b) Advertising artists
   (c) Advertising copywriters
   (d) Assistants to all the above
3. Display staff
   (a) Display director

(b) Display personnel in charge of windows
(c) Display personnel in charge of interiors
(d) Display personnel in charge of shops
4. Sales personnel
   (a) Sellers in all fashion departments
   (b) Department managers
   (c) Area managers
   (d) Alterations personnel
   (e) Beauty salon managers and operators

And so the story is carried from the top level to the sellers who, after all, make everything happen at the point of sale.

Promotional Responsibilities

The promotional responsibilities of the fashion director, as opposed to the merchandising responsibilities, are in a somewhat different league. In some stores the promotional area is the major part of the fashion director's contribution; in others it is a small or secondary responsibility. In a great number of retail operations, however, the promotional efforts and the merchandising assignments are so strongly related that there is no effort or intention to separate them. Both areas, many fashion merchants believe, come under the heading of fashion projection and, therefore, belong together.

Fashion Projection through Visual Presentations
1. Coordinate interiors
2. Coordinate windows
3. Help plan and coordinate boutiques and special shops

Fashion Projection through the Media
1. Coordinate merchandise selections for television commercials
2. Select fashion merchandise and supervise photographic sittings for newspaper ads, catalogues, statement enclosures, and publicity

Fashion Projection through Shows and Exhibits
1. Formal departmental shows—in store
2. Trunk shows—departmental, in-store (see Chapter 12)
3. Informal modeling—departmental, tea room, etc.

Public Relations Responsibilities

In some stores this area is primarily the responsibility of the fashion office to such a degree that the fashion office is included in the publicity division. In other cases, the responsibility is awarded to a publicity director, advertising agency, and/or public relations director or public relations agency. Whatever the system, however, the fashion director seldom can escape a certain amount of involvement. The type of public relations efforts that must, of necessity, involve the fashion director and her associates include:

1. Fashion shows
   (a) Benefits for charitable organizations
   (b) Women's clubs
   (c) Civic organizations or civic efforts
2. Public appearances
   (a) Speaking engagements—schools, clubs, etc.
   (b) Panel discussions
   (c) Radio and TV appearances
   (d) Judging local competition events (beauty contests, etc.)
3. Miscellaneous
   (a) Answer questions and give guidance to customers seeking fashion and etiquette advice
   (b) Help with the personal consultation and selection of a wardrobe when a customer requests special assistance
   (c) Maintain a people-to-people relationship with the press, and radio and television stations

Afterview

Thus, the fashion director is the store's research expert, advisor, instructor, promoter, fashion authority, spokesman, hostess, and ambassador. All of these, of course, are developed in further detail in the following chapters, but seeing the entire picture pulled together at the outset, as viewed from the top fashion assignment, helps to estimate the amount of know-how involved, and to determine to what level an aspirant can and should strive. Finding one's way to the fashion office, and deciding in which role one would be best suited (see Chapter 3), can be made much easier and more pleasant if the route is better understood. Therefore, knowing how the fashion office came to be included as such an important part of a retail store's operation in the first place, helps establish the entire philosophy of the field, where it began, and where it is going.

❋ *In the Beginning*

Back in the days when the "Brave New World" of America was indeed new and brave, no one could have predicted there would some day be such a thing as a fashion director. Not that women were not concerned with fashion in the days of the early settlements. They were. Always. No matter where they came from or where they settled in the New World, geography did not change the fact that they were women. It should also be remembered that many of the women who came over were very young, so before too long they were ready to reach out for what suited their basic nature best, the promise of riches and new status, the things that brought many of them to these shores in the first place.

The Starting Point

The starting point of fashion in America was the fashions which the women brought with them. This, of course, depended on their place in the society of their homeland before they came over.

The Women of Virginia. The first women who landed in Virginia (ninety young women came in 1619) undoubtedly brought the dress of the Englishwoman in the last years of the reign of James I. This was a transitional period for fashion in England, but it is unlikely that they brought the latest fashions. Some were young widows whose clothes may have been the finely made garments of their trousseaus. But for the most part they were poor maidens looking for husbands and a better life. If one uses the inclination of such women as a guide, they undoubtedly scraped together the finest in whatever fashion their money and means permitted, to help make the best possible impression.

The Women of New England.   The first women to settle in New England came to Plymouth in 1620. Most of these women were from modest or poor backgrounds and without much formal education, similar to their counterparts in Virginia. But, because of a break with the Church of England, some had fled to Holland and lived there for some years before voyaging to America. The combination of the Dutch influence in their dress, and their religious persuasions as Separatists, led them to a simpler and more sober type of dress. They brought "sensible" clothing, devoid of any trimmings, in sturdy fabrics and somber colors.

The Women of New York.   The Dutch women of New Amsterdam looked a great deal like the pilgrims of New England. They wore the short waist bodice and full skirt of the early seventeenth-century Dutch, but their colors were brighter. They loved decorated buttons, embroidered collars, and elaborate, pleated ruffs encircling the neck. Chances are, the garments the women brought with them were soon cherished as Sunday best, for church or weddings, and the sturdier clothes needed to meet the greater demands and hardships of those early days were made at home.

Looms and spinning wheels were among the choicest items of home furnishings. The women would spin, weave, and sew all the clothes for the family. The men contributed by processing animal skins for shoes and outerwear. Their fashion guide? They copied what they had—or what their neighbor had. There was little change in American fashion until the middle 1600's.

Earliest Fashion News.   As soon as the early years of settling and building were behind them, the women's interest turned to fashion; it was to become a very important part of their society. Early in this new society there was an apparent hunger for some kind of guide, to advise them in the fashionable life they were now able to afford. This was especially true of the women in the towns. They were eager to know what was new and who was wearing it. But news about fashion was mighty hard to come by. Many weeks or months of water separated the settlers from the Old World. Eagerly they waited for news from every ship that docked in their harbors. It is not unlikely that sea captains or newly arrived settlers who brought new fabrics, current fashions from home, and stories of what the ladies were wearing in London, Paris, or Amsterdam, were their earliest fashion authorities.

When new fashions found their way to these shores, the changes in some areas were gradual at first. After all, nothing was thrown away. The hand-woven cloth was extremely durable and expected to last a long time. In fact, a beautifully executed costume with handmade lace, precious fur, or some other handsome embellishment, was passed on to the next generation as a cherished gift, used and reused, until only the lace or important trim of the garment was saved as a family heirloom. Also, there was not a change of fashion with a change of season, only a change of fabric, perhaps, from a lighter weight to a heavier one.

Before the Revolution.   By the third quarter of the seventeenth century, fashion in home furnishings and dress had flourished into a long-awaited elegance. Rich fabrics from the looms of Europe and the Orient intoxicated the now prosperous townspeople of all settlements. Their homes were glorious with imported porcelains, magnificent woods, Venetain glass, and rich wall hangings of the finest silks and cottons. All the pent-up desire for lavish living burst forth with a boundless energy and passion. The last quarter of the seventeenth century, until the Revolution, was perhaps the most prosperous and gratifying fashion period in our history.

The First Fashion Director.   London was the fashion dictator (until the Revolution, of course) but direction came strongly from Paris. Fashion dolls, called "babies," played the biggest part in transmitting fashion news from country to country, shore to shore. Dressed by the mantuamakers of Paris in magnificently detailed replicas of the latest fashions, the dolls were sent by fast dispatch all over the continent. Those that traveled to London were next sent to America.

When the "babies" arrived in America, expert dressmakers copied the creations for reproduction. The copies were adopted for their wealthy clientele. The creations were usually too intricate for the general populace to copy, so high fashion remained exclusively for the rich for some time.

Town and Country Fashions.   The greatest difference among the women of the New World, was not so much between the settlements, but between the townspeople and the pioneers in the country. In Virginia, the ladies of seventeenth-century Charleston stunned the women from the somewhat rustic plantations.

The women of Boston and Salem were less restrained in their fashion than the women of Plymouth, but the wives of the yeoman farmers of the New England area might have regarded all the townswomen as "fancy." Even though the Puritans had dropped many of the rigid reforms about dress before they came to America, they still maintained strong feelings about extremes in dress and frivolous nonsense like bright buttons, braid, or plumes. Laws were passed, stern sermons expounded, and lists of names of offenders and prohibited dress were posted, but women still came forth in silks and laces and fur as soon as the opportunity presented itself.

In New York as well, the gap between the rich town merchant and the tenant farmer was tremendous. Adversity and hardships kept the farmer's wife busy with bare essentials. In town, however, where life was more leisurely, the Dutch maidens were famous for their industrious creations of an abundance of homespun fabrics and fine linen. They accumulated their beautiful linen, enough for generations, for their own use and for the dowries of their daughters.

Sunday Fashions.   Fashion was not a day-to-day expression, but, come Sunday the women from the plantations or the farms traveled many miles to attend church, the center of social life, and display their new finery. It was their weekly fashion show. The more prosperous members of the congregation, whose costumes were the latest from London or fashioned after the newest creation dispatched on a fashion doll, strutted in a grand manner for all the parishoners to see.

There was not the slightest concern that such opulent fabrics and magnificent laces and ribbons might not be compatible with the crude and somewhat primitive surroundings. If beautifully hand-carved and finely polished wood was not yet the look of the pews, the wooden plank benches were made all the more endurable with so many beautifully dressed ladies gracing the congregation. One can only guess, but it is a good guess, that church interiors were rushed to glorious revisions to meet the demands of the new life style.

Rivalry in dress was part of this new life style. Clothes were unquestionably a way to announce one's importance and station in the community. Ye Ole Status Symbol, brought over from the mother country, became very big with the colonists.

After the Revolution.   The pattern of fashion changes that history has labeled as "trends during war years" and "trends after war years" had its beginning here during the American Revolution. At this time, the greatest fashion changes took place in the larger cities—Charleston, New York, Philadelphia, and Boston. These centers of the gay social life were also the fashion centers of America. The British occupation added color and a gay social pattern with lavish formal balls and elegant dinners, and when it was over something of a dull void was left.

Naturally, the elaborate social occasions encouraged extravagance in dress. The ladies bared their shoulders and accented the low decollette of their gowns with clusters of flowers, real or artificial. They imported the latest hats from the London milliners or sent for those seen in the Paris fashion books. They brought in beautifully hand-made fans from Paris and the Orient. It was a grand period, but when the music stopped a sobering time evolved.

Women's fashions became more masculine with fitted jackets and vests. The graceful hoops and panniers began to disappear and were all but gone by the end of the eighteenth century. From then on, throughout the nineteenth century, changes in fashion occurred with greater frequency, a momentum that was destined to increase with every decade thereafter.

The Nineteenth Century.   By the middle of the nineteenth century, fashion was taking giant steps in bringing its news and availability to the general population. Isaac Singer patented his new improved sewing machine in 1851, and in 1863, Ebenezer Butterick, a country tailor in Sterling, Massachusetts, cut his first pattern. It started when his wife, Ellen, asked him to draft and grade a pattern for a baby dress for their son, Howard. She suggested that many other mothers would like patterns for their children's clothes, and, thus, a pattern for a Garibaldi suit for little boys became Butterick's first big success.

Women urged Mr. Butterick to create patterns for them, too, and he obliged. Ellen undoubtedly furnished the first measurements. It was the beginning of a big boon to fashion projection for the general public.

In 1864 Mr. Butterick opened a New York sales office at 193 Broadway, with patterns for children's clothes. By 1867, he moved his pattern headquarters, which now included patterns for women's clothes, to larger accommodations at 589 Broadway, an area where women shopped for their dress goods and trimmings at the leading dry goods stores.

The Butterick pattern shop became such an important "fashion bazaar," it merited newspaper coverage. *The Buffalo Daily Courier* in 1869 said, "Every day a line of carriages and throngs of ladies on foot crowd the entrance to this establishment. Here has been solved one of the grave social problems which was tending toward a dissolution of the family ties. The making of their own dresses is an occupation that will prove a blessing

Ebenezer Butterick cut his first pattern in 1863, at the request of his wife, Ellen. (The Butterick Archives, courtesy of Vogue/Butterick Pattern Service.)

In 1864, during Butterick's first year in New York, Nathaniel Currier lithographed the first Butterick advertising posters. The center figure wears a Zouave jacket, a colorful braided jacket popular during the War Between the States. (The Butterick Archives, courtesy of Vogue/Butterick Pattern Service.)

to restless women who in the bane of their idleness have turned after the false gods of suffrage." *Pomeroy's Democrat* in 1871 said, "The sewing machine has done more than the piano to happyize our homes. And following the sewing machine has come the Butterick pattern." In July, 1871, the *Home Journal* wrote, "They should be ranked with the benefactors of mankind, this firm that has worked out the problem of clothes."

Not only did the availability of the pattern help work out "the problem of clothes," but another "blessing to restless women" was the sewing machine. The sewing machine was no stranger to the many women who worked on soldiers' uniforms during the Civil War. The women had sewn regularly in sewing circles on hand-cranked sewing machines furnished by the government.

Expert tailors and dressmakers made the clothes for those who could afford it; others sewed at home. The new patterns, naturally, were a great help to those who did sew, and it was an opportunity for the masses to imitate their idols, the fashionable rich.

Ready-to-wear clothes were in limited supply at first. The clothing manufacturers, at the outset, made garments in only a few sizes, but they were established as an industry by the end of the 1880's. New manufacturing methods soon put the United States ahead of all other nations in clothing production. The American ready-to-wear industry, still unequalled, had an astonishing growth from 1890 to 1920.

Fashion is News.   Many publications in the middle 1800's found fashion newsworthy. As a matter of fact, the day *The New York Times* was born (the first issue hit the streets on the morning of September 18, 1851, for one cent per copy) it included in its first edition of four pages, six columns each, a story of "a furor on Sixth Avenue over a couple of daring ladies' startling new bloomer outfits." This story of a fashion innovation undoubtedly caused a great many eyebrows to rise, but as the press and the reader quickly learned, news in fashion has always been something of an eye-brow raiser.

A national magazine that capitalized on this premise by presenting that which was new in unique ways, was *Harper's Bazar*. On Saturday, November 2, 1867, the first issue of a new weekly magazine called *Harper's Bazar*, consisting of sixteen pages, was available for ten cents per copy, or four dollars per year in advance. The Civil War had ended just two years before (April 9, 1865) creating a new kind of woman, one who had assumed duties outside of the home (for the war effort), a position previously unthinkable. It was to this women, educated, affluent, and fortified with a new initiative, that the new magazine, (introduced by *Bazar* editors as *A Repository of Fashion, Pleasure and Instruction*) was slanted.

Women read in *Harper's Bazar* about women who worked and they poured over large woodcuts of styles, fashion patterns, and serial fiction. They also learned what the prominent families were doing with their holidays and what the ladies were wearing at "The height of the Newport Season."

Vogue magazine began as a weekly also, but a little later (December 17, 1892). This journal was also geared to the fashionable, affluent reader. Women of the upper classes were unquestionably the fashion leaders of the time, and it was the dream of every shop girl to imitate their elegant dress.

The early fashion books, journals, and newspapers were greatly responsible for "getting the word around" about new fashion and interpreting its proper use. For many in those days before the turn of the century, the press stood alone as the only available fashion authority.

The Twentieth Century. The speed with which fashion changed and techniques and technology progressed in the first quarter of the twentieth century was breathtaking. But so was the climate of the new America with everything happening at once and fashion, as always, was the mirror to reflect the times.

The lovely Gibson Girl look that graced the early years was replaced around 1910 by a more severe, sophisticated silhouette—straighter, narrower, wrapped in front—sometimes called the hobble skirt because of the way the tight-at-the-anke skirt caused women to walk. About five years later, tired of hobbling, the skirt did a complete reverse. In fact, it progressed to the first step toward what was to be the most revolutionary period in fashion to date; the skirts became full, and shorter. For the first time, the ankle showed.

World War I. Paris was only half alive early in World War I. People left the city and left homes and shops empty. Despite her problems, Paris continued to create fashion. Many restraints had to be employed because of the war, of course, but new trends evolved. For example, designers turned to velvet, leaving the wool for the soldiers.

At the same time, in the United States, the ready-to-wear industry for women was experiencing great growing pains. Giant stores grew from little dry goods shops as outlets for the new-type fashion business. This was a trial-and-error period for the merchant who was not, for all practical purposes, a fashion expert. Nor was the manufacturer much help. He, too, was struggling for new ideas, and the entire field of fashion was not yet properly coordinated. The manufacturer had excelled in making skirts and shirtwaists, but, with the exception of the wealthy whose dressmakers went to Paris for fashion, there was still a great void in American fashion. The problem was basically the absence of American talent in the field of design. There were no notable "designers," per se, but much was being done to encourage American know-how.

In 1913, Adolph Ochs, publisher of *The New York Times*, ran fashion contests in "The Times," with cash awards for the best designs. About this time manufacturers, having no store of developed designing talent upon which to draw, went to Paris and brought back samples of the latest creations. They began to show a talent which they were encouraged to continue throughout their fashion history—copying and adapting the French creation to American needs.

In 1914, John Wanamaker, a most perceptive merchant who sensed the hunger for new fashion, sent his most outstanding buyer, Mary Walls, to Paris to bring back a collection of Paris originals. Customers swarmed in to see the first collection of its kind in New York.

In addition to John Wanamaker, other giant merchants with an understanding of tailoring and construction and with high-level taste and an eagerness to share it, brought fashion institutions into full bloom in New York. They were men like Edwin Goodman, Paul Bonwit, and Franklin Simon.

Women's Wear Daily came on the scene about 1910, and in the ensuing years became the great liaison of fashion information and interpretation between the cutter, the merchant, and the consumer. It covered the entire fashion world in detail, the like of which was yet unknown.

Still, the general atmosphere of indecision about how fashion was to be projected, what the customer wanted, and how to advise her to coordinate a costume, was the climate that created the need for someone to pull all of this together. A comprehensive program of fashion coordination or guidance was definitely in order. This was the condition that led to the creation of a new, specialized career in the retail field.

Tobé Coller Davis.   Tobé Coller Davis, the first fashion coordinator, went on to become one of the most influential and effective fashion consultants, a business she invented, to service retailers. For one who hated fashion as a child ("I was always being told to tuck in my shirt"), hers is a most remarkable story of an illustrious career in fashion.

Tobé Coller Davis, the first
fashion coordinator (stylist),
who went on to become
America's most influential
fashion consultant for retailers,
a business she invented.

Tobé created Tobé & Associates in 1927 with four clients. Her real growth began during the 1930's depression when business was down and retailers were desperate for help. Her incomparable service, a service that heretofore did not exist, was to research and evaluate fashion trends and translate her findings into workable plans which were suitable for the individual needs of her clients.

In her business as fashion consultant, Tobé was doing what she had learned as a fashion coordinator at Franklin Simon's. She kept her knowledgeable finger on the pulse of everything happening in the fashion world and the world in general. She was perhaps the first to recognize that "front page news makes front page fashion." This fact, plus the philosophy that "clothes reflect the lives we lead," led Tobé to watch headlines, the economy, cultural and social tastes, and everything that would lend a valid clue to what would be new and what would sell. Thus she earned the distinction of being the first person to understand how to predict, present, and merchandise fashion.

Her advice came to her clients in the form of a weekly "Report from Tobé." This confidential report included sketches, swatches of fabric, ad reproductions, prices, resources, and recommendations on how much of a certain item the store should stock. She also went into careful detail on items she felt important, what she expected they would do and why.

What Tobé did and what all fashion consulting firms now do on a large scale for a great number of clients, today's fashion director does for her own store on a smaller scale.

Tobé's Background.   Tobé's background is a matter of record. She was born in Milwaukee and experienced her first exposure to fashion through her father, Oscar Coller, who owned and operated a large men's clothing store. Tobé had a strong relationship with her father over the years, due primarily to the fact that her mother had died when she was born. Even though Oscar Coller married again, he discussed all facets of his business with his daughter; his new wife disliked business talk. Thus was the beginning of Tobé's professional training in retailing.

Tobé graduated from Milwaukee-Downer College in 1914, after which her father sold the store and moved the family to New York. Mr. Coller invested all his money in a men's suit manufacturing firm, an ill-advised investment since the firm soon failed. However, if there is merit in the old adage, ''in every apparent failure there is the seed of opportunity,'' this turn of events in Tobé's life bears it out. Tobé was now faced with the need to earn her own living. She considered the possibilities. Since she was not in love at that time, marriage was out. In college she had studied with a possible consideration of teaching home economics, but that prospect seemed to lack excitement. She chose New York and a job.

If it was excitement she wanted, the first job did not provide it (writing form letters in a mail-order house), but it did provide a lead into her next job. Close to the mail-order house was the office of a man who dominated the ostrich-feather business. Although feathers were on their way out, Tobé was insistent about getting a job there. She urged the feather dealer to give her a job as secretary, even though she could not type or take short-hand. Soon she was helping her boss replace the dying feather business with a soap-and-towel service and a hat-advertising campaign and was assisting with the decoration of a new store in Chicago. She was paid $12 a week in her mail-order job and now was making $18 a week.

Her days with the feather king ended when she took a job for $25 a week selling hats at Altmans and at Macy's. She was dismissed, however, for not flattering the customers. She moved on to a secretarial job for the owner of a specialty shop, and then to a job as secretary and assistant to Richard Hickson, a leading designer of women's suits.

It was approximately at this time, 1918, that Tobé realized that fashion was for her. At this point, she began doing something that was to be the pattern of her fashion life—watching /and learning. She watched what women wore everywhere. She learned everything she could about styling, detail, line, and color. She studied the way clothes were made, and learned all she could about prices, costs, and values.

Tobé left Richard Hickson after a year or so, to open a small dressmaking business of her own. She was joined by another Hickson employee and was backed by her future husband, Herbert Davis, a real-estate broker. Tobé confessed that she did not know how to manage a retail business and went broke within a year.

Fortunately, before she closed her doors she met Franklin Simon, who was one of her customers. He was so impressed with her energy and enthusiasm that he offered her an opportunity to create a job for herself in his store. She scouted the store, visiting the various departments, trying to decide where and in which way she could be useful. The decision was made for her—by accident.

One day Franklin Simon asked his advertising manager (according to a story written about Tobé in *Today's Woman*, May, 1949), "What kind of gloves and shoes will be best with Easter suits?" The advertising manager said he did not know. It was decided that Tobé be sent over to the Ritz, then the town's most fashionable restaurant, to see what the women were wearing. At the Ritz, Tobé found that smart women were not wearing the high shoes and laced-up gloves, as expected, but were showing up in pumps and pull-on gloves. Franklin Simon, one of the master merchants of that day, made his Easter purchases on the basis of Tobé's findings and recommendations.

Tobé's future career was launched, but not until she had served nine years with Franklin Simon. Her job was to see what fashionable people were wearing and then make sure her store had it. Soon Mr. Simon sent her to Paris to spot exclusive features for the store. Her big scoop was discovering a creation by Madeleine Vionnet, a slipover dress cut on the bias and made without buttons or hooks. On her return from her first trip abroad, *Women's Wear Daily* met her at the dock and in their story named her the first stylist. Her work captured the eye of other retailers, who offered her similar jobs.

She was indeed the first fashion stylist. The job and the title caught on.

Soon jobs were created for stylists or fashion coordinators and incorporated in the operation of major retailers all over the country. A new career was born.

What Encouraged the New Career.   Tobé's example started a whole new trend, but it also brought to light a question that had existed for some time—how to sell fashion.

After World War I, a big step in the growth of American fashion began. Things were changing. The ratification of the Nineteenth Amendment to the Constitution, providing for woman's suffrage, brought attention to women as those whose opinions counted. This was not only true at the poles, but also in the department stores.

The advent of the cinema, America's newest form of entertainment, was one of fashion's biggest boosters; its influence was tremendous. The movie queens dazzled and stimulated day dreams in the romantic heads of women everywhere. What the star wore, women from New York to Kansas City wanted to wear, hair styles and makeup included.

Meanwhile, back at the local department store, women came to purchase their share of the new glamor. Their demands came faster than many merchants were equipped to meet. The merchants biggest problem, it seemed, was their inability to understand the "new woman." The more the store provided the more she demanded. It occurred to the perceptive men who headed the progressive department stores that men alone could not meet the needs of the customers, most of whom, after all, were women. What is it she wants? How do we get what she wants? How, when we do get it, do we put it all together? Who should do all this?

The First Stylists.   Following Franklin Simon's example with Tobé, department stores created a job which started out with the title of "stylist." However, since there wasn't such a thing, as far as professional or business training was concerned, they hired fashionable women of their community, usually with good social background and presumably good taste. Their job was to advise the buyers and merchandisers. Perhaps this desperate beginning of a career that evolved into a profession for fashion coordinators, directors, consultants, or administrators, is responsible for a stigma placed on women in these posts, some of which has not yet completely disappeared.

While the lovely ladies serving as stylists had some good taste, it was usually limited to their own social level. They were almost always completely lacking in business knowledge, and, therefore, the advice they gave sometimes translated into a disaster for the store. What the store needed, and often was not getting, was that special style sense translated into merchandising.

The Professional Stylist.   Even with what may seem a somewhat false start, the venture did turn up some outstandingly capable women, women whose names have gone on to be noted in fashion's who's who, and thereby proved that the field for fashion stylists had great possibilities. Guiding the buyers and merchandisers to fashion merchandise with customer acceptance obviously, should be a valuable part of a store's operation.

However, retailers discovered that professional stylists were in short supply. This was the big problem hampering the growth of the profession — a staggering lack of properly trained women. Where would the new stylists come from? There was little or no formal schooling available in this field. What's more, many retailers were not too eager for on-the-job training, until they, themselves, had become more familiar with how a stylist should function.

No one was quicker to recognize the need for specially trained personnel to fill the growing demands in fashion careers than the first retail stylist, Tobé herself. She was unable to find enough qualified people for her staff in her fashion consultant business, and the retailers she serviced came to her with the same problem. Where do we find a stylist? Therefore in 1937, Tobé helped create the Tobé-Coburn School for Fashion Careers. Julia Coburn, then fashion editor for the *Ladies' Home Journal*, looking for trained fashion personnel for the magazine and unable to find it, joined forces with Tobé and was responsible for the operation of the school.

The Fashion Group

Recognizing the opportunities available in fashion retailing but still unable to author the techniques and necessary solutions to the huge task in a fast-growing fashion industry, a small group of early stylists banded together to share their problems and, hopefully, come up with some answers.

Such a group of pioneers (to whom every fashion coordinator working today can be grateful) met one stormy night in 1928 at Mary Elizabeth's Tea Room, between Fifth Avenue and Madison Avenue on 37th Street,

New York. (It is still there.) It was decided that a "club" or organization of some kind was definitely in order for women working in fashion. The club would serve as something of a "clearing house" for information about what was going on. This would be a way, they felt, to share problems, explore ideas, and air everything pertinent to their jobs.

The "group" did not take off immediately, but in 1930, forty-five women met at the Women's City Club in New York to hear Marcia Connor (then associate editor of *Vogue*) talk about the importance of a "fashion guild." The move was on. In her book, *Always in Vogue*, Edna Woolman Chase, then editor of *Vogue*, gave credit to Miss Connor for seeing the idea of the Fashion Group through.

In 1931, seventy-five women attended a luncheon at the Hotel Pennsylvania and the Fashion Group was born. It's original purpose, to promote good taste and serve as a clearing house for current problems and new ideas, still exists. However, the extensive research and comprehensive programs conducted and expanded by the Fashion Group over the years (beyond any of the founders' wildest dreams) have been responsible in a large part for the fashion world as we know it today.

The Fashion Group's Influence.   At the time the Fashion Group was founded, fashion meant mostly ready-to-wear and fashion accessories. But already there were signs that fashion was also interior design and home furnishings. In a story about the Fashion Group in *Charm Magazine*, on the occasion of its twenty-fifth anniversary in 1956, Eleanor Pollock wrote ". . . it would have taken more than a swami to foretell the day when fashion was to mean the upholstery of your new car, the color of your typewriter, the shape of your vacuum cleaner, the design of your kitchen stove, the packaging of your breakfast food, as well as the length of your skirt and the shape of your eyeglasses".

The Fashion Group was highly responsible for bringing together all aspects of the fashion business. They made it possible for fabric people to see what new designers were creating; they encouraged the cosmetic industry to have an awareness of which fashion colors and trends were important; they introduced the hosiery field to the shoe industry. All this interchange of fashion information helped to benefit the entire fashion industry. For example, in the old days the hosiery stylists chose their colors without checking with fabric manufacturers; coordination of fashion, therefore, was difficult.

In addition to the regular luncheon meetings with featured speakers dealing with some phase of fashion, the Fashion Group has become famous for their fashion "spectaculars." Annual fashion shows for members and their guests present collections of the best American designers and foreign designers, as well as shows for home furnishings, accessories, and textiles.

A comprehensive educational program was created by the group around 1954 to help educate girls interested in finding fashion jobs or in improving the ones they had. Proceeds of the Fashion Training Course went to augment the library of the Fashion Institute of Technology.

Fashion Group Chapters. Now, with a membership of over 5,000, (over 1,800 of which are in the New York chapter) the Fashion Group has spread its influence and availability to twenty-four major American cities and five foreign countries. The Fashion Group regional chapters, in which membership is available only to women who have worked as executives in the fashion field for at least three years, include:

		Foreign Chapters:
Atlanta	Miami	Australia
Baltimore	Minneapolis	Melbourne
Boston	New Orleans	Sydney
Chicago	New York	Canada
Cincinnati	Oklahoma City	Montreal
Cleveland	Philadelphia	Toronto
Dallas	Pittsburg	France
Detroit	Portland (Oregon)	Paris
Honolulu	Seattle	Japan
Houston	St. Louis	Tokyo
Kansas City (Mo.)	San Francisco	Mexico
Los Angeles	Washington, D.C.	Mexico City

Afterview

The study of fashion history is extremely valuable, but not entirely for the reasons many students of fashion have been led to believe. For example, there are some conflicting opinions as to what fashion history actually teaches.

Cycles.   Some say that history testifies that fashion changes take place with such predictable regularity, that fashion cycles are as inevitable as "death and taxes." Other proclaim that this is only a half-truth, but repeated so often it has been accepted by many as gospel.

A more reliable truth is that *change* is inevitable (in fashion as in all things), but the *cycles,* try as they may to stubbornly emerge in regular patterns, are often interrupted, jarred, speeded up, or retarded by the economy, wars, science, social, and cultural conditions. These are more realistically the dictators of fashion change, not the calendar. Life cannot be predicted, programmed, or regulated, and neither can fashion.

History Repeats Itself?   Another school of thought proclaims that one can learn where fashion is going by reviewing where fashion has been. In other words, that history repeats itself. To accept this cliché as a truth (when it comes to fashion) is giving history too much credit, or more accurately, the wrong kind of credit.

In fashion, the so-called repeating of history takes the form of revivals. "Revival" is not entirely correct as regards the comeback of a former fashion trend. An impression or an influence, yes, but this is an entirely different thing. The influence might come from any age, country, or culture and still enjoy great acceptability. A draping reminiscent of a Greek toga, an oriental kabuki sleeve, a high-rise Empress Josephine empire bodice, an ancient Aztec or Inca motif, and hundreds of other influences from a time lost in history, return today and tomorrow, again and again.

An influence for fashion is often borrowed from a period similar in temperament to that into which it is resurrected. Timing figures very strongly in the success of a fashion recall. For example, fashion cannot repeat itself too soon after its current reign of acceptance. If a trend is too recent, it would be in the range of passe, rather than from the past. Timing is everything—not just time for a change for its own sake, but time for something frivolous, conservative, seductive, modest, elegant or amusing. Whatever the borrowed trend, it returns not so much as a revival in yesterday's form. Instead, it returns in a form related to the present but smacking of nostalgia.

The Mirror. Fashion is always the reflection of times and places, life styles, and people. If one examines the mode of dress during any period of history, remarkable clues found in the fabric, texture, style, or line, reveal something of the cultural, economical, emotional, and moral attitude of the people of that time. They were gay, extravagant, and reckless; they were restrained, rigid, and modest; they were preoccupied with fashion or anti-fashion. Fashion mirrors the current needs to glorify, dramatize, disguise, improve, or change the anatomy—its look, its line, its size.

Point of Focus. One of the strong revelations emerging from the study of fashion history is the traveling point of focus on a woman's body. Throughout periods of overdressing or underdressing, exaggerating or minimizing, concealing or exposing, usually one part of a woman's body becomes the focal point of fashion. One time the waistline, another time the hipline, the bosom, shoulders, or legs. One area or another dominates and directs the manipulation of fashion, the decision to revive a past trend.

What Fashion History Teaches. We need not look to history to predict fashion cycles, but to expect them. We should not look to history to repeat itself, but simply to record. Fashion history is indispensable when it becomes a source from which to borrow influences. It is the infallible reference to discover the truth about people and their times as mirrored by fashion. It is difficult to speak the truth about fashion—an area so filled with disception and evasiveness—but when viewed in retrospect, fashion speaks the truth for itself.

Chapter 3

The Fashion Office

The fashion office or fashion department, like no other area in a retail operation, is custom designed. Even with similar duties and responsibilities, one fashion director's office setup may differ completely from another's. However, the size of a fashion director's office (we are talking about size of staff, not square feet) is in no way indicative of her power or influence in the store. Not at all. The head of a very large fashion office may have less of a voice in the decisions of the store (not because of lack of ability, but often because of the firm's responsibility structure), than the head of a small fashion office, where the fashion director must wear many hats, cover more bases, and answer to many bosses.

Money Doesn't Count. Also, the size of the store's volume is not always indicative of the size of the fashion office. It is not unusual to find a store with an annual volume of $60,000,000 maintaining a fashion office with the same size staff as a store with an annual volume of $117,000,000. Or, an operation topping $100,000,000 employing a fashion office with half the number of people as another doing only $42,000,000. Dollar volume is not the deciding factor. Again, everything here depends on the store's fashion projection, whether it is fashion oriented or promotional, and the nature of the power structure.

However, there are some universal features all fashion offices share if they are at all worthy of the name or are to

41

justify their existence; they are either very small and bursting with activity, or very large and bursting with activity. Large or small, it matters not, the fashion office is almost always a scene of remarkable action.

The Important Three. Within the confines of the three largest and most important types of retail fashion operations—department stores, chain stores, and specialty stores—the fashion director helps tell the world who and what they are.

Almost all of the one hundred top-volume department stores (ranging in volume from $30,000,000 to over $450,000,000) maintain a fashion office, headed by a fashion coordinator or fashion director.

The large chain stores, of which there are about twenty-five at the top of the list, ranging in volume from $72,000,000 to almost $9,000,000,000, in addition to individual fashion offices in individual stores, lean heavily on national fashion directors. The national offices direct fashion standards in their stores throughout the country and in their foreign branches. Specialty stores, who deal mostly in soft goods, with annual volumes of $8,000,000 to over $200,000,000 are often more "image-conscious" for their total concept and depend on their fashion directors to project that image.

The One-Man Team

The one-man fashion office is not the loneliest job in town. It bears little or no resemblance to any other one-man business office. It is a kind of organized madness. Even though telephones ring constantly and people wander in and out for one hundred different reasons, the fashion director is seldom in her office. She is so hard to find that some associates might not be sure if she is a myth or for real. If one is looking for her, she is nowhere to be found; however, it is easy to bump into her in any one of the fashion departments looking over the new arrivals, fitting a model for a show, gathering accessories for show pieces, running off a fashion report on a duplicating machine, taking some clothes up to adveritsing for illustration, climbing into a window to direct a change on a mannequin, conducting a training clinic on the latest trends for the store's fashion sellers, or preparing to fly off to New York for a market trip.

It's all teamwork, one facet of her personality cooperating with all the other facets. And, in turn, all those facets (that combine and blend into a very diversified "team" that makes up the fashion director) must also combine and blend with all the personalities of the store.

All this she must do in a little area called the fashion office that is impossible to find. If you ask, "Which way to the fashion office?", you may hear "You can hardly get there from here."

The Housing Shortage.   Any resemblance between a fashion director's importance and the quality of her office, is strictly unintentional. Her "office" may be a cubby-hole under a staircase, an ex-fitting room, a former storage room behind a wrapping desk, a partitioned-off two-by-four area in the far, far end of a stockroom, or a loft, high up, somewhere between the second and third floors, reached by a ladder-type stairway. Not all fashion office space is like this, of course, but many a retail fashion director will recognize the description of her office.

Within the tiny area, many a resourceful young woman has managed to arrange a desk, telephone, file cabinet, clothes rack for merchandise in readiness for a show, card table (laden with accessories), and a chair in which no one can sit because it is the catch-all for everything that the table cannot hold. And the bulletin board. There is always a bulletin board covered with fabric swatches, new sketches from the fashion magazines, and tear sheets of her favorite or current fashion ads.

Usually, an alert, ambitious fashion director, whose effectiveness has been recognized, can convince her management that in order to do efficiently all that must be done and still grow, the walls must be pushed out.

In order to appreciate and live with the lack of office space in some retail stores, one must understand that every precious square foot of space is first regarded as "selling space." When one considers that each square foot in the average branch store is valued at something like $60 to $100, and very often much more (evaluation made on the basis of total number of square feet of selling space and the amount of volume enjoyed or anticipated by a particular store), it is easier to see why every inch of footage is carefully allocated to its best use.

Work Alone—Learn a Lot.   Although it has been done many, many times, it is difficult for a fashion director to operate a fashion office alone without having come from another department of the store (so that she has some awareness of the philosophy and inner-workings of the firm), or having been trained by her predecessor, or brought in from another retail operation with similar or applicable experience.

Because a fashion job is a responsibility that requires immediate action (there are usually deadlines of one kind or another to meet every day) it is very important for the fashion director to have a clear-cut idea of what to expect. She must expect the unexpected. For example, an emergency call comes from the sales-promotion director who has just received an emergency call from an important customer advising him that the guest speaker for a city-wide benefit has arrived. However, her luggage is snowed-in in Chicago, and she has nothing to wear. The fashion director is advised that the distraught guest and the program chairman will be right over, and "would you please fit the lady in something splendid for the event which is less than an hour away." Or perhaps a designer's collection, due in today for a special-invitation showing tomorrow, will not be coming because of a transportation strike. The invitations are out and the show must go on. An entire show must be pulled, fitted, and coordinated to replace the missing collection. The emergency-tuned-in fashion director drops everything and rises to the occasion. She is always rising to an occasion; that's her job. Perhaps that is why the one-person fashion office is such a remarkable training ground—she must do everything therefore she learns everything.

The number of stores that maintain this size office is considerable. Excellent opportunities are available for an energetic, enthusiastic person, who is ready to set a new track record and is not a clock-watcher (important requirements for all fashion office personnel, by the way).

In a great number of retail stores, where only one fashion person is employed, the major part of her assignment may be the responsibility for fashion shows. She handles all the details, from booking the show to doing the fashion commentary (see Chapter 12), and if it is a store that believes in a heavy fashion show schedule, she may have time for little else. Some stores may consider their fashion shows important, but book a limited number, leaving the fashion director available for conducting fashion training clinics for employees and giving fashion direction to display and advertising, as well as researching the market. Still another type of retailer, less interested in fashion shows, may consider the fashion director more valuable for his purposes almost entirely in the area of merchandising. She is responsible for researching the markets, working with the buyers and divisional merchandise managers, and being totally conversant with the budgets and aims of the fashion division.

Free-lance Assistants.   It is very often the case, when the solo fashion expert of a store is strongly involved in the merchandising side of co-ordination as against the promotional side, that the store engages a free-lance stylist or coordinator. She comes in on those occasions when a fashion show is scheduled and takes over all the details of putting the show together.

If the store's fashion coordinator has the time to coordinate her own shows as well as execute all her other duties but has little aptitude for narrating the shows, a free-lance personality is brought in for the specific purpose of filling the role of announcer. Sometimes she writes her own commentary, coming in ahead of the show to view the clothes. Sometimes it is written for her. In other cases, a commentator may be closely associated with the store and with the merchandise and, therefore, be capable of taking a look at the lineup of clothes, make simple notes, and just ad-lib the commentary. Many a free-lance or part-time coordinator has found her way into the fashion office as a permanent member of the staff.

Fashion models, too, have very often started on a fashion coordination career this way. The store's fashion director asks the model to help co-ordinate a show, and soon she is learning the ropes of how it is all put together. Next, she may be asked to do the commentary. Before long she may be in complete charge of putting a show together as well as delivering the commentary. She may decide this has a better future than modeling, give up the job of mannequin altogether, and accept a full-time job in the fashion office where she can learn more.

Two for the Seesaw

When the solo fashion director's office is enlarged to a duet, immediately the vibration is much greater than might be expected, not just twice as strong as before but many times stronger. If one is looking for challenge, stop here. We are getting into a very lively operation indeed. The two people, usually a fashion director and assistant, share almost every project under the jurisdiction of the fashion office.

Usually, only the fashion director goes into the wholesale market for research and making contacts in all areas affecting her job, while her assistant is home "watching the store." The "watching," however, is a huge job. Follow-through for fashion office procedure never stops. While one season is in progress, another season is being planned. Therefore, the assistant to the fashion director on the home front may be working on these aspects of the current season:

1. Arranging and staging fashion shows
2. Working with advertising and display on current presentations to insure fashion accuracy
3. Training sales personnel on in-stock merchandise

At the same time, the fashion director, away at the New York market, is working on the coming season:

1. Surveying the market prior to the buyers to determine trends and coordinate fashion direction
2. Working with the fashion magazines on tie-in promotions and editorial credit
3. Working with fiber manufacturers on promotions for the current and coming seasons
4. Uncovering new resources

The Large Fashion Office

The ideal fashion office of a major store would include a complete staff of specialists, each responsible for covering a specific fashion area and each reporting to the fashion office head, the fashion director. That of course is the ideal setup. In many large stores, where the goals and aims are focused strongly toward obtaining and maintaining an effective fashion image or fashion leadership, a highly specialized team is more likely to exist, at least in part. Listed below is a breakdown of such a team of specialists, presented here to show the different types of fashion coordination careers available in retail stores. Not all titles indicated will exist in all stores, but the responsibilities of all indicated here are assigned in some form or other to whatever personnel is available in a specific fashion office.

Who Works in a Fashion Office. Such a staff, as follows, is a fashion director's dream come true.

Fashion Director (Corporate)
   Area fashion coordinators
      Women's ready-to-wear and intimate apparel coordinator
      Junior ready-to-wear coordinator
      Children's and pre-teen's coordinator
      Accessory and shoe coordinator
      Fashion fabrics coordinator
      Men's and boys' ready-to-wear coordinator
   Fashion show coordinator
   Branch store coordinator
   Display fashion coordinators
      Window coordinator
      Interiors coordinator
   Youth coordinator

There are also jobs for assistants to the fashion director or coordinator, to the youth coordinator, and jobs as secretaries for fashion office person-

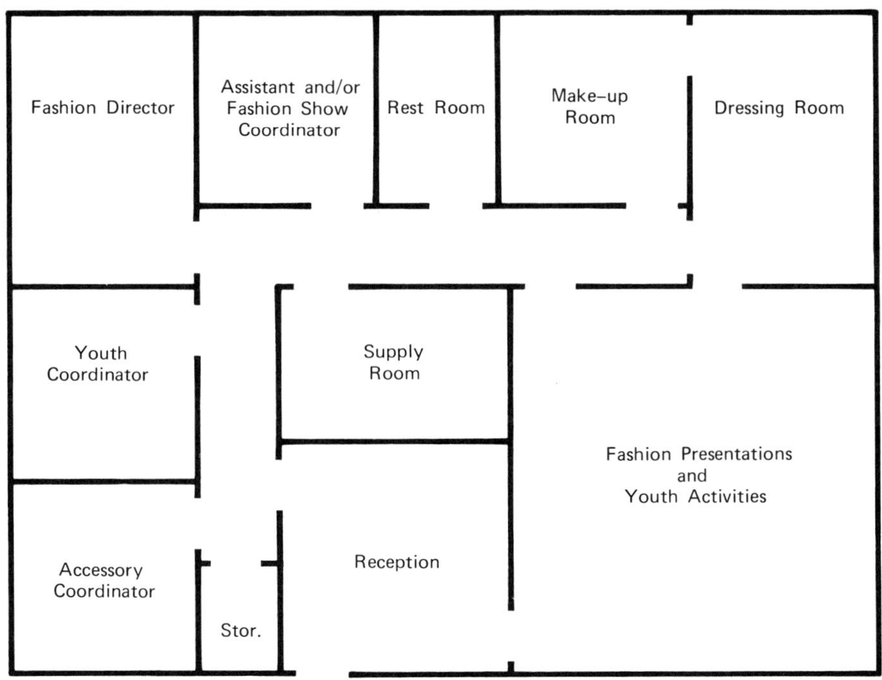

Appropriate fashion office floor plan.

nel, all of which can lead to better positions in the Fashion Office as openings appear or in retailing in general.

In addition to all the above, there is the home furnishings coordinator, who sometimes reports to the corporate fashion director but more often to the divisional merchandise manager or the general merchandise manager of the home division. Where there is more than one general merchandise manager, it is possible that each may have his own divisional fashion director or coordinator. Under this structure, the retailer operates each division as a separate store—men's store, fashion store, home store. The budget or basement store is always separate and sometimes has a separate coordinator as well.

Why Responsibility is Divided

As indicated earlier, it cannot be emphasized too strongly that fashion is in everything and should be expressed and projected throughout the store. Therefore, it would be impossible for all areas to be thoroughly covered in a major store if separate assignments were not allocated to specific fashion people, with clear-cut definitions and directions as to what must be done.

Line of Duty.   Following the outline of the basic responsibilities of the fashion director (see Chapter 1), the procedure of the fashion office and the special assignments of each member of the fashion staff are planned to emulate all the precepts thus far noted and all those yet to be defined. In fact, if one were delegated to set up a fashion office procedure, the following would be a good, fundamental framework to use as a guideline, including those points that fit a specific store's needs and eliminating those that do not.

What the Fashion Specialists Do

Fashion Director.   There is hardly a woman in the country holding this position, if she knows her business and executes it well, who is not a totally remarkable person. It is impossible not to notice her. She sends out vibrations that are electric, and she is almost always, by nature, vital, alive, interesting, and interested. She is an inveterate optimist. When she likes something, she likes it with a passion. ''I love it! I simply love it,'' she says, and then proceeds to share her love of it with every member of management until they are convinced the customer will love it also.

That is the name of the game. Enthusiasm. If, with all the facts available to her, she is convinced a trend is good or big, and if a strong move is in order, she is the first one to generate enthusiasm for what steps are to be taken to make things happen.

Her's is also a people game. She must serve, work with, relate to, encourage, inspire, and forgive a world of people, all of whom are so different there are not enough pigeonholes in the universe to classify them. She does this best when she is sure of her ground. An insecure fashion director is not a fashion director. Because her function is primarily that of advisor and because so much is riding on that advice, the foundation of all her fashion evaluations must be solid.

It is all well and good to be somewhat intuitive, or even to cultivate a "green thumb" for making the right choices, but there can be no substitute for careful, well-planned decisions. There is no place for guessing or gambling when so much depends upon her recommendations. Even with hard facts carefully scrutinized, mistakes can be made because of a number of unforseen developments, not the least of these being the unpredictable acceptance of the consumer. Therefore, guessing is out. With facts, there is less chance of missing; at least one's batting average will be far better.

Once the predictions of the fashion direction for the coming season have been made (and approved by management), the fashion director makes sure that every member of the fashion office is well informed of the entire plan. Each coordinator receives her directions for expediting the plan and reports back on progress and problems.

The Area Coordinators.   The fashion departments of a store are systematically divided into areas. While the separating of areas may differ, it usually follows that women's ready-to-wear is separated from men's and boy's, juniors in another area, children's and pre-teen's in another, and fashion accessories separated from everything else. This does not necessarily mean that these areas are always separated physically but, rather, separated as to classification.

While the over-all pre-season research and evaluation are done by the fashion director, there is a great deal of territory in the market that the assisting coordinator must cover in her own area, concentrating only on that area and reporting back on the highlights or on specifics under question. Sometimes, she will go into the market with the fashion director or a buyer from her area primarily for education or inspiration. The largest part of her function, however, if she works under a corporate fashion director, is focused on in-store coordination and follow-up.

1. She will carefully watch to see that her departments have the merchandise arriving to back up projected fashion plans.
2. She will supervise the selection of fashion merchandise to tie in with interior displays planned.
3. She will make sure each department under her supervision has the desired atmosphere or "look" of the current fashion story.
4. She will select merchandise for the fashion story being carried into the tie-in windows.
5. She will coordinate and accessorize merchandise for the planned fashion ads.
6. She will pull those fashion pieces best suitable for scheduled fashion shows and special events.
7. She will act as liaison on any or all publicity necessary for a celebrity, special guest designer, etc., appearing in her area.

The area fashion coordinator will do all of the above after she has first received the approval of the buyer of the department and an okay from the fashion director.

Example: Miss Area selects three exciting peasant dresses, under the direction of the buyer of Young Designer Dresses. They are to be sketched for an ad on ethnic style of dressing. Miss Area brings them to the fashion office for the fashion director's final approval.

"I think they are great!" the fashion director declares, "The choice of the three different textures is excellent, and the colors coordinate very well. The only reservation I have might be that the green print will come off looking too similar in line to the yellow one. Perhaps it might be a good idea to replace one piece with something that gives us three more completely different expressions of this peasant trend."

On reflection, the area coordinator agrees. She hadn't noticed. Three entirely different interpretations of the look would make a better fashion story. It would give the customer a better idea of the variety of choice and a clearer picture of what the "peasant dress" is all about. It is agreed. The change is made and carried out in just that manner—in the ad, in the window, in the department display.

Another area coordinator, for the junior ready-to-wear department, is busy seeing that her departments are turned into pleasant "peasant villages." The junior area, for example, becomes more gypsy, complete with gypsy tent, and fortune teller, and all the colorful gypsy and peasant costumes are dramatically displayed to tell the fashion story from a younger point of view.

The accessory coordinator, whose responsibilities are the same as the other area coordinators, has pulled every facet of the accessory departments together with a marked ethnic look. Bags, belts, neckwear, jewelry—bizarre and unique with a handcrafted flavor—show the influence of countries all over the world. The woman who selects a peasant gown can find the perfect ethnic shawl to complete the look. A junior customer, who found her favorite "gypsy dress," is enchanted with the gypsy earrings that go "just great" with her costume. It all works. It all goes together. It is fashion coordinated.

The coordinator for the men's and boys' departments is following the "peasant" directive to the letter. Colorful peasant shirts, vests, scarves, and ties, all add emphasis to the importance of the trend.

The store is alive with the ethnic looks of yesterday, as interpreted for the seventies. And so it goes with each and every new fashion story. If it is clearly understood by the store and its fashion personnel, it will be clearly understood by the customer. People buy what is "understandable."

Fashion Show Coordinator. The fashion show coordinator in the fashion office of a major retail store, has a full-time responsibility, zeroing in on this area exclusively. The fashion show coordinator in a small fashion office, however, has other responsibilities as well.

Everything pertaining to fashion shows comes across her desk. She handles all the details pertaining to shows (see Chapter 12) from the booking to the execution of the production. If one needs to know if a particular date is open for a show, they must check with the fashion show coordinator, who keeps the calendar of all fashion office events. In most cases, precedent is given to in-store fashion events. What the store has requested, in connection with the fashion plan, must always come first. After this, if dates are free, shows for benefits, clubs, and the like may be booked. The fashion show coordinator must, like all the other members of the team, get approval from the fashion director on which shows may be scheduled and which refused. Most fashion offices get more requests for shows than the calendar has dates and the energies of personnel will permit.

The scheduling of shows is most effective when tied with the fashion stories planned for a given season. For example, it is at this point that the fashion director might recommend to the show coordinator that during the time the store is projecting the peasant or ethnic looks in all fashion departments, a special "show of peasants" be scheduled in the Young Designer Shop or in the junior area. She might also recommend that informal modeling be offered during lunch time in the store's tea room or restaurants during the week of the special promotion.

During peak seasons, when shows and exhibits are given top priority, everyone available in the fashion office pitches in. This is also the case when other areas have pressure periods. The fashion office "team" bands together for an all-out effort.

Branch Store Coordinator. If the downtown store is treated as headquarters for a retail operation, then the corporate fashion office, along with other executive offices, usually will be found there. However, many retailers no longer regard the downtown store as the flagship and have relegated it to a branch status. In some cases, executive offices are situated in an office building or area relative to the store's distribution center. At any rate, the expansion of retail efforts to branches spread all over the city, in state and out of state, demands that an on-the-spot person oversees and follows up on everything coming out of the corporate fashion office.

This does not necessarily mean that the branches will have the same atmosphere or the same merchandise. Branches differ because the clientele differs. So it is very likely that one store will cater to the more affluent customer, another in the same organization will cater to a younger, more bizarre-loving customer, while others will take the middle-of-the-road and deal mostly in the bread-and-butter items for the moderate-income customer. The location of the branch and the requirements of the customers patronizing the branch dictate the fashion direction.

If the branch is considerably different than the downtown store or other branches in the group, then plans will vary somewhat from promotion to promotion. The branch coordinator, therefore, feeds back information to the main fashion office as to what her needs are, and a special plan is made for her to execute. Also, if a fashion show schedule is different from that of the other branches, the branch coordinator may be responsible for handling all the details of her show alone, including the commentary. Other alternatives include:

1. The branch coordinator arranges all details prior to the show, and the people from the main fashion office go on a tour of the branches with a show that originated downtown, with the same models and same clothes.
2. The branch coordinator fits the show at her own branch, with different models and different clothes (because her fashions may not be available downtown, and vice versa), and someone from the corporate fashion office comes out to serve as commentator for the event.

In still other cases, where there is no downtown or mother store in the traditional sense of many department stores, the responsibility of some or all promotional areas would be handled by the branch coordinator. She would then be responsible for special events, fashion coordination, and even teen coordination and would undoubtedly report directly to the individual store manager. In such an operation, merchandising and advertising are usually centralized for the over-all responsibility of buying and promotion, leaving the responsibility for fashion presentation (fashion events and displays) to the individual stores.

Display Fashion Coordinators. The area coordinator and display coordinator in many stores are one and the same. In firms where they report to the display director but take their direction on fashion correctness from the fashion director, their function is in the area of display only. Under this system, the display fashion coordinator for windows is usually separate from the display fashion coordinator for interiors. Then, to unite their efforts, the display director gets guidance from the fashion director, or requires that his coordinators check all fashion selections with the fashion office. However, for the sake of budget structure and responsibility allotment, the management of many stores prefers that everything relating to fashion projection be assigned squarely on the shoulders of the fashion authority.

In cases where the display fashion coordinators belong solely to the fashion office, they are involved totally in visual presentation of fashion—interiors, windows, shops, shows, and fashion special events. Where the store is extremely large, or these same coordinators are responsible for the branches as well, each of the three visual presentation areas are handled separately:

1. Interiors and cases
2. Windows
3. Special shops, boutiques, etc.

Any or all of the above people may be called upon to handle ramps, staging, production, sets, etc., for fashion shows and special events. These people are responsible for getting the show on the road with lights, sound, technical supervision backstage, and whatever is required.

The Youth Coordinator.   The Youth Coordinator, if the store has one, sometimes reports to the special events director, sometimes to the sales-promotion director, but more often to the fashion director. The youth coordinator is very much at home in the fashion office, because it is a feminine world and the business of relating to young girls in a feminine manner is more accurate here. Depending on the extent of a store's youth program or youth orientation, the responsibilities of the youth coordinator differ in proportion.

1. She might be the same girl serving as area coordinator for the junior department.
2. She might be the junior buyer serving as a part-time youth co-ordinator.
3. She might be a full-time youth coordinator who does nothing but create and execute all youth activities.

In case number 1, she covers the junior market, is in contact with all the young magazines, provides all departments in her area with events of special interest to the specific age group. The part-time youth coordinator who is a full-time buyer (number 2), might work on a seasonal basis only (such as back-to-school) with a Teen Board or school representatives to stimulate interest in her department. But the full-time youth coordinator, if she is to make a valuable contribution, is totally saturated in youth-oriented projects, which include everything from merchandising to fashion shows and special events, to public service and civic involvement.

The Fashion Office as a Unit

The fashion director of a major store usually travels a great deal, and therefore must have well-informed, well-trained personnel in her office to follow through in her absence on all aspects of fashion responsibilities. Although each member of the staff may have specific assignments for which they have total responsibility, there are some general tasks for which all fashion office personnel must be prepared to handle. The job may fall to anyone who answers the fashion office phone.

Telephone Charm.   Fashion office phones ring constantly and when there is a customer at the other end, her impression of the store and its fashion image sometimes can be elevated or lowered by fashion office personnel. Charm. That is a top priority requirement for fashion office people.

"I think it's disgraceful the low-cut dresses you showed in yesterday's show. Don't you people have a sense of responsibility?"

"Can I wear velvet in April?"

"What do I take to Hawaii this time of the year?"

The questions are many and varied. Some are amusing, some tough, but all deserving of some kind of answer. Everyone in the office should graciously answer the question if she can, or kindly suggest that the lady leave her number and someone with an answer will call her back.

Etiquette Questions.   Hardly a week goes by without several calls coming to the fashion office requesting guidance on etiquette problems. When a store telephone operator gets a customer on the line with a question about etiquette (or anything else she cannot clasify) she will very often advise the caller, "I'll connect you with the fashion office. They know everything there." Of course it isn't true, but what a beautiful compliment! It is nice for a fashion office to have that kind of reputation.

Coming up with the right answers for a multitude of questions may become a heavy burden at times, but customers do regard the fashion office as *the* authority on everything about proper dress, behavior, manners, entertaining, weddings, etc. It is important for the entire fashion office staff to be aware of the responsibility to provide answers.

"What are the rules for seating at a dinner party?"
"What do I wear to a garden wedding?"
"What do I wear if this is my second marriage?"
"Isn't it still proper for a boy to go to the door to call for a girl on a date, or is it alright for him to honk?"

If the answer is not known, a good reference library, maintained in the fashion office, would solve most problems. A good beginning for such a library could include:

Emily Post's Etiquette—The Blue Book of Social Usage
(Funk & Wagnalls)

Amy Vanderbilt's New Complete Book of Etiquette
(Doubleday)

Male Manners by Kay Corinth and Mary Sargent
(McKay)

The Wonderful World of Weddings by Elizabeth L. Post
(Funk & Wagnalls)

The Bride's Book of Etiquette by Editors of *The Bride's Magazine*
(Grosset & Dunlap)

Even with demarcations of responsibility, every member of a fashion office is strongly intertwined with every other member. Their effectiveness, their very existence, depends one upon the other. If a fashion prediction turns out big, everyone is excited. If a big fashion event is a hit, everyone in the fashion office feels the success personally. If one sees a highly successful fashion office, one sees a great team.

Sears Roebuck and Company, the world's largest retailer, depends on the Sears Fashion Board, a fashion director and fifteen counselors, for its fashion direction. Pictured with her counselors (each responsible for a different fashion division) Sears Fashion Director Jane Bown (center) created the "board" concept in 1960 to reflect young thinking. (Courtesy of Sears.)

The Chain Store Fashion Office

The mass retailer, such as Sears, Pennys and Wards, have characteristics unlike other giant retail groups. The purpose of their fashion office may be the same, but their structure is somewhat different.

Sears.   A unique example of a chain fashion office is Sears. Directing Sears fashion is a fifteen-member fashion board, headed by the national fashion director. Regarded by Sears as a "unique institution," the fashion board is headquartered in New York. Influencing the decisions on color and silhouette (forecast nine months ahead of a season) the fashion board's power has a far-reaching effect. By guiding fashion buyers of Sears, the world's largest retailer, the influence is felt in the industry at large.

Sears Fashion Board Members.   Each of the major apparel departments is represented on the board by a counselor. Each counselor works closely with the buyers of her division, keeping them advised of fashion board recommendations. The counselor also learns from the buyers about the newest trends in their respective markets. The counselors shop the market, visit sources, work with the buyers in some phases of item development, and are active in selecting merchandise for the catalogs.

In addition to the New York-based counselors, there is a board member who reports from Paris on European trends, and another is based in California to cover the fashion trends from that end.

Two coordinators, one for coordinating fashion pages of the catalog and one responsible for retail programs, are also board members. Three female members of the public relations department are associate board members.

Other Sears Fashion Board Assignments.   What the individual counselor learns from her division she brings back to the fashion board to be incorporated into a composite fashion projection. Together they select the fashion themes for displays, for newspaper press kits, and for the catalog. They conduct workshops for Sears' buyers, and issue the *Fashion Board Newsletter,* a monthly publication to Sears' stores selling fashion.

Afterview

Within the walls of all the responsibility assignments indicated heretofore and those diagramed hereafter, is one remarkable and enchanting fact about the entire field of fashion coordination: each fashion director or coordinator, in addition to her routine duties, can almost create her own job by adding a new dimension through originality and creativity. Fashion is that kind of world. Therein lies the magnificent beauty of the fashion business. It has rules, yes, but all are vulnerable to being broken, provided they are broken gracefully, tastefully, and innovatively. New rules are always in order when trends and times indicate change.

Chapter 4

✤ *How to Work with Management*

The dominant facts that must influence and guide every action of the fashion director or coordinator, are the purposes and objectives of her management. What she reports and advises very often may change the objectives or direction of a store's management, but the decision is theirs.

The Kind of Store. The kind of store, with regard to purposes and objectives, is the starting point for the fashion director.

> What kind of operation is she serving?
>> Department store
>> Chain store
>> Specialty store
> Is it a dominant store?
> Does the store share in a highly competitive market?
> What is the store's primary direction?
>> Completely fashion oriented
>> Highly promotional
>> All things to all people

Is the Store Her Kind? If the store is highly promotional and the fashion expert is not geared for action, nor does she thrive on competition, then this type store is not for her. If the store is primarily high fashion or at least anxious to obtain such an image, the fashion director must relate to this kind of world, or she will not be effective.

It is all a matter of chemistry. If she has a sincere love for the store and its objectives, her management will have no doubt that she is entirely in sympathy with their efforts. This kind of rapport begets trust. It guarantees the result that everyone involved is out to achieve, everyone pulling in the same direction toward the same goals.

What's more, it makes a demanding job more fun. A fashion director works hard, very hard, so loving what she does and having fun with it, is the secret ingredient that makes the whole thing work.

The Store's Philosophy.   When working with management, the fashion director should never lose sight of the store's philosophy. In fact, it is her most valuable guide line. If the store's philosophy is one based on long-standing tradition, and it is trying to change, there are always problems in the process. If the store's policies are designed by a progressive, well-tuned-in management, change will be resisted less, in fact, even welcomed at the right times.

If a fashion director lists the store's purposes and goals, she will discover the direction for her own purpose. Such a list might include:

> To direct all efforts to establish the store as a leading fashion authority
> To guarantee the customer the best value at the best price
> To provide the consumer with everything of fashion importance that is new and to provide it first
> To strive for personal identification with each customer, through specially trained personnel
> To provide the ultimate in services with courtesy and dependability
> To be as involved as possible in community and civic affairs and to make a contribution to the cultural efforts of the community

Of course, not all of these points will apply but where and when they do, it is important that the fashion director understand those areas before she takes her first step.

To Whom the Fashion Director Reports·

Here we go again. Just as her responsibilities differ, her office and type of staff, so it is with whom she calls boss. For all practical purposes there is a choice of three or four top-level management offices, to whom she might report or with whom her activities are greatly involved.

The President.   When the president of a store is also the general merchandise manager, or there is no GMM, per se, the fashion director would report directly to the man at the top. Usually this system exists in a specialty-type store.

General Merchandise Manager.   It is to this office that a larger percentage of fashion directors or coordinators report. The fashion director, along with the divisional merchandise managers who also report to the GMM, helps him fulfill his fashion goals. In some stores there is more than one general merchandise manager, each with his own fashion director, possibly, but the system is the same.

The general merchandise manager has the gigantic responsibility, from a merchandise point of view, of watching the store. All money delegated to each division for buying and selling all goods in the store, is under his control. Not only is he in control of who spends what, but he is the trusted guardian of the store's philosophy, the noble overseer who, if he is a great GMM, surrounds himself with talented people whom he can delegate, teach, and inspire. The real leader in this area knows it is a people business. He knows how to recognize and encourage talent, bring out the best in his associates, and help them to help him make the store great.

A fashion director, reporting to an inspired general merchandise manager, will take on his flavor. But if he is in need of inspiration, the fashion director, recognizing what is needed, can supply it. A truly fashion-oriented GMM, working with an enthusiastic, feet-on-the-ground fashion director, can make a store sing. He needs her authoritative guidance; she needs his power and authority to back her up.

Sales-Promotion Director.   There are two ways to go here. In many operations, the fashion director reports to the GMM and the sales-promotion director. In those where she is responsible only to the sales-promotion director, the store usually regards its fashion director as more effective on the promotional side.

When the store's merchandising team (the general merchandising manager, fashion director, divisional merchandising managers, buyers) fill the departments with the fashion they believe in, it is the business of the sales-promotion director to help sell it. He or she gets the story of fashion to the consumer through newspaper ads, magazine ads, radio and television commercials, catalogues, statement enclosures, special events, shows and exhibits, and visual presentations through display.

How that fashion story is told, however, how continuity of "fashionable" or updated language, theme, and presentation is more accurately accomplished is through the advice and guidance of the fashion director. It is one thing to get the right merchandise into the store, but it is another thing to get the right fashion story to the customer. Because each is so completely dependent upon the other, it is understandable why some fashion directors report to both areas.

Divisional Merchandise Manager.   In another, and perhaps less frequently used system, the fashion director reports to the merchandise manager of her division. In such a case, unlike the above situations, she is not a corporate fashion director, but a fashion consultant responsible only for the ready-to-wear fashion area, only the accessory area, etc. Under this arrangement she usually is a fashion coordinator who concentrates on her area and is not responsible for any other.

The divisional merchandise manager (DMM) has a responsibility of buying and selling similar to that of the GMM, only his is concentrated on his own division. The money and direction his GMM has given him, he now delegates to his buyers. As in any good system of delegated responsibility, the DMM must translate what has come to him from the GMM and the fashion director into a workable plan for his buyers and their associates.

The Store's Specific Objectives

Once the type of store and philosophy of that store are defined, the fashion director can proceed to underscore the specific objectives of the operation and contribute to the accomplishment of the related goals. Management sets the objectives; the fashion director helps fulfill them.

Long-Range Objectives

Before a fashion director can effectively administer her duties on a day-to-day basis, it is good for her to know the plans of the store on a long-range basis. To keep abreast of changing times, all outstanding merchants keep their place in the sun by constructive, heavily researched information about what to expect "tomorrow." Tomorrow not only means next week or next month, but next season, next year, five years from now, ten years from now. No one reads more, keeps a more vigilant watch, or holds his ear closer to the ground than the retailer. Experience has taught him that all things are relative and whatever is happening on the changing scene today will have an effect, one way or another, on what happens in his store tomorrow.

Any number of things may be on the list of long-range plans of a specific store.

1. Upgrading
   Price levels
   Quality levels
   Service
   Community involvement
2. Remodeling
   Renovating or updating existing plants
   Adding or changing departmental shops or boutiques
3. Expansion
   More branches of the existing type store
   Addition of a discount operation
   Addition of free-standing specialty stores
   Additions of twigs or capsules

Anyone on an executive level is concerned with the long-range plans of a store, but to discover exactly how these plans affect a fashion director is the purpose here. We need to indicate to what extent she is involved, and in which way she makes a contribution.

Upgrading

Very high on the list of long-range planning for a store may be the decision to upgrade. This means that the price level and quality level of the store's merchandise is to be moved up, perhaps replacing the low-to-moderate priced goods with moderate-to-good in a specific department. It may mean an increase in big ticket items and a decrease in lower end merchandise in all departments. In other words, the plan may be departmental or store-wide. In any case, the fashion director would have a big job carved out for her.

New Resources.   Her first assignment might be to be on the lookout for new resources when she is in the market. This would mean a line or lines not carried by the store at the time, lines that are coming up important, or those that up to now had no place.

Guidelines for Resource Shopping.   Recommending a new resource to the store requires a careful basis for selection.

1. In which department does it belong?
2. Are there already existing lines in that department that are too similar?
3. Does it fit the kind of customer who shops that department?
4. Is it compatible to the fashion image of that department?
5. Is the price level in keeping with the department's and store's objectives?

If there are several departments for which new resources are being sought in the plan to upgrade, then it cannot be done overnight. In some cases, it would begin as a sampling or testing of a line to judge its acceptability. In an effort such as upgrading, the store cannot throw out the inventory now in stock or that coming in. It must be done with advance planning and the changeover made systematically.

Changing Price Lines.   If the low end of the price line of one women's dress department is too low, compared with its high, the plan would be to drop the low-end, move it to a lower-priced department, and use the money allotted in that area for better-priced merchandise. Thus the process of upgrading begins. The department will eventually become a higher-styled, higher-priced area, completely divorced from the lower-priced look that once existed there.

Changing a Department's Look.   Sometimes the business of upgrading a department has less to do with the price lines than it does with its look. Perhaps it has been decided that department X needs to have younger, trend-setting merchandise, sort of a "here is what's new" department. In such a situation, all goods selected for this area would fit that specific classification—new, challenging, unique, young. The customer looking for this kind of fashion would come to depend on this "showcase" of the newest fashion ideas.

The Total Picture.   To avoid duplication and assure variety, the fashion director must keep in mind the total picture. New resources should supply a missing denominator, not a duplication of an existing one. This does not mean, for example, that shirt dresses need be confined to one department. There may be a variety of shirt dresses in any number of departments ranging in price, daytime or nightime look, misses or juniors. However, too many departments burdened with so many shirt dresses that there is a great lack of other important looks, defeats the secret of balance.

Store Planning—Remodeling

When a store is upgrading merchandise, it is very likely to take a hard look at its physical plant and decide to give it a good face lift, too. It is most difficult to house "now fashion" in a yesteryear atmosphere. If the remodeling is to be major, it most likely will be put on a long-range program, over a year or two, and if the plan includes the fashion departments, management is wise in consulting with its fashion director along with all the other people involved. Having lived with some of the inadequate facilities and antiquated floor plans, she (along with the buyers and merchandise managers) should have some strong feelings about what must be done.

Let us assume that the young fashion customer is not being accurately handled in the existing department. The buyer, area manager or department manager, and the sales personnel are in agreement. The department, they say, is too obscure, badly lighted, lacking in good dressing room facilities, and unattractive and inappropriate in decor with antiquated fixtures for hanging merchandise. The fashion director, while completely aware of all these ills, enlarges upon the whole problem, from a fashion vantage point. As soon as a young customer comes up on the escalator, the view should speak out loud and clear the tempo of merchandise sold here. If it is the young customer who is to be lured, the decor should be alive with a contemporary feeling, with color, with a new art form contributing to the decor. The lighting need not be bright, but it must be interesting and unique. Instead of the usual immobile mannequins, the floor might be

stu7dio

Gleaming chrome. hard. bright. White that dazzles. Mirrored light. All reflecting, revealing today's woman. This is her environment . . . clean, pure, fresh. This is STUDIO 7. A new concept in fashion for the woman who wears 5-15 sizes. For the sophisticate who sees herself in sleek contemporary designs for evening, at-home, career and vacation. Come soon.

H.C.Prange Co.

effective with a feeling of movement. Consider rear projection film or slides constantly changing on one wall, showing the newest fashion trends of people active in the current life styles. Customers could see on film actual, in-stock merchandise completely coordinated. This or some such idea might have been one the fashion director picked up during her last fashion trip at home or abroad. The racks where the new merchandise would be hung, spin and move. The young shopper can mill around easily with her friends, touch everything.

All this, the fashion director offers as a suggestion, if she is asked. A wise management knows that the compiling of ideas often gives birth to new ideas that might not come to light otherwise.

Outdated Classifications.   The teen girl would like to shop with her boy friend at times, so no need to separate the girls' pant looks from the boys'. She would welcome a "Pants Place," where boys and girls can shop together. This the fashion director learned from working with the youth coordinator—another reason why the youth coordinator is helpful in the fashion office.

Perhaps another outdated classification is discovered in the lingerie department. Junior lingerie has been too long absorbed and lost within the women's intimate apparel departments. Time to put it where the young customer has repeatedly asked for it to be put—in her own junior world.

Perhaps trends, classifications, and merchandise plans, when dealing with the young market, come and go faster than one can write them down, but that is the penalty of catering to the young market. A store needs to decide to what degree it wishes to do so, how much bending and bowing it is willing to do.

Request Changes with Caution.   Changing departments and reshuffling classifications is not an easy thing to do. Under the best conditions, there is limited space, and a great deal of advance planning must be expected. The plan should include—making sure that the move is important to the over-all fashion image and leadership of the store and that it better serves

It is difficult to house "now fashion" in a yesteryear atmosphere. A new shop, with fixtures and decor to relate to the merchandise, also provides the format for Prange's ad, based on the look of the shop. (Courtesy of H. C. Prange Co., Green Bay, Wis.)

the customer. Also, can the change be made quickly enough to be effective?

The fashion director's recommendations in store planning are based on fashion effectiveness. She may have influenced a floor change because she alerted her management to the fact that an important kind of department, not existing at present, is very much needed.

For example, she advised her management (the general merchandise manager to whom she reports, and the divisional merchandise manager whose area is affected) that many robe and lingerie manufacturers, who once made merchandise in these classifications only (those things that could not be worn outside the bedroom), were now meeting a great demand for dual-purpose fashions (bedroom and beach, or bedroom and family room), and at-home fashions, not always worn at home but suitable for home entertaining indoors or out on the patio. These fashions did not belong with quilted and terry-cloth robes, nor with sheer nylon night-gowns and pengoir sets, even though they were made by the same manu-facturer.

The home furnishings department was certainly getting the message across. They were aware of a big step-up in permanently-installed outdoor gas grills, enlarging of patios, and increased interest in outdoor "fashion" furniture. The housewares department reported continued interest in barbecue equipment and a greater and growing demand for the newer, more sophisticated utensils, dishware, flatware, and cooking facilities for home entertaining. The home furnishings fashion coordinator incorporated in his spring plans for model rooms, a talk-of-the-town group of specially designed model patios to help intensify the interest.

The more entertaining projected for home—on the patio, around the pool, around the fondue dish, around the home bar, around the fireplace—the more fashions for this life style were in demand. Women didn't want just a pair of slacks from the sportswear department, either. They had had plenty of that. They wanted their at-home clothes to be comfortable, yes, but also glamorous, fun, devastating, bizarre, amusing, whatever the occasion or mood permitted.

"The market is producing a great number of exciting looks to meet these demands, looks we should have," the fashion director tells her management. Management, in turn, recognizes and agrees with her that this is a classification big enough and important enough to maintain on a permanent, year-round basis, to be incorporated into the master "new-department" plan. There would now be a separate "At-Home Fashions" department, separate from robes or sleepwear.

The point is that the fashion director makes her recommendations on well-substantiated evidence of a need. She never recommends big changes just because they seem like a "nice or fun idea." Large or small, major changes in store planning stem from the same direction, or at least should— customer need, customer interest.

When to Live Dangerously.   The foregoing statement does not mean that a fashion person need be a mouse. Far from it. She can be a tiger. She can wander in up to her neck if she dares but only if she knows there is no quicksand. Sure ground, as far as one can determine, no matter what the apparent dangers of sinking, will usually deliver her and her idea safe and sound. She must, at times, live dangerously and take a risk, but only if it is a calculated risk. Otherwise, she would be thwarted in recommending things she believed in.

Store Planning—The Expansion Program

Store planning is not only concerned with remodeling one plant but also with building a new one. Here, perhaps, will be the opportunity to build store or shop concepts not compatible with the parent store or include departments that were not possible because of physical space problems in the old store.

Now the fashion director may be consulted again. Her management may wish to know her view on the best way to handle certain fashion areas, based on the newest fashion direction. What may have seemed a good idea a couple of seasons ago, has not developed as expected and can be safely eliminated. On the other hand, what may have seemed unimportant a couple of years ago when the original plans were drawn up, is showing up now as very important.

Example: Two years earlier, the community didn't have a single indoor tennis court. The only courts available were outdoor in city parks or private country clubs. Now there have been eight indoor tennis courts built and more planned to meet the growing interest in the sport as a year-round hobby. Unlike the outdoor public courts, the new indoor courts require regulation tennis clothes for all members. A pro tennis

The designer boutique or shop, often put together with designer specifications and requirements is an excellent image builder for a fashion store. The Givenchy Nouvelle Boutique, opened exclusively in New York at Bergdorf Goodman. The opening was launched with a Givenchy fashion show. (Courtesy of Bergdorf Goodman, New York.)

shop seems in order if the store is to take advantage of a growing market.

An alert fashion director will bring such a matter to the attention of her management. If the merit of the idea is accepted, the fashion director is requested to locate good, new resources for tennis fashions previously not carried in the community. When the new store opens, it will have the new tennis shop, along with many other departments and shops, conceived and developed in a similar manner. For now, in the new store, there is new space, new customers, new ideas.

Show Place, Kind Sir.   In every sizeable branch store the plans usually include an auditorium or area for shows and exhibits. The store planner recognizes the need of such a place for holding such things as fashion shows. The room might be very lovely, but unless adequate arrangements have been made for staging a show, the facilities fall short of serving their purpose.

A fashion director might be called upon to look over the blue print of the room with the architect and to point out the basic needs for such a room. More than once, areas for dressing rooms for the models were overlooked. Another time a stage was built but plugs for microphones were forgotten. Very often, the builders are unaware of some needs or they forget them.

The well planned presentation hall can be a great asset to a shopping center. Customers will look with favor on the branch as a place to hold or attend special events if the facility is attractive and workable. A fashion director, who has lived through many shows and knows what is needed, what works, and what doesn't work, could be a great help in an advisory capacity in such an instance.

The New Reaction to the Giant Store.   Little dry goods stores into massive, giant department stores grew . . . and grew . . . and grew. The department store grew so large in fact, that a bewildered and exhausted public found itself dashing off to small stores for special attention and less confusion in making decisions. In the big stores' attempt to give great selections and more of everything, they forced the customer to throw up her hands in despair.

Of course, the great selections of merchandise is one of the things shoppers love about department stores. They can find a tremendous range of sizes, colors, prices. But, with this, they have lost the intimate feeling of the family store. After all, the department store tradition began when life was vastly simpler. The basic concept was to bring the customer everything under one roof. However, with the staggering growth of our society and even more staggering growth of our technology, marketing methods, expanded merchandise classifications, and constant, more rapid change, putting everything under one roof is a tough order.

The Shop Concept.   The successful development of the branch stores and shopping centers indicated beyond a shadow of a doubt that "specialty shops" (after all, that is what shopping centers are made of) had a great deal of appeal.

Retailers traveling in Europe found that the women there loved to shop in "boutiques." Paris, for example, was a delight with boutiques everywhere, beautifully done, with strong fashion appeal on a small, intimate scale. This fashion treatment was not new to Paris. The first fine fashion shops for accessories opened in Paris in the seventeenth century.

According to the dictionary, a boutique is a "stall" or small "specialty shop." With guidance of the "word," and the living example as illustrated in Europe, department stores began to put little stalls in the store, and soon the specialty shop was brought inside the department store—a store within a store. The old standbys (the maternity shop, the swim shop, college shop, ski shop, bath shop) have been undeniably successful and a great testimonial to the merit of the shop concept. However, even with all its great advantages, it is literally impossible and certainly not advisable to "shop" everything.

In planning new shops and boutiques, the fashion director can be very helpful. It is important for her to know, however, exactly what makes a good shop, what it takes to make it work, how it is merchandised, and what its primary purpose is, before she can advise and guide in this connection.

What Makes a Boutique Work?   Undoubtedly, there are several reasons why some boutiques take off like the wind and others never get off the ground. But basically there are less chances for failure if a check list, similar to the following, is reviewed carefully by all involved before action is taken.

1. Does it fill a strong customer need?
2. Is it in keeping with the objectives of the fashion department to which it will be added?
3. Will the profit margin justify the space, cost of operation, cost of promotion?

These answers must come first, and the answers must be yes to all three, no matter how fascinated the fashion director may be with her new shop idea. Remember the precious selling space and costly square footage. It must pay off.

Even after the above points have been justified, there are still more factors to be considered. It is one thing to have a great idea, but it is another thing to have a good plan. Without it the chances of success are slim.

To throw a shop together, helter-skelter, just because a competitor has one or one has "heard" of one someone else has in New York or London, is to court disaster. After all, if the new shop is not better than the competitor's not much is gained, and what may have worked in New York or London may not be feasible at all in Mobile or Denver.

But after all things are considered, the shop idea does rate the effort, then it should be included in the fashion plan, with certain provisions. A shop concept works if, and only if, it offers:

1. A clear-cut fashion message
2. The right merchandise to back up the message
3. The right accessories (in merchandise and decor) to punctuate the message
4. The location, atmosphere, and decor blending in to make the message ring true

The ski shop is a timeless and excellent example of how a workable shop is put together. The shop is set in a rustic area, perhaps with ski lodge decor, a warm fireplace, comfortable chairs around a table for sipping and after-ski conversation. The shop has everything the ski fans need, a great selection of ski fashions (for men and women), after-ski fashions, ski boots and after-ski boots, gloves, scarves, caps, face masks, and goggles. Also, there is a choice selection of famous-brand skis, ski poles, ski books, travel bags, travel folders, and information on all the ski lodges and special ski trips available. There is even a choice selection of lotions and moisturizers and other skin treatment products designed especially for the skier. Skiers love to come to this shop because they know they will find everything that is new and everything they need right there. If the skier is a beginner, he will know that the sales "pro" knows exactly what to recommend.

It is all there. Check the foregoing four points. Now, with good promotion and follow-through, such a shop is likely to succeed.

The Twigs. The "twig" shop or "capsule" unit is a shop offering edited versions of the store's full stock of some accessory and/or fashion departments. They appear in shopping centers or in concentrated commercial areas away from the parent store, perhaps even in communities located elsewhere in the country. The size might be anywhere from 3,000 to 20,000 square feet. The accessory and cosmetic store (twig), starting in size at about 3,000 square feet, was pioneered by Dayton Hudson Corporation. This first such twig was scheduled to be built in Milwaukee's Southridge Center. National brand cosmetics and women's fashion accessories, including handbags, belts, scarves, costume jewelry, hosiery, and intimate apparel, were all planned in the new concept to "tailor an individualized fashion look for each customer," the corporation president, Kenneth H. Dayton, said in a story for *Women's Wear Daily*, December 7, 1970.

The pioneer of a 17,000 square foot capsule unit, bringing together a concentrated selection of merchandise categories sold in their larger stores, is Lord & Taylor. April, 1971, was the opening of the first capsule as an experiment in the Burlington Mall, Burlington, Massachusetts.

Such shops are always geared in a strong fashion direction to exemplify the fashion image or leadership of the parent operation. If a fashion director is involved with the buyer in helping decide on the selection and presentation of such fashion merchandise, she will, of course, be guided by the purpose of the shop and the existing fashion image of her store.

The Free-Standing Specialty Shop.   In the free-standing specialty shop, be it a furniture store or a women's ready-to-wear store, the fashion office might be called on to help "pull" suitable specialty items. Specialty shops excel in fashion treatment, so this would be a place where the fashion specialist could advise and direct a fashion idea and execute her responsibilities in exactly the same way as in the parent store. A fashion coordinator, from the fashion office, may be assigned this special responsibility along with her other duties. If the specialty store is devoted to furniture and home furnishings, the home furnishings fashion coordinator would have the entire assignment.

Seasonal Objectives

Many of the projected plans under "long-range" could be included under "seasonal," because it is by taking a step or two forward each season that some of the long-range plans are finally accomplished. Seasonal planning, therefore, should contribute to the long-range plan.

Work Ahead—Far, Far Ahead.   One of the greatest contributions the fashion director can make to her management is to plan far in advance of the coming season. Six months ahead, she will have started her research on what's coming, and five months ahead of the season, she will make her initial presentation to management with recommendations of her findings (see Chapter 5).

It is from these early evaluations that management is able to anticipate what steps of action are to be taken. If, for example, the coming fashion trend justifies a new shop concept, buyers' budgets can be set up for it, the display director or store architect can be enlisted to design for it, carpenters can be booked to build it, and new arrangements can be made for the merchandise coming out of that area to make room for the shop. It all works together, and all because the fashion director assures her management that this is the way to go.

Immediate Objectives

Everything that deals with in-season or current season fashion projection comes under this heading. The merchandise is in, the windows and interiors are decorated as planned, the ads are scheduled, the radio and television time is bought, and the sales personnel has been trained to interpret the fashion trends to the customer. All is in readiness. Everything that was planned for months ago has arrived. It is now the fashion director's job to see that all those well-laid plans do not run amuck. She and her staff coordinate all aspects of the fashion projection to the customer with continuity and dramatization.

Afterview

In understanding how to work with her management, in relating to the philosophy and objectives of her store, the fashion director finds the clue to what makes her presence on the team important.

She is not concerned with pleasing just one boss, because in theory she has many. She serves every level, every area, and if she does it well she is never like the waitress in a restaurant who says, "Sorry, sir, but this is not my station." All executives in merchandising, all fashion departments, all divisions, are indeed her station.

So, to whom she reports—the president of the store, the GMM, the

DMM, the sales-promotion director, or any other—it matters little. Her effectiveness is still felt by all of them. She may not always be sure who is her boss, but her management will never have any question about who is the fashion director.

Chapter 5

* *Influence of the Fashion Office*

The fashion director is a messenger. She brings back to her store the fashion message gleaned from her research. She and her staff refine, document, and interpret the message for the store. Once approved (and purchased), she and her staff translate and dramatize the message to be carried to the customer. Thus, the influence of the fashion office is a buying influence and a selling influence.

Buying Influence

When merchandisers and buyers go into the wholesale market to make their selections for the coming season, they are greatly aided in making an astronomical task less so, and certainly more efficient, if they are fortified with advance information.

When one considers the tremendous numbers of resources available for every departmental classification and the multiple numbers of choices at each resource from which to select a bushel-full of fashion trends, it staggers the imagination to know how it can all be covered, how decisions can be made on what to buy and what to pass up. As if this were not enough, the buyer has limited time in which to make selections, and limited money to cover those selections. A strong buyer, capable of evaluating recommendations made on fashion trends, will be delighted and eager to take the fashion director's predictive information right along with her as an authoritative guide on which way to go.

Every buyer in a specific division, may accept the fashion plan with enthusiasm—every buyer, perhaps, except one who defies the whole thing and proclaims that it is not for her department, not for her customer. She may be right, or, perhaps, only partially right. In any case, the final decision on which way to go rests with the buyer, unless she is so far out of line that intervention by the merchandise manager is in order.

When the merchandising staff, including the merchandiser, the buyer, and sometimes the assistant buyer, has a definite direction of what the store believes in as far as (1) trend-setting fashion and (2) dominant-sell fashion, they are in a better position to come home with the right kind of merchandise to back up the fashion plan.

Trend-setting Fashion.   If a retail merchant wishes to obtain or maintain fashion leadership wherever his store or stores exist, his organization must be geared towards what could very well be called a fashion store's creed. In effect, the creed might state that one of the store's goals is "to recognize and include all the newest, most important fashion trends appearing on the fashion scene—and to have them first."

New fashion, incorporated early and effectively in a season's inventory, comes under the heading of trend-setting. A dependable performance, season after season, of providing the consumer with "everything new, and providing it first" establishes the customer's confidence in the store as a leader.

It is very likely that the competition will have the same type merchandise eventually, but the store that has it first has the ingredient for leadership. Everyone follows the leader, the customer certainly and the competition inevitably. In both cases, it is the endorsement of success and the ultimate compliment.

Volume or Dominant-Sell Fashion.   Along with the customer who wants to be first in her circle to show up in something new and different, there is the customer (and very often she is one and the same) who wants fashion that is established and accepted. Such merchandise comes under the heading of volume or dominant-sell fashion. This category includes fashion which came in as a trend and through strong acceptance grew into volume selling. A good example of the big dominant or volume classification is the pant suit trend that appeared in the late sixties and became dominant-sell fashion in all departments, at all price ranges. Thus, successful trends become dominant-sell or volume items.

Bread-and-Butter Merchandise. There is still another group and it has been around much longer. Sometimes, it is merchandise which is not necessarily regarded as good taste—the "dumb coat," the "nothing dress," carried season after season because the customer demands it. And, sometimes, it is good-taste merchandise but not necessarily "fashion-y."

In retail circles fashion which is established and accepted is often referred to as bread-and-butter merchandise—a term borrowed from the food business. In a food market, such staples as bread, butter, milk, and sugar, are always available to the customer, no matter how many other food products or gourmet items are added to the shelves. So it is with fashion. Regardless of how many fashion innovations appear, the good old basics that sell day after day, year after year, must be stocked. True, there is the usual amount of updating each season—a newer fabric, a slight revision of line, the latest color, but still and all, a shirt is a shirt, a skirt is a skirt, and a jumper is a jumper.

Of course, there are strictly bread-and-butter stores and there are shops that are strictly gourmet. But, in any sizeable operation, catering to a wide variety of customers, with price lines running the gamut from high to low, all phases of merchandise need to be represented.

Balancing Fashion Merchandise. Recommendations by the fashion director about what merchandise to buy must be based on the extent of fashion trend-setting and the amount of dominant-sell involved in a specific store. Keeping the two properly balanced is perhaps the most important factor involved. Too much bread-and-butter merchandise overwhelming every fashion department, could leave fashion trend-setting merchandise so smothered as not to be noticed. Even when trend-setting departments are completely separated from bread-and-butter departments, the scales can get out of balance, and the store takes on the flavor of the stronger weight.

If customers say too often, "They never have anything new in that store . . . just the same old things . . ." even the "same old things" won't sell as well. Customers will, strange as it may seem, buy the same old things from the store that has fashion leadership if the prices are reasonable rather than patronizing a store with no leadership at all. Undoubtedly, this is because they feel safer with a "fashion authority."

Fashion Leadership vs. Image. In the early days of merchandising fashion, image evolved accidently or deliberately by perceptive merchants, especially during the thirties, forties, and fifties, when catering to the customer who regarded clothes as social security. Images were born through snob appeal, status ratings, or just plain sensationalism.

A store's image is very often recognized or saluted during gift-giving occasions such as Christmas. One is often impressed by the name of the store on the package when giving or receiving a gift. "A gift from Tiffany's! How grand!" A compliment both to the giver and receiver. Christmas catalogues with impressive gift suggestions have made some stores famous, bringing them into the news year after year. For the person who has everything—what about a solid-gold bathtub? Or perhaps his-and-hers airplanes? Neiman-Marcus of Dallas was repeatedly in the news for just such fabulous gift ideas.

A store's image, however, may project so strongly that many customers are afraid to walk in for fear they may be slapped with a cover charge. In the times when status-seeking customers make their selections on the basis of store and label, the combination is perfect. The arrival of the seventies, however, brought a strong indication towards "antistatus" and many an astute merchant recognized the fact that customers today buy merchandise not image. That is, customers will not buy from a store because of its image alone, but because the merchandise is right.

Therefore, if the store's image shouts "expensive" or "exclusive," its fashion direction naturally follows that line. If a store is regarded as a young store, a conservative store, or whatever, they are invariably obligated to back up that image if it is to be maintained. However, many leading merchants on today's scene have recognized "you can go broke trying to live off of an image."

It is all a matter of timing. When times change, the fashion story (always the mirror) changes with the times. For example, there was a time when mink was very high on the list of status symbols. At first mink was only for the rich. However, imitating the rich has long been a practice of the general populace, and the bigger and stronger our upper-middle-class population became, mink began wrapping multitudes of women. A working girl might walk up four flights to a little two-by-four apartment, to save money to pay on her mink, her status symbol. However, when the mink stole became a "uniform," showing up on everyone, everywhere, and when the maid was wearing mink on her day off, it was time for the lady of the house to turn to something else.

At the outset of the seventies, flaunting status symbols, such as haute couture designer labels, not only were resisted but were considered downright vulgar. There were too many issues of grave importance on the scene.

Whatever is socially acceptable during a given time affects the peaks and valleys of so-called image stores. But stores with fashion leadership, as against image, usually are in a position to better serve a changing society. Leadership is always in fashion, image not necessarily.

Thus, the fashion director should always keep leadership uppermost in her plans, and in cases where it is necessary, urge and inspire her management to accept the role of leader.

Buying for Special Events.   In some stores the fashion director does no buying at all. She may only suggest and guide. In other operations, the fashion director may be given some "open to buy" money, to be used for "sampling" pieces for testing, for consideration of a new line, a new look, a new item.

In other situations, the fashion director buys, or requests the buyer to include in her orders, special pieces necessary for fashion shows or special events. An entire show or a scene in a show, may depend on a specific fashion illustration. It would be necessary, therefore, to buy especially for that show. Fashion show pieces sometimes must be purchased for a specific model—size or type. This is more likely to occur when a guest model (important customer, club woman, etc.) is representing the store in a show rather than a professional model. It is imperative in such a situation to buy what the non-professional can carry off, what her particular figure problems, personality, or age will permit.

Sometimes, "show pieces," not as readily salable and therefore not usually carried in stock, are necessary to add excitement and emphasis to a fashion production. Also, for an important show or promotion, part of the impact is to present pieces previously unseen in the department.

Windows also come under the heading of special purchases by the fashion director. When a theme or promotion is big and important, it is often more efficient to have the fashion director actually pick and pass judgment on those things necessary to carry out her fashion idea for the store's windows.

When the unique or bizarre are part of the fashion impact, these special fashion pieces are excellent as illustrations or attention-getters. The buyers, however, cannot always sacrifice precious dollars from their "open to buy" allotment to contribute to show pieces. Thus, the fashion director's show budget is established, so she may do the buying.

The Predictive Presentation

Perhaps the most important thing a fashion director or coordinator does for her management is the predictive presentation. It is through this effort that she exerts her greatest influence on buying.

After the fashion director's research has been accumulated, refined, and evaluated, it is time for her to share all her findings with top management and all executives of the merchandising staff. This first, all-important, predictive presentation is submitted before the merchandising staff goes to market to shop and place their orders. It is here that all findings for a coming season, from all fashion market areas, are brought together and submitted as a guide before the market opens. It is also material that must be kept confidential. At this point one does not share the store's information on future plans with any personnel other than those immediately effected and responsible. Thus, this first meeting is devoted to those in decision-making positions only.

Who Calls the Meeting. The fashion director sets the date for this presentation, checking with the store calendar and travel plans of those expected to attend. Since this meeting is seldom repeated, it is important that everyone involved be present. Those invited must be advised far enough in advance to firm up the date and to insure the best possible attendance.

Advance Preparation.   In addition to the research done by the fashion director, there is much preparation before the future fashion story is ready to be revealed. She has tabulated her findings, censored and evaluated all proposed recommendations (see Chapter 1), and now she is ready to interpret and translate all the facts into a workable plan.

Since there is so much territory to cover, and limited time in which to relate the entire story, the utmost of discipline should be exerted to reduce the whole thing down to a succinct, comprehensive presentation. An economy of words and an extravagance in illustration is most desirable. It should be understood that there are places where there is no substitute for oral explanation, but where visual illustration can assist oral explanation, it should be strongly included.

A brochure or booklet written by the fashion director and, if possible, illustrated by a member of the fashion office or an artist from the advertising department, serves as a most valuable aid in many ways.

1. As a text to follow, and perhaps, as an outline for taking notes during the presentation
2. As a way to review highlights of the presentation before going to market
3. As a reminder or reference book to take along into the market

How to Make a Predictive Presentation.   It is possible for the booklet or brochure to be used as a format of procedure for the meeting. That is, each page can relate to the facts and points presented if it has been compiled in the order of presentation.

At the very outset of her presentation, the fashion director should give a brief and revealing summary of what the coming season has to offer. Setting the "tone" and "temperature" of what can be expected is most helpful to those following the details presented later. This tone-setting summary should be a blanket comment, all embracing, and certainly inspiring. The inspiration should come right from the beginning. Such an opening comment could sound something like this:

"The coming spring-summer look will be long, lean, close-fitting, soft, easy, and uncluttered.

The head will be small, the neck long, free, and open. The waistline will be in great demand.

A direct line of communication on what is happening in fashion at Sears, what to look for in new stocks, plus highlights and evaluations of trends, is supplied in a monthly newsletter from the fashion director, to Sears stores everywhere. (Courtesy of Sears.)

It will be a seaon of stabilization after a season of experimentation. Those fashion ideas that tried their wings last season, flew too high for a while, then quickly fell, exhausted, over exposed, and over done, will not be around. The spring fashion skies will be filled instead with floating lines that move gently and easily.

It will be a "soft" spring. Fabrics, colors, silhouettes. All softened.

There will be a great stress on easy-care, packable fabrics in garments for people on the go. There will be great respect for fashion items that live a double life. Double-duty clothes are important for busy people. Less clutter. Easy to transport. Easy to live with.

Easy. That's the key word. Easy and soft. The kind of spring we have waited for. The kind of spring that should have great sales acceptance."

The mood is set. Everything that follows will enlarge upon and illustrate that opening statement. From this point on, the more illustrations, samples, models, and visual aids used, the better.

Although trends change from season to season and year to year, there are certain basics that must be covered in all predictive presentations, all of which help mold the format. Consistently, the format should include:

1. Presentation of Predicted Leading Fabrics
   Illustration: Use fabric swatches, mounted on a board, or on several fabric posters. Each poster can tell a different fabric story.
   Point out: (a) Which fabrics are new, which are in greater demand, which are important in which markets (couture, better, budget, women's or juniors)
   (b) Which fabrics will be trend-setting
   (c) Which fabrics will be dominant-sell
   (d) What the new fabric combinations will be
   (e) Which fabrics will be the leaders, and what seems to be showing up as best choices for promotion
2. Presentation of Important New Colors
   Illustration: Use color swatches of fabrics or color charts. Separate charts for each color family are best to show to degrees of color changes.
   Point out: (a) Which colors are showing up as most prominent
   (b) Which colors are trend-setting
   (c) Which colors are dominant-sell

(d) What new color combinations are in the offing

(e) Which color is the number one color and which ones are the colors for leadership

3. Presentation of New Textures and Patterns

Illustration: Fabrics, leathers or colored sketches

Point out: (a) If it is going to be a season of soft, pliable textures as against former bulky, rougher ones

(b) If it is going to be a good year for polka dots, stripes, or prints, (If it is going to be a good year for prints, for example, the merchandising staff needs to know what kind of prints—petite and delicate, large and bold, abstract, nostalgic, muted, etc.)

(c) If more than one kind of texture will be combined with another in the same garmet (For example, leather, real or simulated, combined with knits could be included as an important fabric combination)

National fashion magazines supply the retail fashion director with seasonal kits of sketches, illustrating the most important fashion silhouettes of a coming season.

These are suitable for fashion
presentations and training
sessions. They can be duplicated
or blownup and used as a
visual aid.

    (d) Which texture and/or patterns will evolve as most important

4. Presentation of Furs and Leathers

Illustration: Samples or leather ''chips'', mounted

Point out: (a) Which furs will be used—real or make-believe

(b) How furs will be used (body, trim, accent, etc.)

(c) Which leathers will be important, and what the new fashion colors will be

(d) How leather will be used (body, trim, accessories, etc.)

Visual Aids.   After the fabrics, colors, textures and patterns, and leathers and furs have been revealed and evaluated, it is time for a brief forecast of the trends that will continue strong, those falling away, and those coming up new. Sketches, color slides, or film of the new looks should be presented now to illustrate what will be seen in the showrooms when they go into the market. It is one thing to see the fabric and the color, now they need to see how it will be manipulated.

Dividing the Markets.   Even though leading trends filter through all markets in degrees, it is important to the individual buyer that the presentation be divided according to separate fashion areas. Each buyer, therefore, can be more confident about what he or she should personally look for in specific markets.

For example, the coat and suit buyer needs specifics about special treatment of coats, ensembles, and suits. Will they be full or narrow, belted or unbelted, cuffed or uncuffed, lined or unlined? Will there be capes? Will there be prints or solids? The dress buyers, on the other hand, need an entirely different set of facts about what's new, as do the sportswear buyers, accessory people, etc. Therefore, the presentation, with explicit facts, affecting each area, should be divided and presented in a manner such as this:

> Coats, suits, ensembles, rainwear
> Dresses
> Sportswear
> Junior fashions (coats, dresses, sportswear, etc.)
> Accessories (bags, belts, jewelry, etc.)
> Shoes
> Intimate apparel, lingerie, at-home, or loungewear
> Cosmetics
> Wigs
> Children's fashions

In each category, during or after describing the new fashion looks on the color slides or sketches, the top fabrics, colors, and silhouettes showing up as important, should be clearly indicated. Each classification should also include recommendations of new resources worth considering, or resources now being carried whose new collections look good.

Live Illustrations.   There is nothing like a live illustration of a new fashion look—a costume worn by a live model. For now everyone can see how it falls, clings, floats, moves, whatever. They can also see the costume accessorized to get the total picture from head to toe. This is how their customer will look in the forthcoming season. Whenever it is possible to get samples (at this early stage it is not always possible), it is obviously a great advantage. Obtaining samples before merchandise is in stock, is only possible through a personal contact of the fashion director, who might be able to get a manufacturer's salesman to loan them to her for one day.

If the actual merchandise is not available from a manufacturer, then filmed models, moving in the new fashion expressions, are equally helpful. These films may sometimes be begged or borrowed from fabric mills who have developed them for their own fashion presentations. Color slides are often available early from the fashion office of the store's resident buying office.

Recommending New Ideas.   Along with the incoming trends, the fashion director should pass along any and all ideas that are significant to updating lines or departments.

> If a new cosmetic line is appearing on the horizon and she has obtained some significant facts and figures to prove its effectiveness, the cosmetic buyer might appreciate her information so he can look into the matter further when in the market.
>
> If a new jewelry designer, just beginning to get reaction to his new creations, looks good, it behooves the fashion director to pass along the word to the jewelry buyer.
>
> If she has learned that a leading fashion designer is planning a new subdivision, with a completely new and different line to supplement his higher-priced couture fashions, perhaps with a younger and more moderately priced look, the buyer affected should be advised.
>
> If a new shop idea fills a gap the fashion departments have been needing, she should accumulate all the information (theme, resources, price lines, space needed) and present the idea for consideration in the plan of major additions for the new season.

Everything of importance, or seeming importance, available for the coming season, should be passed along to management and the merchandising staff for consideration.

Well, Almost Everything.   A certain amount of censorship, of course, must take place. After all, there is just so much time, so much money, and so much space in the store. The fashion director must be aware of what could not possibly be utilized in her organization. These things, out of good judgment, should be eliminated from her presentation. However, there are exceptions in this connection. There might be something, even though it could not possibly be utilized in a store such as she serves, which could contribute to her management's being well-informed about what is happening or help influence other decisions.

Promotional Recommendations.   After relating the complete fashion story for the coming season, listing each and all facts as they relate to the whole picture, she is ready to present her recommendations for promotable, trend-setting fashion stories. She will do this in three parts.

1. List the leading fashion stories—those best suited as top promotional ideas for the store
2. Indicate which are best as store-wide promotions, and which are best as departmental promotions
3. Note clearly what is the recommended timing for all promotions

The fashion director will submit under the foregoing points, three or four, or maybe a half-dozen, top fashion stories, listed (as she sees them) in the order of importance. Everything she has been able to learn in her pre-market research indicates that this is the way to go.

In addition to the major fashion stories, she will recommend top "item" promotions. Every season a great many items pop up that merit promotion on their own.

The Fashion Plan.   At the conclusion of the presentation a summary of the predicted highlights evolves as a suggested fashion plan for the coming season. The plan will spell out the direction the store's coming season should take, with new fabrics, colors, trends, silhouettes, promotional themes, and promotional items, plus new accessory treatments. New shop concepts, new classifications, perhaps resulting from new fashion trends, will also come to the fore. Management, evaluating all they have seen and heard, will decide the final direction. They will meet, consider, and formulate with the fashion director, a new season fashion plan.

The Total Picture.   This predictive presentation may be the only time the entire merchandising staff and management will see and hear the entire fashion picture of the coming season.

Remember, the junior buyer goes only into the junior market. A jewelry buyer sees only the jewelry market. It is most revealing and most advantageous for all fashion buyers and merchandisers to get the prediction of all markets in order to see how one relates to the other and what the possibilities are for the total store. After all, the jewelry buyer will certainly have more confidence selecting jewelry for the neck, if she knows about the new necklines. The shoe buyer will not be led down the garden path, if he knows in what areas he must be covered in order to relate to the new skirt lengths and new lines.

Thus, the buying influence of the fashion director is one of guidance and fact finding. It is one of stimulating in her management reaction and action for those important fashion facts. However, as they say in the trade "we buy to sell," so her work has just begun.

The Fashion Director's Selling Influence

It is thrilling to find great fashion trends, believe in them, and buy them. It is even more thrilling to see all those efforts succeed; they succeed when they sell.

No fashion director worth her salt will drop the ball at this point, not here, where it really counts. She will very likely sit close at the elbow of her general merchandise manager and sales-promotion director during planning meetings for the coming season. She will hope that she made her points clear enough and strong enough to encourage them to include exciting advertising programs, display plans, and good exposure in the radio and television media for the fashion trends recommended. She will hope also that they will schedule all their trend-setting action early, in order to be first in the community with the important fashion news.

Telling the Fashion Story to the Customer.   The fashion director's first step is to help guide the store in getting the right fashion merchandise into the departments. Her next step is getting the fashion story to the customer.

Fashion-impact newspaper ads and fashion magazine ads will help; radio and television commercials, carrying waves of excitement over the airwaves, will contribute; inspired windows and interior decor, displays, and vignettes will help. Fashion shows and special events bringing the story to life, help tremendously to repeat the fashion story to the consumer. But the most important help of all comes at the point of sale. If the selling staff does not have the fashion story down pat, the whole network of effort could be wasted.

Fashion Presentation for Sellers

As carefully as the predictive presentation was researched, planned, and presented, so must the fashion presentation for sellers be coordinated.

Every fashion seller from every department and every branch should be scheduled to attend seasonal fashion training sessions. At the top of the season (when the new season's merchandise is arriving), the meetings should be scheduled to educate the selling staff on everything that is new, how to sell it and how to put it together.

How to Make a Seller's Presentation.   The sellers have not been to the fashion market. They have seen none of the samples, heard none of the predictions. Perhaps a few rumors have filtered down to them, or perhaps they have picked up bits and pieces of fashion news, but it is very possible that the bits and pieces have not been properly interpreted. Also, there is no way for the seller to know, at this point, what the merchandise in her department will look like throughout the season or what her store's fashion point of view will be. It is up to the fashion director's presentation, therefore, to provide all the answers.

First, a short summary of the general "flavor" of the coming season, much like the one she gave in her predictive meeting to the executives, is in order. She might explain:

"You have had bulky springs and bright springs, daring springs, but this year will be different. Spring will be a little 'soft' this year."

She should paint a picture, stir the imagination, light a fire, incite their interest. She might continue to explain that the fabrics, colors, and lines will all go "soft." Whatever words she chooses, whatever techniques she applies to describe the season they are about to sell, she must be sure she projects enthusiasm and belief in the fashion direction the store has taken.

Since this is not a decision-making body and the plan has already been formulated, many of the details offered at the predictive meeting should be omitted. In the interest of time, and to eliminate the risk of confusing the group, it is usually best to present only the top or leading features in each category. For example, she would present:

1. Leading fabrics
2. Leading colors

3. New fabric combinations
4. New color combinations
5. New fashion trends
6. New accessory treatments

Illustrate Everything.   Illustrations, many of the same kind used at the predictive presentation, are most important. At this date, however, when merchandise is already arriving, plenty of samples should be available from stock to model and coordinate.

When selecting merchandise for a sellers presentation, it is most wise to use samples from as many departments as possible. There is no finer way than to have many departments represented, so the sellers can see how their own particular fashion pieces look on a completely accessorized model.

Assume Nothing.   Advise them about all promotions which will help influence their thinking. The promotions also encourage them towards inspired selling and help them know to what degree their efforts are backed up. Fill them in on any new shops affecting their area. Nothing is more demoralizing to personnel than to walk into their department one day and find it dismantled, with no warning about what is going on. Include them in your philosophy of what fashion should be today, how the things you show are to be worn, and where if it is not obvious.

Assume nothing. The story is not new to the fashion director; she has been living with it for weeks. But it is all new, surprising, confusing, and perhaps resisted at first by this audience seeing the season put together for the first time.

A selling job is part of the fashion director's efforts here. Before the fashion seller can *sell* the customer with conviction and understanding, the fashion department must do a bang-up selling job itself. Sometimes selling the sellers on a new idea is a gigantic challenge.

Something to Remember.   Whenever possible, supply all the sellers with a brief résumé or booklet on the highlights of the presentation. It should be simply done, easy to understand, (all new trends clearly identified) and illustrated for easy reference. A booklet about the size of the seller's salesbook is usually welcome; it can be tucked in the back and always be handy for reference.

Color slides are ideal for showing close-ups of details on new trends. Jewelry, shoes, accessories of all kinds, and design details, such as seaming, trims, pockets, fabric patterns, and textures are great close-up material on slides or film.

Question-and-Answer Period. Even after the most comprehensive presentations, there are bound to be questions. In fact, the asking of questions is a good sign. It indicates that the fashion director has stimulated their interest to debate, challenge, contribute, clarify, and seek further information. Great ideas come out of such sessions, and involvement is a vital part of a presentation. Since the audience may not volunteer questions, it might be wise for the fashion director to mention at the outset that a question-and-answer period will follow. It is an ideal time to clear the air, for the fashion director to learn what points did not hit home, for the audience to express their feelings about the season, and for all present to hear what the other person is thinking.

Presentation for Advertising, Display, and Publicity Departments

These three specialized fashion people, the teams responsible for delivering the fashion message to the consumer, should be included in all presentations—the predictive, the sellers, and for emphasis on specifics that do not necessarily affect other associates, a special presentation might be in order.

For example, a special session in the fashion director's office, exclusively for members of the display department, is often scheduled at the start of a season and repeated at regular intervals as needed, when new merchandise comes in or new promotions are ready for execution.

In a session for display people, examples of how the new looks should be draped, worn, and accessorized is most vital. The tone or theme of a promotion will influence the kind of mannequins used, props, decor, style of presentation. If any fashion directive needs clarification in this connection, this is the way to do it. The fashion director can review any fashion points regarding the windows, interiors or shops. The exchange of ideas here may turn up something that heretofore had not been considered.

The Language Barrier. A separate session for the advertising and publicity staffs takes another direction. In addition to hearing the entire story in the predictive and selling sessions, these creative people need to be filled in on the new language. Along with every big fashion change, with every important fashion story, the terminology changes.

Nothing is more damaging to the presentation of a new fashion story than incorrect or uninspired language. If new fashion trends are presented with "old hat" tag lines, descriptions, handles, or banners, the power of the new impact is watered down. It would be laughable to call an umbrella a parasol, or a hat a chapeau, unless, of course, they were used deliberately as a put on. Language must be updated in all copy as quickly as stocks in the departments are updated. The two must be compatible.

Language is one of the most effective tools used to educate the consumer about new fashion. When peplums in jackets and dresses came back into fashion in 1970, young fashionables asked, "What's a peplum?" Never having seen this flare treatment at the waistline in their fashions before or never having heard the word, it needed to be clarified with illustration and identified with the fashion language. Soon they knew what to ask for when shopping.

In the late sixties and early seventies, words like mini, midi, and maxi were fabricated by the trade to identify specific fashion looks. *Women's Wear Daily* projected these words and others to underscore a new fashion trend. They created the word "longuette." They identified what formerly had been called shorts as "hotpants" when they appeared during the winter of 1970 and spring of 1971. They had a new look, these hotpants. They were created in every fabric imaginable, from satin to velvet, brocade to fur, cotton to corduroy, and they now had a new purpose—evening attire for parties and dancing, where once they were confined to active sportswear. They were no longer shorts, no longer just for joggers or the gym. Therefore, shorts were not hotpants, and vice versa. Things change. Words change.

What's Wrong with this Picture?   There was a time in fashion magazines and ads when the models stood in a stilted manner with their hand on one hip. This was fine in the day when she had a parasol in one hand. The hand on the hip seemed to belong with the hour-glass figure. It was the attitude of the day. However, figure lines and body movements change with time and dress. The look of the posed model, as against the natural or candid model, went the way of all dead trends—into the archives. Thus, sketched or photographed illustrations must have the look, pose, and motion of the current trend. The fashion director, watching the fashion story from all angles, must be sure everyone knows the score.

Being a Selling Influence by Example

It is only natural that customers and business associates alike should look to the fashion director and members of the fashion office to serve as a fashion authority by what they do as well as by what they say. Usually when a new trend is evolving in fashion, the "fashion people," coordinators, buyers, and models, are among the first to lead. If they do it well, their example is readily followed. They add emphasis, inspiration, and endorsement for those less courageous.

Taste, Above All. Often, fashion pioneering takes courage, but for a fashion person to wear what is new just for the sake of doing so, whether or not it is suitable to her own personality and figure, is a number one sin. She should be a good example in the censorship of dress as well as endorsement of dress. Everything is not for everybody. What is right for her adds flavor to the trend; what is wrong for her creates distaste. Many a fashion person, overwhelmed by a sense of responsibility to join, defeats her purpose. In any given season, there are many great fashion stories to choose from, enough from which to pick only those that are a good influence.

If a fashion director has a great high-fashion look, if she is dramatic enough, tall enough, and lean enough to get away with most difficult-to-wear trends, she is wise to capitalize on this fact. Adding impact to fashion in this manner, particularly through personal appearances, can be very rewarding for the store.

All fashion stores prefer all their employees to show up in the latest trends as soon as possible. To encourage updating of work wardrobes, many retailers provide generous discounts on fashion merchandise. It is much easier to indicate to a customer that this is a fashion look she must have if the people selling it are also wearing it. Overdressing, however, is a danger. One should not outshine the customer any more than a hostess should outshine her guests.

Influence on the Young Customer

Along with the fashion office's buying and selling influence, comes its influence on the young customer. The influence on the adult or mature customer is covered in every aspect of this chapter and throughout the entire text (whether it be through advertising, displays, shows, or special events), but a special area must be set aside for the young customer. This potential customer of today, and hopefully in the years to come, is a completely different consumer, whose interests require special attention. Many stores depend entirely upon the effectiveness of its fashion office to attract and influence the teen customer.

The Teen Customer.   Perhaps the first awareness a young lady has of herself is in regard to her appearance. "I look fat. I look skinny. I look tall. I look pretty." She is concerned about what to do with her hair. She looks at makeup with mixed feelings, wondering how to use it, if to use it and what kind to get. She pours over *Seventeen Magazine*, her fashion bible, identifying with the lovely young models throughout the issue, wondering how she would look in something like that. The next thing she knows, she is wandering through the junior department of a store, spots something she saw in the magazine and tries it on. Her fashion rapport has begun.

She is a little unsure of herself at first. However, there is usually one thing about which she is not in the least unsure—she would like to be a model. She has heard her friends at school talk about modeling schools and modeling classes. She has heard them talk about the fashion boards at the store. Everybody, it seems, "comes to the store" for almost everything.

This may be one of her earliest experiences as a young adult in associating with "the store." And it seems to follow, that if there is something that she wants, in the way of information, a course, a service, advice, news, or instruction, she will call the store. They will undoubtedly have it, know the answer, or know where to guide her to get the answer. The store may grow a little weary (foolish if it does) of being expected to be all things to all people, but it is this image that is indispensable, especially in gaining the housewife or career woman of tomorrow, as well as the buying power of the youth of today.

Give the Young Customer what She Wants.   Since the young consumer

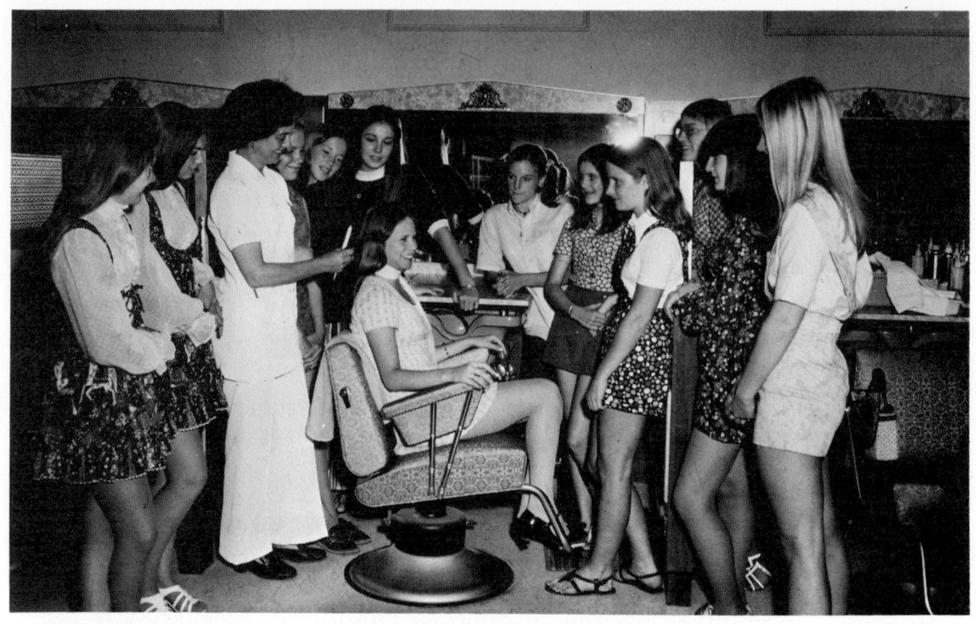

Students get advice on beauty care from the *Seventeen* **Beauty Work Shop. Hair-styling session at Casey's Department Store, Williamsburg, Va.** (Courtesy of *Seventeen* Magazine.)

is enchanted with the idea of fashion modeling, and the retailer is enchanted with the idea of getting her into the fashions he has for sale, the offering of a modeling course serves a dual purpose. Such a service is especially advantageous to the retailer, as revealed during an anti-fashion period (appearing in the late sixties) when "grubbies" reigned supreme. This was a rare opportunity to expose her to now fashions, much of which she was strongly avoiding. Invariably, if she is a young lady with an interest in fashion or modeling, she will find her way to the fashion office.

"How can I sign up for your modeling course?" she will ask.

"Right here," the secretary-receptionist sings. "Just have a seat and I'll call the youth coordinator (see Chapter 3).

Most applications come by telephone or mail in answer to an ad about a new course beginning.

The Educational Program for Youth.   The youth coordinator, responsible for all events pertaining to the youth market, is also an educator. In the case of special classes offered for the girls, she will usually follow a procedure, something like this: She decides what kind of classes seem most in demand and draw the best attendance:

1. Modeling classes
2. Good grooming and beauty classes
3. Sewing classes
4. Interior decorating classes
5. Fashion know-how classes (on latest trends)

The youth coordinator will select from a list that includes such courses, and discuss with the fashion director which have been most successful in the past, which should be eliminated, and which new ideas should be incorporated. Much depends on the trend of interest at the time. What was good last year could be losing ground this year and completely out of the picture for next year. There is very little loyalty, either in interest of activities or in the store, where most young people are concerned. It is imperative, therefore, that they be captured again and again. When the

Teen girls at Bergdorf Goodman, New York, for the launching party of ''Bigi Does It,'' the store's young handcrafts boutique, opened as part of *Seventeen's* ''Needlemania'' crafts promotion (Courtesy of *Seventeen* Magazine.)

decision has been made, the educational program for young customers for the coming season might include:

1. An eight-week course combining modeling, good grooming, and beauty care
2. An eight-week course on a current new interest in knitting and needlework (instead of a sewing class because most girls are getting good instruction in home economics classes at school)
3. A one-day seminar on the new way to coordinate the new young fashions
4. A weekly exercise class on how to shape up for the new fashion trends
5. A makeup clinic to learn the new techniques of makeup
6. Skiing instruction

Scheduling the Classes.   Timing, of course, is of the utmost importance in scheduling the classes under the youth program. There is a greater interest in exercise classes, for example, preceding the bathing suit season, or at the beginning of a new fashion season where the new looks are more revealing. Sewing or knitting classes make more sense in the cold months; this is indoor activity.

In addition to scheduling the right classes at the right time, the rest of the fashion calendar must be consulted. Too many events must not be scheduled at the same time, both from a standpoint of personnel need and space availability. For example, a store may use the same people from the fashion office to do a number of things. One could not lecture a class and conduct a fashion show at the same time. As to space, a store may have only one auditorium or classroom, therefore, space must be reserved far enough in advance to avoid conflicts. Other departments in the store also have activities, meetings, classes, etc., which require space.

When the schedule of classes is firmed up, copies of the intended program should be sent to everyone in the store who might be affected. Communications with the buyers of the young fashion departments is especially important; buyers and their salespeople are asked most often what is being offered. A calendar of events, posted in all the young departments, announcing "what's going on and what's coming up" of special interest to the young customer, will be most helpful.

The Instructor for the Classes.   The youth coordinator very often finds herself the teacher. In courses where her background and experience qualifies her as the instructor, the job is hers. In situations where the instruction is specialized (such as knitting, makeup, skiing, etc.) a qualified person is brought in to teach just those classes.

Many stores prefer, however, because of the demands on the time and energy of their youth coordinator in other directions, to employ a part-time instructor for youth-oriented courses. Such a part-time person would teach all the fashion-related courses, including the modeling and grooming and beauty classes, leaving the so-called specialized projects to the skilled people in those areas. An instructor from the needlework department in the store, for example, might help with the youth program by conducting a special course.

Very often, experts in a field come in from outside the store to instruct on a public relations basis. A physical fitness expert from a local gym or beauty spa might come in to direct a class on exercising for health and beauty. Occasionally a national celebrity will be making a swing around the country to publicize a book on exercise and diet for young figure problems and will be available for a three-day session, perhaps appearing to conduct classes at three different branches. The cosmetic companies are most effective in this regard. There are many occasions when national representatives of cosmetic companies geared to the young market come into a store for a full week of makeup instruction, with classes scheduled and enrollments made through the store in advance.

Fees for the Classes.   While the store encourages activities such as a youth educational program for the purpose of public relations, most courses (especially those that run several weeks) carry a charge or at least a registration fee. The charge is usually nominal, perhaps enough to help offset the overhead of the instructor's fee or help justify the youth co-ordinator's expanding an already ample program.

The student, too, is benefited. Attendance is always much better and more faithful when an investment has been made, no matter how small. Also, there are supplies that often are included in the course, and the tuition usually covers all the required work tools. A charge also guarantees the limited number permitted in a class, making room for those who are really interested rather than those who might just drop in out of curiosity.

Fashion Boards.   For many years, fashion boards on high school and college levels were very high on the list of importance in youth activities offered by retail stores. The idea started in 1943, in a store in San Diego, Walker-Scott, by Catherine Wueste, then associated with the store's advertising department. Miss Wueste started with eight high school girls representing various high schools in San Diego, and she called them the High Debbers. The High Debbers worked in the store on Saturdays, helped with two or three big events during the year, their own local radio show, a dance at Christmas, and a jamboree. The jamboree was held at a local movie house which in those days still had a stage for live performances as well as a screen. Miss Wueste developed a mailing list of 15,000 local teen students, and promoted the preview of a new film. On stage, before the showing of the film, the store's board presented a fashion show. At the end of the year, a scholarship was awarded by the store to one student as "the outstanding girl of the year."

This beginning was soon picked up and used successfully by almost every large or small department store, specialty shop, and chain operation in the country. *Seventeen Magazine* gave great emphasis to youth programs and helped refine and expand their purposes and activities. To be selected for membership on the teen board was an honor. After all, to represent one's school as the leading "fashion example" of a sharp, well-dressed young lady, was a mighty nice feather to wear in one's cap. What they learned as student members of the fashion boards, it was hoped they would take back to their classmates at school.

The College Board.   With many retailers, the College Board began as a fashion advisory board. A membership on the College Board very often meant a summer job, working in the college shop, where all the new back-to-campus clothes were shown. Besides selling, the job incorporated the role of "advisor" or guide for in-coming freshmen on their way to campuses everywhere, on what to take, how much to take, and what was to be worn for what (campus, class, dorm, social, etc.).

Along with the job in the college shop was the opportunity to participate in back-to-campus shows. This, perhaps, was the biggest attraction; here was the College Board member's chance to model. She appeared on a ramp in the young fashion departments, was seen on a stage in the auditorium, modeled in the tea room of the store, was photographed for the store's newspaper ads, and appeared on television. It was great fun and great experience. She made a little money and learned something about fashion and the retail business at the same time.

The Pre-Teen Boards.   Although not as many stores were involved in this area, many did give a try, for a time, to fashion boards for pre-teen girls. The girls learned about fashion appropriate for them, had field trips, slumber parties, contributed to civic needs (sang Christmas carols during the holiday season, delivered pumpkins to orphanages during Halloween, and gave food baskets to the poor at Thanksgiving). Their little fashion shows were usually held in the pre-teen departments, usually before Easter and back-to-school fashion periods, and they were a joy to behold, especially for their parents and grandparents.

Some of the Pre-teen Board members eventually graduated to the store's high school fashion board, and the high school members sometimes continued their association long enough to join the College Board. The entire picture was a very worthy, wholesome kind of undertaking. Everybody wanted to be a part of it. Everybody seemed to have a good time. Everybody benefited.

The Changing Scene.   No one will deny that the entire life-span of the teen fashion boards, from the middle forties through the sixties, had a remarkable record of excellence in public relations for the store, and were good training grounds for young people who excelled in interest and involvement. The record clearly shows that many a Teen Board member, getting her first taste of the retail business, decided this was the field for her. Some of the finest youth coordinators and fashion coordinators had their start in retailing in just this way—as a member of the store's fashion board.

In the late sixties, however, the scene was beginning to change and the seventies brought a new kind of young student into the picture. She was far more sophisticated. She literally preferred to go to summer school or tour Europe. There were more distractions, more demands on her time. There was evidence everywhere that she was more concerned with the real issues of the world and her environment. Her social conscience was showing. She not only knew what was going on in the world, but wanted to do something constructive about it.

The college student was becoming a deep concern to retailers—"anti-fashion." She thought less about what clothes to take to school with her than she did about what political group she would join and what social cause she would support. There was less shopping at home for the customary back-to-campus wardrobe. After all, rules about campus dress had long since fallen away. Pants-dressing for girls, once forbidden, met approval everywhere. Jeans and "grubbies," once deplored, were now applauded by both men and women students and accepted in the classroom. If she needed any clothes, she picked up things in shops where she was going to school. She felt she knew it all when it came to fashion, and what she didn't know, she made up. It was easy to do; fashion had become an original, individual thing.

The New Boards.   An awareness of what changes have taken place directs what changes should be made internally in the store's program. This is a very big part of the youth coordinator's function, because it is she who is in a good position to keep a constant finger on the pulse of the young market.

The new boards were made up of student body delegates or representatives who were no longer enchanted with doing a little fashion show, throwing a party, or holding a dance. This new group was happy to show up at board meetings at the store, if, and only if, they felt they were doing something important.

The New Programs.   The seventies brought ecology programs all over the country. The fashion boards were excited and delighted to meet and plan what to do about pollution. They went door-to-door, distributing educational literature on the pollution problem, collecting protest signatures, even appearing on the floor of their state legislature to speak out on behalf of the youth of the community about what the problem meant to future generations. Many of the letters written to soldiers in Viet Nam and prisoners of war came from fashion boards of department stores. Many made a valiant effort to see that mail reached the boys on a regular basis. They even raised money to send delegates to the Paris Peace Talks and carry their mail to the proper liaison officers abroad protesting the treatment of the prisoners of war. Many similar social programs (raising money for medical research, for the handicapped, for the underprivileged) became the work of fashion boards. They met to discuss sex, overpopulation, religion, poverty, and racism, none of which were treated with anything but the greatest concern.

Even if fashion *boards*, per se, be outmoded, fashion *programs* never will be, as long as the program fits the time and the need. Fitting the time and the need is what retailing is all about. Therefore, whatever it takes to keep abreast, to be in touch, to be of service, that is what must be done more immediately in this area—the youth area—than in any other. For, here, is where the temperature rises and falls most quickly in reaction to what is happening.

Afterview

Since presentations to management and store personnel are such a major part of the fashion director's contribution—for which she must write

Dressed in their board uniform, the High School Fashion Board of Brandeis appeared en masse at the Nebraska State Legislature, while one of their members spoke on the floor, asking for reforms to reduce pollution. (Courtesy of J. L. Brandeis, Omaha.)

directives, booklets, brochures, or releases; for which she must write an effective format, organizing and presenting reams of material in a succinct and comprehensive manner—it is advantageous for her to have an aptitude for writing, to have studied creative writing, or to have had some journalistic background. Not imperative, but helpful.

Also, because she must speak before astute and knowledgeable bodies often, including her management, personnel, the consumer, and the listening and viewing audience of the media, and because she must address groups, clubs, and audiences of all kinds interested in her views and reviews on fashion, it is most desirable that her speaking voice be pleasant and listenable. Her speaking ability should be cultivated and professional. Many a fashion director has done this by acquisition, by training, by just plain inborn talent. In any case, education in speaking techniques or voice cultivation is worth considering.

The qualities of speaking and writing are secondary, of course, to her qualities of taste, judgment, vision, and enthusiasm. With these, her influence on buying what is right for the fashion departments, and helping to sell what is right for the consumer, is undeniably vital, needed, and when executed with dependable accuracy, it is welcomed.

❊ *Chapter 6*

❊ *Covering the Market*

Everything the fashion director does is related to, affected by, and the result of how she covers the market and what she finds there.

Definition of "the Market." In retailing, "the market" is anywhere manufacturers and designers (also referred to as resources, vendors, or cutters) offer their wares for sale at wholesale, to merchants to sell in their stores at retail. For buyers the initial time to "shop the market" for a coming season is during the so-called "market week" or whenever the market opens. It is at this time of readiness that the designers and manufacturers show their proposed collections or lines from which the buyers make their selections and place orders.

While the giant retailers may cover all the domestic markets from New York, the largest and most important, to California, Los Angeles and San Francisco, many merchants may concentrate their purchases in two or three strong markets and by-pass the others. For example, all retailers may not cover the Dallas market or the Miami market, but at some time during the year, almost all of them cover the New York market. Therefore, this chapter will deal primarily with covering the New York market, a procedure that is applicable to all other markets.

The New York market, for women's ready-to-wear, is for the most part concentrated on two famous streets—Seventh Avenue and Broadway. Seventh Avenue has become

109

more than the name of a street; it is the phrase that is synonomous with American fashion. "Seventh Avenue says . . . ," or "Seventh Avenue predicts . . . ," or, as *Women's Wear Daily* reports, "SA believes . . ." Even though many outstanding designers are to be found elsewhere in America, Seventh Avenue has the image as the American authority for New York's couture, designer, and better ready-to-wear. Broadway, on the other hand, is where more of the mass or volume cutters have their showrooms.

How a Buyer Covers the Market

It is important for anyone in the fashion coordination field to understand how a buyer buys, what makes her tick, what problems she must face, before the fashion director or coordinator can establish a good rapport with the buyer and provide a good service. If communication between the fashion director and the buyer breaks down or does not exist the goals and objectives of both can be seriously impaired. It is nice for a fashion director to have a buyer's respect, but it is more important to have her cooperation.

The buyer comes into the market with a plan. It is primarily a two-sided plan—how much to spend and how much to select in each classification. Naturally, the system the buyer follows to formulate a buying plan differs with the type of operation, chain, specialty, or department store. But as a guideline the market plan of a buyer of women's better dresses in a department store would be indicative of how a fashion buyer works.

How a Buyer Draws Up a Market Plan. "Forget the past," may be a nice philosophy for anyone wishing to get off to a fresh start or a better life, but the past, as far as a department's sales performance is concerned, is what every buyer has to live with.

Before the buyer makes the first scratch on the proposed buying plan, she must check her open-to-buy, stock condition and sales performance of the comparable period last year. Guided by this past of units and dollars only, the buyer sets down what she expects to buy. Classifications such as street dresses, ensembles, social occasion dresses, daytime pant-dressings, dressy pant-dressings, etc., are different every season. Some classifications are strengthened, some shortened, some added, and some completely eliminated. The decision of what the new classifications will be depends on the new trends, those undoubtedly predicted and recommended by the fashion director. Each classification is identified by a special number, and each number awarded a certain number of dollars. The total of all the classifications makes up the amount the buyer feels she must spend to fill the stock requirements of her department or departments for a given period.

Let us assume the buyer is going into market in February. At this time she will spend March and April money—possibly seventy-five percent of March, and fifty percent of April, holding back enough for expected reorders and new developments. It would be sad, indeed, for any fashion department, if something hot or new showed up, and there was no money left to cover it.

However, before the buyer gets the money, so to speak, the plan must be submitted to her divisional merchandise manager for consideration. It is very likely that the DMM will take her plan and all the other buyers' plans in his division to the general merchandise manager for approval. When the buyer's plan is approved, the DMM gives her the go-ahead, and she is off to the market.

A Day in the Market.   If the fashion buyer is with a department store that is associated with a resident buying office in New York, she undoubtedly meets with the merchandise representative (MR) of her area before doing anything. The resident MR is a specialist. She knows her buyer's area thoroughly; she also knows the buyer's store and its needs. Therefore, she is in a position to say to the buyer:

"I feel you should drop resource X this season; it is not looking good and they are overpriced. I feel, on the other hand, you should take a look at resource W which is new and catching on very well. So-and-so is doing very well with them and they are a store like yours."

Both the buyer and the fashion director can take advice like this, check it out and decide if it applies to their store, their customer.

Next, the buyer probably sits down at the telephone and starts calling to make appointments for showings of all the manufacturers or resources on her list, both those with whom she has been doing business and those she wishes to check out as possible new resources. She calls the Oscar de la Renta showroom. She identifies herself by name and store. If she is going to attend the showing alone she reserves one seat. Next, she calls Donald Brooks, Bill Blass, Dior-New York, Geoffrey Beene, Chester

Weinberg, and many, many more. The appointment book is filled. Showings are booked at least an hour or an hour and a half apart (most shows last about forty-five minutes, but seldom start on time) leaving only enough time for lunch (sometimes) or more phone calls. She is on Seventh Avenue from early morning until the market closes, about five o'clock P.M.

During each show, while carefully scrutinizing each model, she makes good notes so that when she goes back later—if she is interested enough to go back—she will remember the pieces she would like to consider.

Writing Orders.   Viewing the collections in formal shows and reviewing lines in a showroom is only the beginning for the fashion buyer. Now the real work begins. Another round of telephone calls. The buyer calls back to the resource whose show she has seen and liked well enough to consider buying some pieces. Again, when she calls, she identifies herself by name and store. "I would like to make an appointment to write," she says. "Eleven tomorrow morning? Fine. Thank you." When she arrives the next morning at the showroom, she is seated behind a desk, well supplied with order pads, pencils, and is offered a cup of coffee. The representative or salesman with whom she works, after making sure the buyer is comfortable, brings over the racks of clothes to be reviewed and considered.

The buyer may wish to look at the entire collection once more before making any final decision if she is planning on buying in depth, or she may wish to look at only those numbers she noted on her program during the show. When shopping the better houses, it is not likely that there will be much "in-depth" buying. At the urging of the fashion director, or a decision of the DMM, she is more likely to select only the choice pieces of many manufacturers, thus giving her department a more "item" look. The customer can then enjoy greater selection with less duplication.

Leaving Paper.   As those pieces she requests, or those recommended by the salesman, are presented for review, she may write on her order pad the color, size, and number of pieces of each style number she might buy. After she has reviewed and written the line, she may do one of two things. She may sign the order blank made in duplicate, rip it off (keeping one copy for herself), and hand it to the salesman, thus fulfilling what all manufacturers love and prefer—the business of "leaving paper." Leaving paper means to leave the order on the spot. Many buyers, however, may take the order away with them, either to reconsider their selections as compared with other selections in other houses, or to submit the order, along with all others she plans to place, to her divisional merchandise manager to approve and sign.

Whether the order is left on the spot or mailed in later, the amount of paper the manufacturer receives on a certain number determines whether or not it will be "cut." In other words, if a particular creation does not stimulate enough interest from all the buyers who have seen it, it will be eliminated from the line completely and not be put into production. That is why sometimes after a buyer has gone home, she will be advised by a manufacturer that a number or two she has ordered will not be available. The success or failure of a style number in a line, or of the entire line for that matter, depends on the buyers who leave paper.

The paper work a buyer must do in order to expedite her responsibilities is considerable. Many evenings, after covering the market all day, are spent in a hotel room writing orders, rewriting orders, reviewing notes, and changing decisions. All of this is part of making sure her department or departments are covered as planned.

How the Fashion Director Covers the Market

To a buyer, covering the market means *her* market or *his* market. For example, to the shoe buyer it is the shoe market; to the hosiery buyer, the hosiery market; to the junior buyer, the junior market; to the coat buyer, the coat market. Each covers his or her own market, and that market only.

When a fashion director covers the market, it is a different story. She is not only interested in each buyer's market individually, but in all of them collectively. It is only by seeing the entire fashion picture, piece by piece, department by department, and then put together, that she is able to interpret the strength and direction of coming fashion trends. Differing from the buyer, the fashion director does not come into the market with a buying plan; she comes in with a routine.

Before the Market.   Before the buyers come, before the market opens, before she is able to make recommendations to her management and the store's merchandising staff, the fashion director begins with research (see Chapter 1) on the stuff of which fashion is made—fabrics. She not only discovers in the fabric market what important fabrics are available, but learns what designers are selecting.

Designers go into the fabric market, to see what is being produced—colors, textures, fibers, treatments, and weights. They want to know about performance of a new fabric, perhaps get a pattern confined and, therefore, get an inspiration from the goods with which they will work. How it can be manipulated, combined, and disciplined, very often influences a designing trend.

The fashion coordinator, or director, is very much like a reporter out to uncover a story. She follows the line of action. She traces the story line back to its source. Thus her routine is formulated.

The Routine of Appointments. Like the buyer, the fashion director lines up appointments, by mail or telephone, identifying herself by name, title, and store. Wherever possible, not knowing in advance how much time will be necessary to cover each source, she leaves enough time between appointments to avoid overlapping or arriving late. It is also helpful if appointments in one building or area are made consecutively; much time is lost in travel between addresses.

Time is a valuable commodity, not only for the visiting fashion director, but for all those people who are making space on their calendar to see her. A respect for the time of those granting the interview is a must; it is best to be a little early and wait. If an unavoidable conflict arises, the original appointment must be notified as soon as possible and a new time set up. To make an appointment and not appear, regardless of how justifiable, is unforgivable. Next time, that door may not be opened as readily. Since a fashion director can use all the help she can get, diplomacy, good manners, and expressed gratitude for all aid extended (even if it is their job to do so) is not only good business, but will make her next trip to the same source more pleasant and more valuable.

The First Stop. Before the fabrics comes the fibers that go into the fabrics. Therefore, to track down clue number one, she calls on giants like DuPont, Celanese, and Monsanto as well as other fiber people whose research experts have done an amazing job of anticipating way ahead what will be in demand or what will be accepted. The fashion director asks them first "what's new." The fiber authority may take the fashion director into a fabric room stocked with swatches, panels, and books of "what's new." She will also learn what is getting the action, what the mills are producing, and what the cutters are buying. From this area she will get a clue or indication of several things:

A new fiber appearing on the market
A new color projection
A new texture
A new weight

The people at DuPont, Celanese, Monsanto, or wherever might tip her off as to where they discovered a certain color or texture. Perhaps it came from a brick color of a castle in Spain or a men's shirt fabric in a Florentine boutique, great ideas to copy for women.

Things worth noting are beginning to show up—new trends, a strong comeback of an old trend, a repetition of a currently established trend. Conclusion: if everybody has caught on to these trends and is incorporating their new treatments, new colors, new textures, and new weights, there must be something going on indicative in the fashion designer's studio and in the manufacturer's cutting room. At this point, however, no de-

Buyers and fashion directors take notes at a preview showing at Du Pont of knitwear in Du Pont fibers. (Courtesy of Du Pont.)

cisions are made by the fashion director, nor is she permitting herself to jump to any conclusions. She has hardly seen or heard enough to evaluate the picture, but she has a strong indication of what to watch for.

The Second Stop.   Her next stop will be to an assortment of fabric people. What the mills are making is all important. If major mills are producing a certain fabric in huge volume, it is very likely they have good reason to believe in it and/or the cutters are buying it. Heavy purchases of an item by manufacturers is a most dependable clue.

Indicated earlier in this text was an example in which the fashion director learned from one mill that the demand for denim was so great it appeared as though there would be a shortage. Another season panne velvet caught on so well, suppliers ran out of the velvet before the manufacturers could fill their orders.

The fashion director does not ignore the lesser trends, those that look big or good, even if they are not giants. It takes more than one fabric, one color, and one look to make a season or fill a store.

The Chains.   In addition to working with stores or store groups, the fabric producers (the mills) work very closely with the chains. Very early, the fabric people make presentations to the fashion departments and merchandising executives of the chains. An exchange of ideas takes place. The chains learn what the mills can and will do, what they believe in and why. On the other hand, the fashion department of the mills learns what the chains feel strongly about, what direction they might take, and what specifics they might like developed. What such giant retailers regard as important is always worth noting.

Leather Sources.   Leather producers also work far in advance of seasons, carefully evaluating colors, textures, and marketing possibilities. Will total garments, in addition to coats and shoes, be expressed in leather? What about accessories? What new combinations will be acceptable? Here again, it is imperative to check and see if the designers are including new uses or new expressions of leather. In which way? To what degree?

Designers Come Next.   Good contacts among good designers can be invaluable. Even though they may not be in a position to reveal everything about a collection, they might agree to give you a glimpse or a feeling

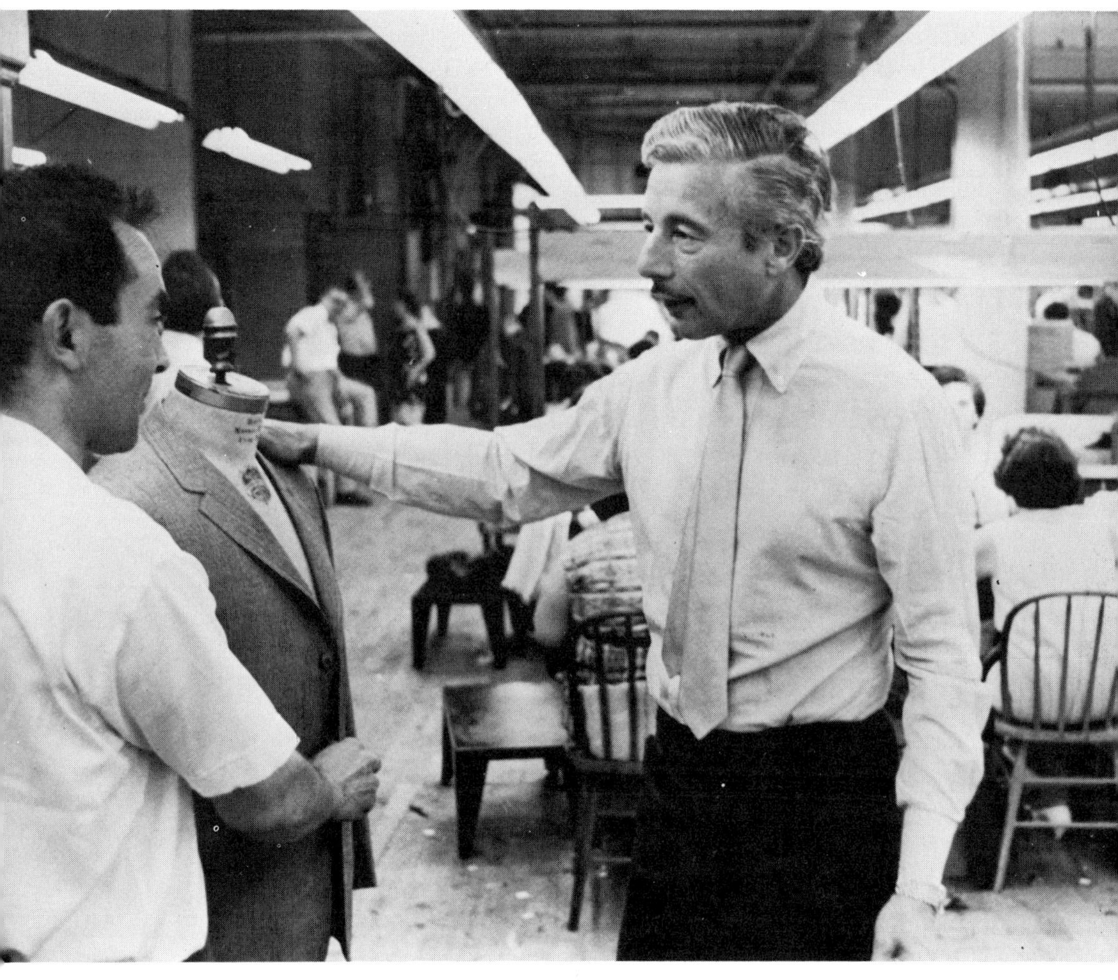

In addition to talking with important designers, it is helpful to visit
a cutting room for a better understanding of what takes place. Oleg
Cassini consulting on the fit of a piece in his line. (Courtesy of
Oleg Cassini.)

about what trends look promising. "Almost all of my new collection
will be soft. All fabrics will be manipulated into soft lines; the fabrics
themselves will be soft in texture, soft in color," one designer might
confide to a visiting fashion director. He may express thoughts about
which silhouettes he has faith in and which he feels are not good or not
for his market. The fashion director, as part of her routine, makes good
notes of all she sees and hears. She is getting the picture.

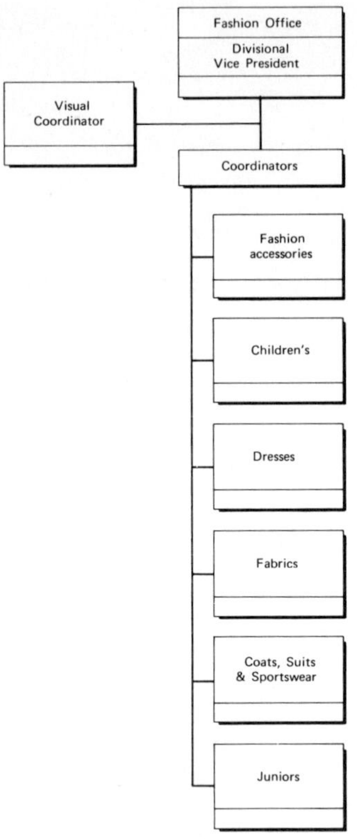

The fashion office structure of Associated Merchandising Corporation. Fashion directors of member stores may receive advice and guidance from these fashion office coordinators.

Consultations with the Buying Office. If a store belongs to a buying office that provides its members with good predictive information, the fashion director is greatly aided. The staff fashion director of a resident buying office in New York has had the market thoroughly researched and is in a position to advise fashion people from member stores about their findings. This advice may be shared in personal conference with the individual fashion director or in a group meeting. Group meetings, designed especially for fashion directors to carry back to their management, usually are held semiannually; one for predicting spring and summer, one for fall and winter. Predictive information from the fashion department of a resident buying office is made available to member fashion directors far in advance of the market openings, approximately three or four months ahead.

Perhaps the most complete fashion office of any buying group at this time is the Associated Merchandising Corporation (AMC). The fashion office of AMC, for women's and children's apparel, intimate apparel, and fashion accessories includes six fashion coordinators, each responsible for a separate fashion area and reporting to a fashion director (divisional vice president).

In the semiannual predictive fashion directors' meetings, each AMC coordinator presents her findings and evaluations of her specific market area. The stores' fashion directors attending the meetings, who see at least eight or nine different fashion presentations (separately covering fabrics and colors, sportswear, dresses, coats and suits, juniors, children's, intimate apparel, shoes, and fashion accessories) have an opportunity to see how the coming season might shape up. These predictive presentations are made with the aid of sketched illustrations of actual merchandise, fabric and color samples, live models wearing samples from influencial designers, guest speakers from the industry, and individual evaluations of each classification by the fashion coordinator responsible for it.

The Composite.   At this point, the fashion director, in her effort to get valid advanced information about a coming season, has interviewed leather sources, fiber companies, fabric mills, designers, and attended meetings and conferences with fashion people in a resident buying office. Each area and each interview has provided her with another piece of information, another point of view, relating to coming fashion trends. Still her work is not finished.

Look and Listen.   Along with a good, sturdy pair of legs for the endless work of calling on, tracking down, and chasing after anyone who has new and reliable fashion information, the fashion director also needs a good pair of eyes.

Reading reams of printed information, predicting, forecasting, and revealing what's to come, helps supplement other information or add impetus to those clues that have surfaced thus far. A fashion director is wise to have such subscriptions of material as *Women's Wear Daily* sent directly to her home. She is likely to find there is more time for leisure reading away from the office interruptions and busy phones, a better chance to concentrate and reflect on the steady flow of material.

Talking with other fashion directors, magazine editors, merchandisers, buyers, and anyone related to the fashion business provides a fashion person on a hunt with an undeniable "feel" for what is in the air.

Also, it is very important for her to talk with the big cutters. If the big fellows are putting big money on a trend by "putting the knife to it" (that is, actually cutting the numbers) she will get closer to what is actually happening.

Shopping, another aspect of the leg work, helps to enlighten and educate the visiting fashion director. New York, or wherever market trips are made, provides examples of good merchandising in the local stores. Boutiques, too—elegant, unique, kicky—provide excellent indications of trends in taste. Shopping uptown, downtown, on the Avenue, in the Village, and in out-of-the-way places, provides new clues and new inspirations. It is the composite of all this activity that adds to the validity of a fashion director's recommendations.

How to Work with the Buyer in the Market

Everything the fashion director learned before market she has shared with her management and merchandising staff before they all go off to market. All of this she documented and presented in her predictive presentation, and, so, with the sanction of management, everyone is off to buy according to plan.

When the fashion director accompanies the buyer to showings during market the buyer calls to make reservations for seats. "I would like to reserve two seats at a showing of your new collection," she will say when calling a designer, "one for our fashion director and one for myself."

The Show Begins.   At each show, the buyer and fashion director take notes on impressive features and numbers of possible purchases. "Number 1412," the designer or showroom representative announces as a model enters the showroom filled with buyers, fashion directors, merchandise managers, and store presidents. The announcer will repeat the number, sometimes identifying it with the amount of the wholesale price. On occasion, there is no announcer at all and the model may announce the number of the garment she is wearing. There is rarely any description other than that provided on a printed program, and even that is seldom.

Retailers review the Bill Blass collection during a New York market showing. (Courtesy Eleanor Lambert, Inc.)

Sometimes a designer will appear to greet the audience, make an opening comment or two, and then disappear. Sometimes the designer will be called to take a bow at the end of the showing.

The showings are usually fairly long; the models move quickly in and out to a background of appropriate music. The professional people watching soon get the message of what the designer is trying to say. Since most buyers buy by items, rather than entire collections, especially in the better markets, the notes they make are to identify, for later reference, those pieces they feel will fit into their fashion departments. By choosing only items, the buyer gets the choice pieces from every collection, those best suited to her department's customer, and also builds a stock that has greater versatility and better selection. If the buyer's notes include many numbers, it is a good sign she has a strong interest in the collection. If she has noted only a couple, she may consider it unsalable or unsuited to her needs.

If the buyer and the fashion director are sitting next to each other during the show, they may compare notes, exchange opinions, and express ideas. Perhaps they are sitting at opposite ends of the room because of a seating problem (shows are very often overcrowded). It is also possible that, due to conflicting schedules, the buyer and fashion director do not attend the same performance of a showing. In the latter case, they might compare notes at a later time during the day after all the showings have been completed, but almost always before they return home.

Showroom Presentations.   Not all lines are viewed in formal shows. Many are viewed on racks in the manufacturer's showroom one piece at a time, presented for consideration by a showroom representative or salesman. Occasionally, a piece from the group will be shown informally on a live model. The buyer may feel she cannot judge the line of a certain garment on the hanger and request it shown on a live model.

When accompanying a buyer at a show or showroom, the fashion director takes her own notes and is wise to sit quietly while the buyer does her work. She does not interrupt or contradict an opinion or conversation the buyer and showroom representative may be having.

Why the Fashion Director is There.   When accompanying a buyer, the fashion director keeps a watchful eye on what she is seeing and hearing, always remembering why she is there. It must be reiterated that the buyer is seeing the market from her vantage point only, but the fashion director is seeing it total store. Because of the fashion director's premarket presentation, the store has decided upon certain trends in which they believe, and the fashion director is here to see that merchandise is being selected to back them up. She is also on hand to select from the lines she sees, certain provocative pieces that are great examples of a trend and that will lend drama or excitement for windows, displays, and fashion shows she has planned to help sell it.

"I'd love to have that for a fashion show," she might say to the buyer during a showing.

"Then you should buy this group of three pieces," the showroom representative might suggest. "It would make a great window."

The buyer and the fashion director might or might not agree. They sometimes do buy a group for display or window illustration, but they also might select separate pieces from separate lines to do a better job of telling their fashion story.

The fashion director is also on hand as advisor. A buyer may be undecided about certain pieces or about an entire collection. She may, after viewing a line, turn to the fashion director and ask, "Does this group have the look you were talking about?"

"Frankly, I do not feel that they are doing the new look as well as some other houses. Also, I feel they are overpriced."

"I am inclined to agree. What's the alternative?"

"I ran across a new resource that might just fill the bill. Would you like to look at it?" the fashion director might suggest.

The discovery of a new resource might come from any number of directions; from the resident buying office, or from other fashion directors who have seen the line, and report, "If you haven't seen this line you should. We might even open a special shop featuring this collection. It is that good." A new resource might be one that the buyer formerly was familiar with, one that went out of business and reopened under a new label. She knows his workmanship. She knows his reputation.

"Let's take a look." They call for an appointment. It may prove to be the greatest line yet; it may prove to be completely unsuitable for their needs. However, if the fashion director has done her homework well, she will not recommend any buyer to sacrifice valuable time to look at a line that would not be suitable for their store. First on her list of evaluation would be, "Is it right for us?" The fashion director is a merchant. She is interested in seeing buyers and departments involved with merchandise that is right and salable. She is careful to keep herself out of it, to regulate her own personal tastes and prejudices. Her personal likes and dislikes don't count. When working with buyers in the market, the fashion director keeps her eye on the fashion objectives.

The Fashion Director's Objectives in the Market

1. To be sure enough good fashion items are being selected to cover the new fashion stories.
2. To watch for good coverage to back up the promotions planned.
3. To see the right kind of merchandise is selected for windows, displays, and fashion shows.

In addition to the above, if a new trend, a sleeper, or a hot item seems to be showing up, the fashion director must check it out (as she has other trends) and immediately advise merchandisers and buyers of its importance. She must, if her conviction is strong, urge the buyer or buyers to include the new item. She would be wise, of course, to advise the DMM and/or GMM also, in case additional money or change of plan is involved.

Covering the Import Markets. Just as New York was used in this text as an example of covering the domestic market, the European market will be the example for the import fashion market. The procedure is applicable to most other foreign markets.

Similar to New York, the couture market in Europe opens ahead of the ready-to-wear market. In Europe, the couture collections are introduced in January and July, the prêt-à-porter (ready-to-wear) in April and October.

In addition to viewing the collections abroad, it is helpful to talk directly to important designers. The author with Pierre Cardin in Paris.

At the outset of the seventies, the haute couture of Europe (primarily Paris) failed to give the fashion direction for which it has always been famous, for which it has always held leadership. Throughout our modern experience with fashion, leadership and direction has always migrated from the top, the haute couture. But the sixties started a new influence, from the bottom—the Village in New York, communes in San Francisco, Kings Road in London, the Left Bank in Paris, and boutiques in Copenhagen. Influence came, in fact, from everywhere, anywhere, on almost any street, except where fashion had always been born and bred, Paris and the other fashion capitals of the world.

The European fashion leaders, instead of being creative, began to get their inspiration from the same places—the streets, the discoteques, and the scattered communities of rebellious youth. Thus, the looks that started out as put-ons, or antiestablishment were picked up by the so-called fashion establishment, endorsed, sanctioned, and glorified.

It was in such a climate, together with the grave issues of the day (Vietnamese War, racial issues, pollution, overpopulation, inflation), that created an antistatus atmosphere. It was a climate that turned people away from any extravagant display of "show." Even with those who could afford it, that which was extremely expensive in fashion seemed unnecessary. Fashion dictation from the European haute couture, therefore, seemed to have another strike against it. And, since little direction was offered, little direction was taken. In addition to this, the life style of the people had changed, and there was no longer the same need for couture leadership.

The prêt-â-porter showings, on the other hand, held more interest. They were ready to compete with Seventh Avenue, and Seventh Avenue (strongly dependent upon inspiration from European couture) was challenged to come up with originality of its own. Thus was the flavor of fashion direction at the beginning of the seventies. The growing importance of the prêt-â-porter market of Europe merits attention on these pages.

However, this trend in no way indicates that the haute couture is to be overlooked. Never. Smart fashion researchers overlook nothing. Fashion being what it is, the entire power structure could turn around tomorrow. Couture on top again. New designers on top. Those who have dropped down, pulling up. New reasons, new life styles, and new needs.

European Travel Schedule.   Travel plans are guided by the dates of the prêt-à-porter openings. Usually Paris takes the lead, setting its dates first, then the others plan accordingly. When the schedule comes through, it might include:

Florence—April 8 to April 12
Paris—April 14 to April 18

The first stop, then, is Florence. Unlike the showing of collections in New York, viewed one at a time in the designer's own showroom, as many as sixty or more collections may be seen at one place, the "Sala Bianca" of the Pitti Palace.

When the buyer and fashion director arrive at the Pitti Palace, they find it to be exactly that, a palace, an ancient palazzo converted into commercial use. Although surrounded with automobiles, the long walk up three flights of wide marble steps (attended by beautifully costumed "guards"), reassures visitors they are indeed in a palace. In the foyer of the salon, where the shows are held, juice, rolls, and coffee are served to guests waiting for the doors to open. When entrance is permitted, each guest must take the seat assigned to her. Every seat is reserved. The shows are presented with style in the Sala Bianca, a white salon with crystal chandeliers. The physical setup is excellent, an extremely wide ramp-stage extending through the center of the room, with viewers seated on three sides. The rows are tiered so everyone can see perfectly.

Brought to Florence for the showings are Italy's leading high fashion houses, boutiques, and high-fashion knitwear collections. The visiting buyers and fashion directors follow the procedure from printed programs and from announcements made by the commentator, both of which are very brief. The commentator merely reveals the collection by name: "The collection of Princess Irene Galitzine." And, then, as each model appears, the commentator reveals the number of the piece in three languages, French, Italian, and English. When the Galitzine collection is over, it is immediately followed by another collection. Where it applies, the announcer will also tell the audience what designer furnished the shoes or other accessories for the collections. "Makeup by Helene Rubenstein," she will say.

The work has just begun. Part of the time is spent at the Pitti Palace for the shows and part is spent at the Strozzi Palace where floor after floor is filled with showrooms of Italian designers. Here the buyers may view at close range the pieces that are of interest, see additional pieces modeled by a showroom model, and discuss price, and expected date of shipment.

When shopping an import market, price must be very carefully noted. There is, first of all, FC or First Cost (the wholesale price of the garment). Then there is LC or Landed Cost (what the garment will cost shipped to our shores). The total cost of bringing a garment into the store must be considered. Next comes the store's markup. If the retail price justifies the the purchase, it is worth the trip.

In addition to viewing the collections at the Pitti Palace and reviewing the lines at Palazzo Strozzi, the fashion director gathers additional information and inspiration from the community. She visits the boutiques, searching for special boutique items that will be exclusive and unique. She carefully notes how the women of Florence dress, in fact, every city she visits will be excellent ground for research on what women of the world are wearing for what occasion and how they are putting it together. Once again, the fashion director becomes an observer, a reporter. What she sees she reports to the buyer and to her management back home.

The Next Stop, Paris. Prêt-à-porter is the French phrase for ready-to-wear and the French collections are paraded for American merchants at Porte de Versailles. In addition to selecting merchandise, it cannot be overlooked that a trip abroad is a tour for inspiration and education.

When collections are viewed in the salons of the individual designers in Paris (Saint Laurent, Cardin, Dior, Ungaro, Ricci, Givenchy, Patou), the presentations are not too unlike those presented in New York. Buyers seated on straight chairs in every available nook and corner, usually spread over more than one room, view the interpretation of a fashion season by the great names. Music is in the background. Models carry the number of their costume, or an announcer calls the number aloud in French and English.

After all the collections are seen and lines reviewed, the decision of what to buy follows the same pattern. Do we have the customer for this look? Will the customer pay this price? Is it in keeping with our fashion image?

Again, shopping the boutiques in Paris (the fashion world's greatest), observing what the people wear, where they wear it, and how they put it together is extremely valuable to the fashion director. She must come

Christian Dior

prie M ....

de lui faire l'honneur d'assister à la présentation

de sa nouvelle collection à partir

du ....

Il lui demande d'avoir l'obligeance d'indiquer
la date qui lui conviendrait, soit par téléphone, soit
en lui retournant le talon ci-contre.

30, Avenue Montaigne
Elysées 93-64

Vendeuse. ....

Voir au verso une précision importante

A sample invitation admittance card to a showing of a Christian Dior collection in Paris.

home and interpret the new fashion looks and their treatment for management and for the customer in shows, displays, windows, and advertising.

The Fashion Team. Teamwork, exemplified through relating to the efforts of each, is essential to the effectiveness of the buyer-fashion director relationship. In some organizations a buyer is rated on his or her ability to use the fashion director. The buyer is way ahead who understands that the fashion director's goals and her goals are one and the same—to select merchandise the customer wants, to keep the cash register ringing, and to make a profit. The fashion director, on the other hand, needs to understand the road the buyer must travel to arrive where they are both going. The buyer is faced with space problems, open-to-buy limitations, goals for growth, pressures to make figures, concerns over deliveries, personnel problems, and customer acceptance, to name a few. The fashion director can read vibrations and anticipate trouble spots by asking questions relating to those trouble spots, and working closely with the buyer on specific plans and promotions. A little personal attention indicates sincere sympathy with the buyer's efforts.

For example, a strong trend of zodiac and astrology prints and patterns are turning up on a number of important silhouettes, many done by leading designers. In her eagerness to see the buyer have a good season, the fashion director might say; "You represent a strong fashion authority with your department, and I would love to see you be first with the exciting impact of this trend. What do you think of the idea of flying in a few pieces of zodiac-printed fashions, including some of Pierre Cardin's 'wear-your-own-astrological-sign' creations. We can banner the ads, the signing in your department, a window, and perhaps even do a capsule show in the department on 'you were born for beautiful fashion' or 'your fashion future.' What do you think?"

The buyer likes the idea. She agrees. She has been inspired by the fashion director to promote a trend or look, a new attention-getting item. She will now depend, almost entirely, on the fashion director's enthusiasm and initiative to follow through on the proposed promotional idea to make it work. A good fashion director can be worth her weight in gold to a receptive, fashion-minded buyer. The buyer who knows how to use a fashion director, has a huge plus in her corner.

Afterview

More than any other time in the history of retailing, buyers are extremely busy people. They have many more tracks to cover than ever before. Besides the initial duties of buying merchandise and supervising the operation and personnel of their departments, they have many more branches to visit, cover, and protect. The more branches, outposts, specialty shops, twigs, and whatever, the more paper work and, of course, responsibility. These busy people need help.

With trends firing in and out, up and down, it is vital to the lifeblood of her area to call upon the fashion director for advice and guidance to help her select the most effective merchandise, and help her get the fashion message over to the customer and the department's personnel. Also, the fashion director, keeping on top of all trends, knowing when they have peaked, supplies a much-needed service to the buyer.

The fashion director, if she is one who can look and really see, listen and really hear, will be unafraid to take a position on that in which she believes. She must urge her management to recognize what is needed. If she must push hard to convince the skeptical or the unseeing, then she must. If it is an important fashion issue, she is duty bound to see that her management or the buyer in question understands it is important. If the fashion director sees the goal as attainable and profitable, and if customer interest is indicated, she may have to fight the buyer for the sake of the consumer. The customer comes first. To take a position with conviction takes courage, but it helps make the store authoritative.

On the other hand, if the fashion director is new with a store, or new in the job, she is wise to permit a good buyer to be her teacher in many things, how to cover the market, what to look for, etc. Many a fashion director making her first trip abroad, has some generous buyer or merchandiser to thank for showing her the ropes. The best way she can repay the buyer is to learn her lesson well and some day give her the assistance she will need to make a good fashion department better.

Chapter 7

❀ *Sources of Advanced Fashion Information*

A fashion director has a world of unseen friends. They are scattered everywhere. Some she knows personally, some she never meets. Nevertheless, she receives constant communications from all these friends, who are dedicated to helping her keep on top of every aspect of current or coming fashion trends.

These remarkable fountains of valuable information flow from such sources as national fashion magazines, trade publications, fiber companies, fabric institutes, leather industry, and cosmetic industry, most of which are unsolicited but generously dependable. Also, indispensable information flows from resident buying offices with which a store is associated, from fashion consultants whose services the store employes, and from organizations of the industry to which one may enlist membership, such as the Fashion Group, National Retail Merchants Association (NRMA), etc. With a little help from friends such as these, in addition to her own organized scratching, there is very little that should escape the perceptive fashion director.

Resident Buying Offices

Why Stores Belong.   In a business that is as highly diversified and fast moving as is retailing, memberhsip in an effective buying office is a must for the progressive merchant. While the services and purposes of a resident buying office are many, the most universal advantages include:

1. An opportunity for all member stores to exchange information. Ideas, experiences, and plans can be shared.
2. An opportunity to share figures. A chance to learn what items or trends are doing well in other stores.
3. A place to receive up-to-the-minute information on market research from people who are constantly on the scene.
4. A way to save buyers endless leg work. The buying office staff, through advanced market research might tell a sportswear buyer, "Out of these hundreds of sportswear resources, this group is not for you, but these you must visit."
5. A system of keeping pace with departmental structures which are subject to revisions due to the changing fashion scene.

The sharing of ideas, plans, and figures is not a problem with stores regarding competition within a buying office membership, because each buying group represents only one store per city.

Types of Buying Offices.   Actually, there are three major types of buying offices.

1. *Cooperative*—Member stores share ownership and own stock (i.e. Frederick Atkins, Inc., Associated Merchandising Corporation).
2. *Fee*—Member stores pay a fee for membership, based on the volume of the store and services rendered (i.e. Mutual Buying Syndicate, Inc., Arkwright, Inc., Felix Lilienthal & Co., Inc.).
3. *Chains*—Chain stores own and maintain their own buying offices (i.e. Allied Stores, Associated Dry Goods, May Department Stores, Macy's Corporate Buying Division, Gimbel Bros., Sears Roebuck & Co., J. C. Penney & Co., and Montgomery Ward & Co.).

Some buying offices maintain facilities on the east coast as well as New York, and some stores belong to a west coast office to take care of their needs at that end. In fact, west coast buying offices such as Harry and

Sidney Arkin, and Davidson, also act as California offices for other buying offices (i.e. members of Frederick Atkins, New York, would use Arkin, California).

A top source of fashion information should be constantly available from the fashion department of a resident buying office. A unique and excellent example of a most comprehensive setup for such service to the fashion directors of member stores, is the Associated Merchandising Corporation.

AMC's fashion office, complete with a fashion director and divisional fashion coordinators working in concert with the merchandising staff of AMC, provides all of its stores' fashion directors with up-to-the-minute fashion information. AMC's philosophy is that disclosure of all fashion information to the store's merchandising and executive staff "should go, initially, through the store's fashion director so that she may decide, along with her merchandisers, what part of the fashion message will be emphasized to the customer. Any predictive ideas that may initiate with the merchandisers, need to get screened through the fashion office, where the decision will be made, in general agreement with the merchandising staff, as to the AMC position on news in fashion and the timing of its release."

Realizing that such responsibility must be fortified with accurate fashion information, a network of authorative guidelines is provided. It is on the basis of this system that the AMC fashion office provides, immediately and in explicit detail, those vital guidelines for fashion leadership. Such guidelines come in the following forms:

Fabric Book—Issued semiannually. Forecast for spring/summer and fall/winter. Includes swatches of complete fabric market in terms of important color families, patterns, prints, and classified textures.

Advanced Colors—Issued semiannually. Forecast for spring/summer and fall/winter. Colors presented in categories by hue and new color combinations.

Advanced Leathers—Issued semiannually. Same as colors.

Holiday Color Report—Issued annually. This area needs specific treatment insofar as it differs from the other fashion seasons.

In addition to these, other published material comes semiannually in the form of a Paris Report, a Europe Report, and a report on American fashions (as a seasonal forecast), all supplemented and kept up to date with weekly development reports on all fashion trends in all areas.

In the New York office, where the AMC fashion office headquarters are located, a Fabric and Fashion Library is maintained so that a store's fashion director may study and review pertinent fashion information. If further guidance is needed, the AMC fashion director or any of the divisional fashion coordinators are available by appointment for consultation.

All resident buying offices, whether they service independent stores or store groups or chains, work through their own system. Their purpose, however, is relatively the same—to provide their stores with advanced guidance for their activity in the market. Since the fashion office of a store is responsible for the evaluation and interpretation of the facts provided, she can never be exposed to too many facts from too many sources. It is the composite of them all that help her function accurately.

Fashion Consultants

Not all stores subscribe to the services of fashion consultant firms. They feel capable of doing their own research of trends, or depending on the combination of their own fashion office and that of a resident buying office. However, those who do subscribe might use such reports as religious authority or as supplementary information.

Reports from fashion consultants, if they are used as supplementary material by the fashion director, can provide another viewpoint or a different opinion. A fashion director is wise to keep an open mind. It may be just the viewpoint that is "different" that uncovers a sleeper.

The fashion consultant firm usually has a staff of fashion coordinators who give their full attention to a specific area in the same way that fashion coordinators' in a buying office work or the area fashion coordinator of a store operates. Each covers a specific market, and feeds back the information necessary to make up the report. The fashion consultant is especially effective in dealing with specifics concerning a particular store. "This item is a natural for you." "This is not your cup of tea." "This is the way to go to provide the best results for your type store."

Confidential, Please.   The material provided in reports from any service, is regarded as highly confidential. Subscribers, after all, are paying for an information service to help them obtain fashion leadership. If it is shared with anyone who is not directly responsible for its utilization, its purpose is not served. One is not in the business of educating or training one's competition.

The fashion director carefully reads the reports from the fashion consultant. She might consult with her management on certain points to obtain their reactions and compare them with her own. "This bears careful watching," they might all decide. In such a case or, in fact, in all cases of fact finding, she will keep a sharp lookout for other references in this connection and check out everything she finds on that specific area. That, in essence, is the beauty of all the pieces of advice that come across her desk. It helps her decide: "Is the idea just a fluke? Or is the smart money really gung-ho on it?"

Fiber Companies—Fabric Companies

Very early on the scene, usually six or eight months ahead of a forthcoming season, the fiber companies announce their predictions. The fiber people release their findings sometimes a year in advance, but most fashion directors find the six-month forecast of more immediate use. The chain stores, however, along with buying offices, consultant firms, designers, mills, and converters must have predictive information much earlier. However, if a particular specialty or department store is planning on confining a special pattern or print as "our very own," it is imperative to work much further ahead. In such a case, the fashion director, along with the buyer, will be greatly involved in the research and selection of what that confined fabric look will be.

Color Cards. If advance color information is a vital issue for a long-range projected promotion or special event, the fiber and fabric people are good early sources. It may be necessary to know a year in advance if yellow will be good, and, if so, what shade of yellow will be the best choice. A review of the fiber and fabric color cards, leather chips, and predictive information from sources such as the National Cotton Council or American Wool Council, would turn up some pretty reliable suggestions.

Whether a year in advance or six months in advance, all the color cards and releases come up with a rainbow of new and impressive names, even for standard colors. A brick color becomes Spanish Tile, Red Fox, or Hot Ginger. A blue becomes Ink, Blue Persian, or Blue Night. When the brick or the blue has a new hue that is a bit different from a season or two ago, it must also have a new name. It is all part of its "image." Some very good suggestions of what to call a new color come from releases of the leading fiber and fabric producers.

Mademoiselle Magazine once editorially identified a new color which combined tones of brown and green as "Breen." Manufacturers and retailers who had been at a loss as to what to call the new color that was neither green nor brown, picked up the inspired idea of *Mademoiselle Magazine* and used "Breen" extensively in their promotions.

The Fabric Books.   Swatches of every conceivable fabric anticipated in the fashion market come in fabric booklets or charts from the fiber and fabric sources. Again, these are usually unsolicited and provided at no charge. The fabrics are identified as to trend, texture, and use. For example, a page on sheers with swatches showing examples of chiffons, voiles, batistes, and silks, might be classified as the new "soft trend." A page might be classified as the "new nubbies," with swatches illustrating these new textures. And, as examples of uses of the fabrics, pages or groupings might point up "the new skirtings," "the new shirtings," "the new coatings," etc. All the presentations are very comprehensively prepared for effortless reading and easy reference.

Additional Fashion Information.   It would seem service enough if the fiber and fabric people saw fit to supply retailers with color and fabric forecasts alone. Surprisingly, the service does not stop there. Their printed presentations also include their version of the fashion trends in ready-to-wear silhouettes, accessories, hair fashions, and cosmetics. Naturally, the total picture gives more authority to their fabric and color predictions, but it also helps to relate these predictions with the over-all fashion picture.

Color slides, too, are often available for the fashion office's use, showing the predicted fabrics, colors, and fashions from resources using their ingredients. These are usually available upon request for use at training meetings or fashion shows.

The Cosmetic Industry

Helpful information comes from almost every imaginable area of the fashion world. In cosmetics beautiful and imaginative releases pour forth to keep

The Cosmetic and fragrance industry keeps the retail fashion director informed with what's new through merchandising kits and news releases.

the fashion office of a store "au courant" with the important beauty innovations. Some of the most enchanting adjectives and inspired product or color titles emerge in romantic glory from releases and forecasts of cosmetic companies and fragrance houses. New and never-before-so-effective, never-before-so-glamourous, for-the-first-time-natural-beauty secrets are announced dramatically and poetically in kits addressed to the fashion director.

It is a most worthy service. The fashion director notes that the fabric color charts show a strong interest in new shades of warm beige for a coming season, and then along comes the cosmetic forecast that tells of "the new bronze face for the new warm beige fashions." Someone has done his homework. Esteé Lauder personally goes to Paris to get fashion direction, even before the couture market opens. Charles Revson and his staff make the European fashion scene, as does Pablo, creative director of Elizabeth Arden. All the leading cosmetic authorities seek fashion guidance from the experts to assist them in making decisions about what the new fashion face will be. All of this is an excellent illustration that the entire fashion industry is coordinating its fashion direction.

Such coordination makes fashion what it is. If the trend is towards a soft look, makeup should be soft. If the colors and textures are bright and heavy, soft pastels in makeup might not be as suitable that season. It is necessary to emphasize "that season," because what might not work one season might be just the ticket another season. At any rate, one needs to know what is being planned for a coming season and how it all goes together.

In the cosmetic forecast, along with the glowing names and inventive descriptions of forthcoming new products, comes the cosmetic industry's version of the coming fashion trends, as they relate to the new "faces." If exotic fashions are expected to be important, the exotic eye might be in order. If the "little girl look" is to be a fashion trend, makeup for the "little girl" must be created. The exotic eye certainly wouldn't suit the little girl look. Naturally, all cosmetic companies will not be doing the same thing, but in one way or another, the leaders will all manage to be fashionably accurate and well informed about the future of fashion.

It would be quite disturbing for the fashionable woman to buy a costume in the new "berry tones" and be unable to find a lipstick that would match or blend. The perceptive fashion director, while scrutinizing the fashion forecasts she trusts, from all areas of the industry, will discover that, sure enough, if "berry tones" are going to be good in ready-to-wear, there will be "berry stains" in lipsticks. This revelation points out another fact for the fashion director. The color is being picked up by many areas. There seems to be a great deal of confidence in it. What's more, what they are doing with it, developing its image and enhancing its potential, makes it a good possibility for a promotional color. At least it is one to consider, something to watch.

In addition to color, texture plays an important part of the cosmetic fashion story. For example, the look and hand of fabrics or their special use in our life styles, influence the "matte face," the "shiny face," the "dewy face," or the "transparent face." When see-through fabrics and fashions were making the scene, "see-through makeup," and "see-through lipsticks" were created to tie in. A fashion director and all members of her staff, would do well to check cosmetic releases for just such clues.

Besides color, besides textures, and besides silhouettes, the cosmetic industry gets into the act with seasonal fashion. At cruise time—skin bronzers for tan without getting in the sun. At ski time—skin moisturizers and protectors against the winter elements. The season, the look, the trend, and the mood are all translated by each fashion area of the industry to relate to the other.

The Consumer Magazines

In the process of accumulating factual material for their editorial pages, the consumer magazines have developed fashion editors and fashion departments whose reputations are synonomous with fashion authority. Even though all retailers will not agree with all magazines nor recognize the extent of their influence, there are few who will deny that as documents of record, interpreters of total fashion, and innovators of fashion presentation as an art, they are incomparable. In the area of fashion presentation, the magazines, especially the high fashion books, have been accused of soaring too far over the average woman's head. They have not been accused, however, of talking down to women.

It would follow, therefore, that a medium which regards fashion as something of an art form and is so articulate in glorifying its creations, would certainly be worthy of a fashion director's attention, especially when it is help they are offering.

From Whence Cometh Your Help.   In their eagerness to be valuable, perhaps even indispensable, to the retailer, the consumer magazines reach out a helping hand in many forms. Choice information on advanced issues is one of them. These advanced information kits come thoroughly documented, usually with illustrations or tear sheets, along with a complete explanation of what fashion direction the issue is taking, what will be shown, who makes it, how much it is (cost and retail), what the promotional opportunities are, and suggestions for windows, displays, ads, and fashion shows.

Whether or not the fashion director is in a position to accept an offered promotion from a magazine, she is benefited greatly by the information passed along in the process. It is hoped, therefore, that even when the official promotion is not consummated, the fashion director can advise the customer in other ways concerning how she feels about the authority or advice of a magazine. Perhaps in the commentary of a show or in a television interview she might relate, *"Harper's Bazaar* feels so strongly

A complete promotion kit from *Seventeen* Magazine, includes glossy reproduction of the cover, mat for newspaper use, fashion points, fashion show plan, and ideas for windows and displays. Many fashion offices and youth coordinators lean heavily on such assistance. (Courtesy of *Seventeen* Magazine.)

about this new look they are devoting a large part of their April issue to it. Watch for it." Or, "*Seventeen* says this is going to be the new girl on campus. You will find this merchandise tagged 'Seen in *Seventeen*' in our junior department."

Magazine Foreign Reports. Twice each year, following the couture or prêt-à-porter collections in Europe, traveling magazine editors who have been on the scene to cover the foreign import markets, share their findings and feelings about trends with retailers. Fashion directors find reports from such fashion editors a welcome plus. A Paris Report from *Harper's Bazaar*, for example, might not only include the highlights of trends in fabrics, silhouettes, accessories, makeup, and hair fashions, but even such revealing information as preoccupations and conversation in Paris at the time regarding art, food, and health. All of this additional information provides clues to direction of life styles, moods, and appetites, all of which affect fashion.

The stacks of advanced fashion information supplied by national magazines helps the fashion office of any store keep an effortless finger on the pulse of their thinking, endorsements, and interpretations. These, incorporated into her other stacks of information, either underline what she already believes or emphasize something she might have felt more or less lukewarm about before reading another point of view.

Magazine Fabric Reports. Unlike the other materials and information provided free of charge, the magazines do require a subscription fee for their color and fabric reports which are prepared twice a year for spring/summer and fall/winter. The charge is something like $10, $15, or $20 per copy. In addition to retailers, buying offices and fashion consultants buy the magazine fabric books, undoubtedly to keep a close check on what all fashion people are thinking and doing.

Seasonal Seminars. Before market, most of the leading national fashion magazines that headquarter in New York send out invitations to store executives and buyers to be their guests at a seminar or predictive presentation of a forthcoming season. One magazine may make their presentation at a traditional champagne breakfast, another during a coffee hour in a morning session or cocktail hour in an afternoon session. Others may be held in strictly formal meetings. Usually, reservations need to be made as to which session is most convenient.

At these sessions, which usually never last more than forty-five minutes, one or two editors preside, showing color slides, films, sketches, or actual merchandise to be featured in a forthcoming issue. In addition to the visual presentation and the editor's comments, each guest is usually provided with printed resource lists advising exactly what will be incorporated in the issue, piece by piece. Each piece is identified by manufacturer, style number, and wholesale cost. In this way the magazine acts as liaison between manufacturer and retailer. The manufacturer gains additional exposure and prestigious attention while the retailer gets an opportunity to know in advance what merchandise will be featured editorially and, therefore, consider including it in their orders while in the market.

The magazine seminars also have good educational value from a "how-to" point of view. How to accessorize a new look, how to merchandise a new idea, how to combine new proportions. Thus, an important part of "covering the market" for the fashion director includes "covering the magazines." From the magazine resource lists she can indicate to the buyers that here is a house worth checking out, here is a style number or two they might like to consider. "It looks very good and is priced right. Let me know if you buy it, and we'll get you magazine credit."

Also, before or after the seminars, it is possible to have a consultation with a magazine editor, to discuss any questions or problems regarding their service or their promotion plans. It is not necessarily the business of the magazine to decide what will be big or important in fashion; it is their function to point up those things in which they believe and those things they regard as fashion, according to the magazine's philosophy and readership. They will tell you, however, when asked how enthusiastic they are about any given area of fashion.

In-Store Presentations.   Occasionally, some of the leading fashion books have sent regional editors to stores outside New York to make seasonal presentations. *Harper's Bazaar* has maintained field editors to service the larger cities or top retail stores. *Mademoiselle Magazine* was one of the first of the fashion books to establish regional offices outside of New York (in Chicago and on the west coast) with traveling editors to cover those regions. Through these regional editors, closer contact with the retailer is made possible, and on-the-premises presentations make it possible for all interested members of the store's fashion division to attend en masse, get a united exposure to the magazine's fashion philosophy, and at the same 'time help the magazine get a closer contact and identification with the store.

Arrangements for in-store presentations by a magazine editor can come about by the fashion director contacting the magazine and making such a request. However, when an editor is making a swing around a territory, it is very likely that the magazine will contact the store.

The New York Fashion Productions

Of all the sources of education and inspiration provided by the industry for the industry, the major fashion productions, such as those staged in New York each year, are highlights of most retailers market trips.

In their New York editorial offices, retailers can see *Seventeen's* display ideas, as well as fashions from future issues. Pictured, how to display kits, fabrics, and crafts to attract young customers. (Courtesy of *Seventeen* Magazine.)

The Magazine Shows. Perhaps the single most effective and impressive effort on the part of the young national fashion magazines is the "June Show." Geared to their August issue, specifically a back-to-campus issue, and the September issue of fall fashions, the June Show is a major fashion

Each year, *Seventeen* holds a June show, to acquaint retailers with new looks and trends in young fashions, from the August and September issues. In a multi-media fashion production retailers were alerted to make their stores a place where girls like to shop. The show even included a "group therapy session" (pictured above), on attitudes, behavior, and buying patterns of young customers. (Courtesy of *Seventeen* Magazine.)

The annual June show of *Mademoiselle* Magazine has run the gamut of a major fashion production, a filmed presentation, to a huge party with big-band music and fashions modeled informally among the guests. Above, a *Mademoiselle* spectacular held in the Waldorf-Astoria grand ballroom. (Courtesy of *Mademoiselle* Magazine.)

Below, finale scene of Milliken Breakfast Show. (Courtesy of Milliken.)

presentation held in New York during the June market week. Embellished with all the professional know-how of show biz, the June Shows, presented by *Seventeen* and *Mademoiselle Magazine*, primarily, are fashion events all retail executives make a special effort to attend. Over 1,800 store executives pay approximately $20 per ticket to see a staged version of what these leading magazines have to say about fall fashions for young women.

Each member of the audience is provided with a detailed program which includes, in order of appearance, a breakdown of scenes or categories and the manufacturers and style numbers represented therein. A retailer can follow the show, item by item, making notes and selecting numbers for consideration.

Usually, only tie-in stores are eligible to attend such major efforts. While the show stimulates interest in the new looks and educates how they are to be coordinated, the retailer has the additional privilege of coming to the offices of the magazines any time during the following week or two after the show, to closely examine the merchandise to be included in the magazine's August and September issues.

The Bridal Magazine Show.   Twice a year, *Bride's Magazine* is host to a black-tie dinner and fashion show for the trade to exemplify their part of the fashion picture. Since almost every fashion store and, therefore, every fashion office is responsible for bridal shows for their own customers, these bridal magazine events provide a glimpse at the new looks from a wide selection of top bridal gown manufacturers, and perhaps suggest a new fashion show idea.

Fiber and Fabric Shows.   The most unique and stimulating fashion show experience of its kind is the famous Deering-Milliken show, known as the Milliken Breakfast. Given a thoroughly Broadway-musical treatment, with original book and lyrics every year, plus big name stars, the event runs for two weeks (end of May, early June) to packed houses in the giant ballroom of the Waldorf-Astoria Hotel in New York. Breakfast is served at 7 A.M., the show starts at 7:55 A.M. and is over before 9 A.M. when the retailers must go off to the market. A fashion director, attending a trade show, such as the Milliken Breakfast, can come away with an eyeful of new fashion looks and a headful of inspiration.

What a great way to present rainwear!
What a charming idea for our next show of children's fashions!

What a unique way of bringing on models!
What a stimulating way to merchandise a new fashion look!

One idea may beget another, suitable, of course, for a specific store under specific conditions. Nevertheless, most ideas are adaptable. While the buyer attending the show is getting a strong message about Milliken fabrics and what resources are using them, the fashion director is enchanted with the style of the presentation, fashion story line, and interpretation. What's more, she has no difficulty thinking of Milliken as anything but gay, spirited, alive, inventive, and exciting. A mighty nice image to have. She remembers this. Her own shows should, in their modest way, also project an image to be remembered warmly, happily, and elegantly, whatever the store's message might be at the time.

NRMA Spectacular. The National Retail Merchants Association, to which retailers look for the latest information available in their field, presented for the first time a fashion spectacular during their January, 1970, national convention in New York. Staged by Walter Hazeltine, models were moved into the audience on a conveyor-runway. The top American designers, whose creations were featured in the show, appeared in person on the conveyor behind their models. It was an innovation. This live fashion show was the climax of the afternoon. It followed a multi-media, giant-scene slide presentation and guest speakers who discussed the state of fashion, where it was, and where it is going.

Fashion Group Shows. Members of the Fashion Group (see Chapter 2) enjoy a wealth of professional analysis of fashion trends. One of the outstanding ways the Fashion Group of New York analyzes and interprets fashion is through an annual schedule of remarkable fashion productions. Twice a year, Paris couture shows; twice a year, American collections; special shows for all the other fashion divisions—fabrics, children's, sportswear, home furnishings. In addition to these, each year brings showings of newly-spotlighted imports which are special fashion impacts.

The fashion director has the advantage of viewing together, such as at a Fashion Group's American collections show, all the leading American designers showing their choice style numbers. Seeing a composite of the American market all in one show, is without a doubt an excellent way to appraise the look of the market.

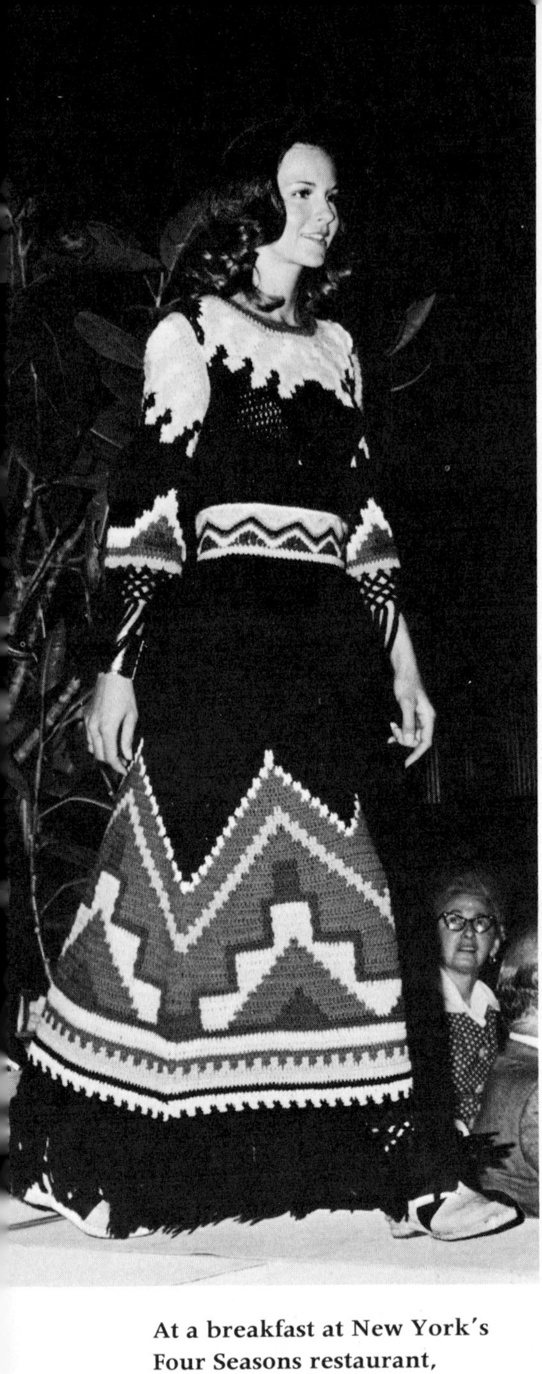

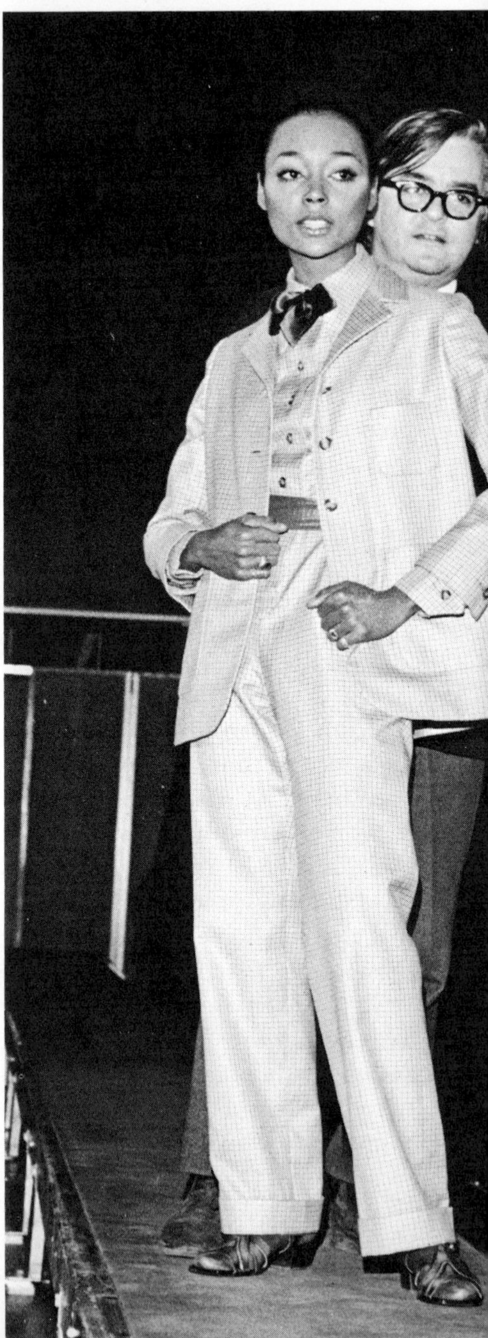

At a breakfast at New York's Four Seasons restaurant, co-sponsored by The American Wool Council and the National Hand Knitting Yarn Association, retail executives saw hand knit fashions by leading designers. Above, a Georgio di Sant'Angelo dress. (Courtesy of American Wool Council.)

Below, designer Geoffrey Beene appears on a conveyor-ramp with his model at NRMA's Fashion Spectacular, to 4200 people in the Americana Hotel Imperial Ballroom. (Courtesy of *Stores* Magazine.)

Salute-to-Fashion Shows. Show-and-tell is magnificently done in the world of fashion. The cosmetic and fragrance industry, for example, relating intimately to the fashion world, has made outstanding contributions to fashion through lavish productions to salute the talent of fashion design.

Perhaps one of the most famous and the most coveted awards in this area of the fashion industry is the Coty American Fashion Critics' Award,

The Fall Import Show, presented at the New York Hilton by The Fashion Group for members and their guests. (Courtesy of The Fashion Group.)

founded by Coty, Inc., in late 1942. Presented each year to American designers whose work during the previous year has had a significant effect on the American woman's way of dressing, the presentation is accompanied by a fashion extravaganza to a black-tie audience. Under the direction of Eleanor Lambert, the productions are the ultimate in fashion glamor. From the first Coty award winner, Norman Norell in 1943, every influential name in American fashion (couture designers, leather designers, milliners, furriers, designers of lingerie, children's fashions, men's fashions, fashion accessories, and cosmetic and makeup creators) has received an award for distinguished contribution.

An alert fashion director, whether she attends such award shows or not, will consider such news-making fashion events worthy of her attention. Award winners get there through great efforts and are recognized by panels of astute judges. Therefore, the special interest created for their designs, from the store's and the customer's viewpoint, has undeniable merit. The promotional value is obvious.

The Coty American Fashion Critics' Award "Winnie" statuette. (Courtesy of Eleanor Lambert, Inc.)

Other Trade Shows.   Everything is fashion. Even the linen and domestics industry has related their creations to the fashion world. For example, Fieldcrest brought new fashion emphasis to their industry in the spring of 1966 with a unique fashion show of specially designed, one-of-a-kind fashions made from their new collections of towels, sheets, and bedspreads. The event was staged at the Four Seasons restaurant in New York. In 1968, another Fieldcrest fashion show, held at the Plaza Hotel in New York, introduced a new collection of designer towels and linens to point up the

Fieldcrest stressed fashion in their products with a fashion show of designer clothes, made from their sheets, towels, blankets, and bedspreads. Left, created from shower curtains and a blanket. Right, an Anne Klein design with towels. (Courtesy of Fieldcrest, Inc.)

fashion elegance of the colors, patterns, and fabrics. Later, the collections were available to tour department stores that carried Fieldcrest merchandise for use in community fashion shows.

Put it all together; it spells fashion. And show business is a big, big part of it.

Afterview

One might get the idea, after taking a look at the avalanche of advanced information that pours down on the fashion office, that making decisions about what should be incorporated into a coming season would be a snap.

Not so. Judgment is still the most important factor. A barrage of predictions could cause a bad case of confusion if the fashion director has no judgment, direction, or personal touch with the facts. But a fashion person who is well indoctrinated with her own research and taste and who has an awareness of consumer needs and desires, can intelligently evaluate everything that comes from her mailbox.

What is good for one store, one market area, is death in another. Although the differences are not as great today because of the onslaught of immediate communications, life styles still differ from one community to another. Even though the differences are slight, they are enough to make one fashion look sell well, another not so well.

In a store where a fashion coordinator is new in a job, accidently falls into it in an emergency, or is hired into a fashion job in a store where one did not exist before, sources of fashion information, such as those noted in this chapter, come as a blessing. A fashion director, from one of the most highly regarded fashion store's in the country, interviewed for the purpose of this text, exclaimed: "I would have given anything if someone had spelled out for me, where to go for information or guidance, what to look for, and how to use what I found. Having it all set down, even if you are knowledgeable, is like having someone hold your hand. The touch of a dependable hand is not a bad idea. Especially in this business. Who doesn't need it?"

 *Chapter 8*

Planning Fashion Promotions

Fashion promotions help build acceptance. That is what fashion needs. That is why promotions are born.

Up to this point, the fashion director has guided her management toward the important fashion trends, the buyers have gone out and bought those important fashion trends, and now it is time to tell the world about them. How much customer acceptance is enjoyed depends a great deal on how well the merchandise is promoted. Clearly, dramatically, and uniquely. Whatever it takes.

The fashion director, highly responsible for the fashion content of her store, is also responsible for helping promote it. From the instigation of a fashion promotion, to its planning and execution, the fashion director is strongly involved. Although the fashion director is not involved in sale promotions (clearance sales, special purchase sales, etc.), a store with a good fashion and quality image is very likely to experience better results. In other words, a sale by a store that knows and promotes fashion has great meaning. The spin-off from a good fashion promotion is indisputable.

A fashion promotion cannot simply mean that just because some new merchandise has arrived it is time to run an ad. Running an ad is running an ad. But running an ad, or a series of ads under the umbrella of a "theme" with all visual presentations corresponding to that theme, or perhaps presented as a campaign, that is a promotion. That is what we are concerned with here first, the fashion promotion (large or small) that helps build acceptance.

How Fashion Promotions are Selected.   The selecting and the care and feeding of a fashion promotion is one of the special thrills of the retail fashion director. At least, it should be. In this endeavor creativity can blossom. All her groundwork, the research, the recommendations, and the planning, is on the threshold of fruition. When the racks and counters and cases are filled with those things the fashion director said were good fashion, the great reward is to see those things coming out because happy customers are saying "I'll take that."

Fashion promotions come from at least three different directions. Some are automatic, some are created, and some are offered. For example:

Automatic
Holidays—Valentine's Day (see Chapter 1), Mother's Day, Father's Day,
   Christmas, etc.
Seasons—Spring promotion, summer, fall, cruise, back-to-school, etc.
Offered
National magazine tie-in promotions
Vendor co-op promotions
Fiber companies, fabric mills, ingredient institutes
Created
New trends
New colors
New fabrics
New accessory treatments
New products

The automatic promotions literally write themselves into the promotion calendar and very often serve as another slot to promote those listed under created promotions.

The offered promotions are of special interest to the fashion director. If what the vendor, magazine, fabric mill, or fiber company offers is in line with those promotional ideas that the store will be "creating" during a given season, then the offer might be encouraged by the fashion office. If it is completely contrary to the fashion plan, then the offer might better be passed up. It is very tempting for a store to accept a promotion that offers co-op money, that is, money offered by a supplier to help pay a part of the advertising campaign (ads, display, fashion shows, etc.) to encourage the promotion of their product. However, even very large stores can handle only a certain number of promotions per season, and being selective is part of presenting the best fashion image.

The promotions that are specially created or tailor-made for the store's needs and season's specific fashion trends, are of most concern to the fashion director. It is this type promotion that is the offshoot of the fashion director's recommendations. She insisted that denim was big and important, and the market testified this was true. She claimed that the ethnic influence in fashion was explosive and the market underlined the belief with great selections. She applauded the return of the classic suit in new soft fabrics, and the buyers, equally enthusiastic, brought it in strong. The new season is coming; the new merchandise is coming. Promotion-planning time is here.

The season's fashion promotions are selected from the original list of fashion promotables, trends, and items presented by the fashion director in her predictive meeting (see Chapter 5). The list was appraised and refined by management before market and perhaps again after market to include hot items that popped up.

How to Work with the Sales-Promotion Director

In meetings with the GMM and the sales-promotion director, decisions are made as to which promotions take precedent over others, which will get the big treatment, and which the small. Some will go store wide, some divisional, some departmental.

The fashion director and the merchandising staff provide the sales-promotion director with ammunition on which to base a promotion, advising him on what the fashion story is and helping him decide how the story should be told. The sales-promotion director is responsible for selling the store and the merchandise therein. Working with the merchandising staff and the fashion director, it is his responsibility to pull all the facets of a promotion together and supervise its execution.

At an initial planning meeting, called by the sales-promotion director to get the promotion planned and into the hopper, everyone involved makes a contribution. Those present would undoubtedly include the merchandising staff of the fashion division, the GMM, the fashion director, advertising director, publicity director, and display director. All of these people are indispensable to the promotion department.

For example, the promotion in question is a western-type country look.

"In which departments will you have this look?" the sales-promotion director would ask the DMM.

"In all of them," he might answer.

This indicates that the promotion should cover the entire ready-to-wear division from children's to adult's. To the advertising director this means that a series of ads will be necessary to cover the story for the whole division. To the display director it means that decor throughout the whole division must tie together with the theme of the promotion. Establishing that theme will come next. But first a word from the fashion director, on the request of the sales-promotion director. He would like her to reiterate, for the benefit of all present, exactly what the trend or look is.

"The look is predominantly country-girl, country-boy flavor, with influences of early prairie ladies, young milkmaids, country hoe-down fashions, and frontier fashions. It is very spirited. In the young departments it is quite authentic, sometimes costumey, and in the adult areas it is mostly an influence, in fabric, patterns, and trimmings, sometimes a bit more elegant but still a gay, relaxed look."

From what the fashion director has said, everyone present gets the idea that the promotion must be handled in an easy, light-hearted manner.

"Absolutely," the fashion director agrees. "It should all be cooked up country-style for country folks."

That's it. The theme. From this astute group comes a number of suggested titles. "Make Mine Country-Style," "Country Folks," "The New Fashion Frontier," "How the West Was Won," "It's a Free Country." The fashion director cautions that the last title suggested is more patriotic, a better Fourth of July handle, but this fashion look is not that at all; it is *folksy* American.

The whole promotion, it is decided, will be very folksy. The whole concept must be completely unpretentious, cozy, and friendly. Everyone

The fashion promotion of a trend—"Country Girls." A window display inspired by the look. (Courtesy of Filene's of Boston.)

is caught up in the excitement now. Enthusiasm projects from all sides of the room.

"Why don't we have some live country music on the opening day of the promotion? Maybe country rock?"

"Let's turn the entire store into a country store."

"Let's bring in a country or Grand Ole Opera star."

And so it goes. The fashion director watches in all directions, just as she did with the title, to be sure the theme is kept in line with the fashion look. It is her job to see that the terminology in ads and signs and the decor in display tell the fashion story accurately. The sales-promotion director will note all suggestions and contributions offered in the meeting and later draw up a finalized promotion plan which assigns everyone to his or her responsibility. He will request the fashion director to direct all fashion aspects of the promotion, to be certain that the fashion theme rings true and does not get lost in the shuffle. She will meet with her fashion office staff and delegate their assignments.

The area coordinators will be responsible for all details in their area, and the display coordinators will be given explicit details of the plan. The fashion show coordinator will be advised that a ''show of country folks'' should be held in the fashion departments where the clothes originate, and informal modeling should be scheduled in the restaurant areas of the store every day at lunch time.

All this is why the fashion director was in the market with the buyers. She saw what the buyers selected, she knows what will be coming in, she knows what she can count on for windows, ads, interiors, television, and shows. The promotion is thus coordinated.

The Divisional Fashion Promotion.   We just ''sat in'' on the formulation of a divisional fashion promotion. In this type of effort, a single division (the women's ready-to-wear division, in this case) is the recipient of the entire coordinated program.

Since the biggest responsibility of a promotion is to generate excitement, it should be (1) worthy of the spotlight and (2) handled with the pzazz it deserves. A fashion promotion worthy of the name should feature that which is new, different, and important. If the promotion is successful, the merchandise should become wanted, needed, and loved. In fact, the entire division, including those things that are not involved in the promotion, should benefit.

The Store-Wide Promotion.   Fashion leadership, as stated earlier, is a month-after-month business. Promotions of all kinds are necessary to perpetuate excitement, stir up enthusiasm, and generate interest in those products the store has for sale. One of the most effective tools for encouraging traffic is the store-wide promotion.

The automatic promotions, such as national holidays and new seasons, are natural for store-wide exposure. The general public literally expects the retail store to embellish a holiday with inspired interpretations in decor, merchandise, and entertainment. They can actually take their cue from the store as to when it is time to shop for a holiday, a season, or an event. The store tells when it is time to think of Christmas, time for spring, time for the cotillion ball. These are automatic because they happen every year.

The store-wide promotion that is "offered" is very instrumental in getting over a fashion idea that might not otherwise be so thoroughly expressed. An excellent example of this type is a promotion offered by a fiber company such as Du Pont, Celanese, or Monsanto. A Du Pont promotion might include "Du Pont on every floor," from, hosiery, intimate apparel, and ready-to-wear for every member of the family, to the fashion fabric department, home furnishing department, housewares department. A Celanese promotion, geared strictly to fashion, would, nevertheless, wander from the ready-to-wear departments to carpeting, drapes, and upholstered furniture. Scheduled to run for a week, the promotion might cover a different aspect of "Celanese Fashion" each day.

How the Fashion Director Contributes to Store-Wide Efforts.   Whether the fashion director is corporate or divisional, she will be called upon to coordinate with the fashion coordinator of the home furnishings division when a store-wide effort requires their combined talents. Each will check their resources to see which products contain Celanese fibers in order to make them eligible for the promotion. Celanese will be most helpful in this area by advising each division what resources are available for their products. The divisional merchandise managers will clue in everyone involved as to what departments and what items they wish spotlighted.

The home furnishings fashion coordinator, guided by Celanese and his or her DMM, might project that division's fashion image by creating model rooms, containing fabrics made from the promoted fibers. He may also do a fashion window, dramatizing the man-made fibers with carpets, drapes, and furniture from his area. He will select those pieces to be illustrated in the newspaper ads and those items to be used on television.

The fashion director of the ready-to-wear area will meet with the home furnishings fashion coordinator to learn what he is doing. Now she will execute her part of the promotion in a similar manner. She will make a list of possibilities to feature Celanese from her fashion point-of-view, and she will help tie the whole scheme together.

1. She may put a live model, wearing Celanese loungewear in the model bedroom on the home furnishings floor.
2. She might put a mannequin in the home furnishings window, draped in Celanese fabrics from the fabric department, or perhaps request a complete window of Celanese fabrics.
3. She may arrange for a special Celanese fashion show in the fashion area.
4. She will pull and coordinate Celanese fashions that the buyers and DMM wish included in newspaper ads, television commercials, and display areas.
5. In all cases, she will see that all merchandise is properly accessorized.

All of this she will have checked out with the sales-promotion director who might give the entire program his blessings or add an idea or two of his own. It may be his wish, for example, to invite all sales personnel in the areas involved to a preview clinic which will educate them on the facts they need to know to properly answer the customers' questions. The fashion director might be called upon to expedite such a meeting. She will undoubtedly invite the Celanese experts to supply the necessary information and visual aids. After all, they know their own product best. She might arrange for models to show the fashion pieces that are Celanese, advising the group about the performance of the fabrics. The Celanese people will instruct on how to care for their products.

All is in readiness. The right goods are in the departments to back up the promotion. The in-store areas involved have been decorated, signed, and displayed to speak out "loud and clear" about what is going on. A bank of windows has been devoted to the promotion. The ads, illustrating merchandise selected and accessorized by the fashion office, are scheduled. So radio and TV spots are scheduled. The fashion director has arranged with the advertising director to publicize the special Celanese fashion show. The fashion sellers have been educated. The store-wide promotion, selling Celanese fashion, is under way.

The Fashion-Inspired Store-Wide Promotion. Some of the most exciting store-wide promotions are originated in the fashion office. If the GMM and sales-promotion director are in sympathy with the idea, it is very likely to get the big treatment.

Take, for example, a fall season that reveals a newly-expressed interest in leather. The import markets (Montreal, Copenhagen, Spain, and Israel) are coming up with some exciting fashion innovations, new colors, new combinations, and new silhouettes. The cutters on Seventh Avenue and Broadway, in California and St. Louis are turning out inspired expressions in their collections of leathers and suedes. The classic leather looks are taking a back-seat to the new expressions in leather for night as well as day, in every imaginable fashion trend, all sizes, all prices, all departments.

It is big enough, the fashion director may advise, to warrant total store treatment. It is agreed. Men's, women's, and children's ready-to-wear divisions, the accessory division, and the home furnishings division are in accord to "leather up" for a store-wide promotion.

The sales-promotion director, after learning that imported fashion and accessory items will be an important part of the merchandise picture, arranges to have personalities brought into the store from abroad and to have exhibitions which lend color and excitement to the fashion story. To add drama to the promotion the store might bring in personalities such as a leather expert or designer to demonstrate or lecture on the new artistry of leather, a shoe display showing the step-by-step creation of a shoe, perhaps an exhibit or film on the various types and stage of leather treating and dyeing (suitable for visits from student groups).

The fashion director's responsibility is, again, to coordinate all the fashion aspects of the promotion, the shows, ads, displays, windows, and commercials. She will supervise the new way to accessorize the new leather looks; she will teach the sellers, display, advertising, publicity departments, and her own staff what the new leather message is.

A fashion promotion of this type is a busy time for area coordinators. Each is responsible for seeing that her department has the "look of leather." Also, it is during such promotions that subordinates in the fashion office, in need of learning the ropes, can latch on to an assignment, no matter how

a nice girl like you
a nice girl like
a nice girl like
a nice girl like you...
a nice girl like you...
a nice girl like you...

A departmental promotion umbrella, ''A Nice Girl Like You,''
based on the store's philosophy that the 18–25 age junior-size
woman wants a more sophisticated look in sportswear, coats, dresses,
lingerie, accessories, and shoes. The signing for advertising and
displays, done in typewriter type, to relate to the young career
woman. (a) The displays. The mannequins (females always in the
company of males) are indicative of how the young modern woman
sees herself. (b) The shopping bag. The look of the contemporary
junior woman who would shop the ''A Nice Girl Like You''
departments. (Courtesy of The J. L. Hudson Company.)

small, and discover another aspect of fashion coordination. Every event
produces a new wrinkle. Even if the beginner is only typing up a bulletin
or directive of procedure for the promotion, she can take notice of the
words she is typing and observe later as it all unravels—how it started,
how it developed, and how it all turned out.

Departmental Promotions. The promotion that concentrates on a
specific fashion department is the one that is most dear to the heart of the
buyer involved. It is her baby! The enthusiasm she exudes is a joy to

behold. If there is ever a time for the fashion director and buyer to be buddy-buddy, this is it.

The idea for the promotion might emulate from the buyer, the DMM, or the fashion director. The DMM may have requested a fashion promotion in a given department, wanting to see "more action," or wishing to promote a new collection, a new designer, or a new shop concept. The buyer may have originated the idea through her associations in the market. A designer or fashion celebrity may have offered to come to the store during a tour around the country.

The fashion director, whose job it is to keep a steady fire burning under the store's fashion pot to be sure that something is always cooking to perpetrate or stimulate her store's fashion position, might offer to create a special fanfare for a departmental fashion promotion.

She would talk with the buyer first. "If we can get everybody's blessing, how would you feel about our doing a fashion promotion with your merchandise exclusively? Your department could give us the kind of leadership we need for the looks we will be trying to promote." The conversation might have been prompted by the fashions they both saw in the market earlier, or it may have come about at the prospect of a new shop opening or a new trend that is unique to that department. If the buyer is in accord, the fashion director might submit the idea, either verbally at a forthcoming promotion meeting or in writing to obtain the necessary "blessing."

To: Mr. General Merchandise Manager
         Mr. Divisional Merchandise Manager
         Mr. Sales-Promotion Director   cc: Mrs. Buyer
From: Miss Fashion Director
Subject: Fashion promotion
         Designer shop only

This shop is new. We feel that a lot of beating of the drums will be necessary to attract the right customer. We submit to you the following promotion plan for your consideration:

1. A grand-opening kind of event in late August or early September—such as a sit-down brunch and formal fashion show, by invitation only.
2. Informal modeling every day for a week in the department, publicized

by department fashion sellers, signs throughout the store, and newspaper ads.

3. Informal modeling at peak hours and peak days, for the rest of the month, in the department and throughout the store.
4. Personal appearances of attention-getting young designers with their collections. With each designer, extend some type of hospitality (coffee, tea, etc.) to customers for a sit-down formal show followed by informal modeling the balance of the day or days the designer is in the department. These might begin late August and continue through October.

I have discussed this with Mrs. Buyer and she is eager for our help. She is willing to contact whomever necessary to get the right designer into the department to help push the pieces and collections she is buying. We anxiously await your prompt opinion regarding the above. Any suggestions or amendments you can offer will be greatly appreciated, but I strongly feel we must get the consumer as excited about this new department and our new fashion direction as we are.

Timing Is Everything. Timing, one of the vital three magic words in a fashion director's life (see Chapter 1), is everything in the business of planning fashion promotions. All promotion ideas must be dreamed up and submitted for consideration far in advance of execution day. If the plan for a store wide promotion is due for execution in August, it should be in the making in May or June. If a divisional spring plan is under consideration for March, January is not too early to start. Two to three months ahead, for an important divisional promotion, should be the minimum time allotted for preparation, four to six months for store wide promotions.

It cannot be repeated too often, however, that if a strong and unforseen trend climbs up, all conditions for latching on must be go. Flexibility, another magic word, is indispensable to meet the unexpected and is part of the fashion director's challenge. Rigidity, or jealously-guarded, neat little plans cannot coexist with the unpredictable nature of fashion, neither can they coexist in the nature of the fashion director. Flexibility is a must.

As stated, store-wide promotion plans are usually projected about four to six months in advance. This long range plan, of course, would include all types of promotions (special events, fashion promotions, volume promotions, and sales) for all divisions. It is into this major plan, established to be elastic, that special, indispensable, and unanticipated promotions are interwoven.

Approval of the Fashion Promotion.   When management examines the merits of a proposed promotion, they analyze the idea in much the same way that a good newspaper story is appraised. Does it explain who, what, when, where, and why? A review of the fashion director's proposal will show that it does answer these questions.

> Why—explained in the first paragraph
> What—listed in points No. 1 through 4
> When—indicated in points No. 1 and 4
> Who—noted under point No. 4
> Where—mentioned in points No. 1, 2, and 4
> The less pertinent information follows in the last paragraph

Following such a format, brief and to the point, when writing or submitting promotion plans, will alleviate a great deal of delay and guesswork. Members of management are busy people. They need to read concise, uncluttered commentary in all business communications and are usually grateful for it. Evaluation and approval, therefore, can be expedited promptly.

When approval of her promotional idea for the designer shop comes through, it very likely will be with a complete "go ahead." It may also come through with a request to meet and discuss the plan further. There would be need, for example, to make decisions about budget, how much should be spent for food, show production, music, flowers, etc. In any case, once the decision has been made, the fashion office takes over.

Steps of Procedure.   The first step would be to book all the proposed events for the designer shop on the fashion office calendar. Copies of the calendar are sent to all store executives, a month in advance, to keep them informed or reminded of what has been scheduled and what is coming up.

Next, the fashion director would call in and meet with all personnel pertinent to expediting the proposed promotion. When all have heard the story and have had an opportunity to voice their opinions and offer suggestions, the fashion director is ready to share the total plan (so that all involved understand what they must do and the right hand knows what the left hand is doing) in the form of a responsibility sheet.

Purpose of the Responsibility Sheet.   A good responsibility or work sheet, designed to record the details of a promotion, makes life more pleasant for everyone concerned. Again, brevity is the key, but above all— ASSUME NOTHING. Therein lies the secret of having all bases covered without a hitch. A fashion director, like a good teacher, would do well to place these words, big and bold, in full view of everyone in her office. Assume nothing, then nothing is likely to be overlooked. To "assume" that the printer knows when to have the invitations printed and delivered (He can see the date of the event on the copy, can't he?) is unfair. To "assume" that every model knows there will be two performances of the show instead of one (We usually do it that way, don't we?) is a grave mistake. Spell it out in delicious detail. It saves such a lot of grief later.

Drafting of the Responsibility Sheet.   Every promotion is different. A responsibility sheet, directive, or work sheet, whatever a department wishes to call it, is a tailor-made document advising everyone involved about what is needed and what is expected.

Continuing with the departmental promotion for the designer shop as the example, each idea on the approved promotion will have a separate responsibility sheet. The following is for the first event, the grand-opening brunch and fashion show. Copies of the following, sent out from the fashion office, will go to all executives mentioned, plus the GMM, DMM, sales-promotion director, publicity director, and everyone in the fashion office.

After all concerned have their assignments, one person in the fashion office, usually the fashion director's secretary (a good training spot for a would-be coordinator), draws up a check list and follows through, right up to show time, to be sure every objective has been accomplished.

The Item Promotion.   We have examined illustrations of the store-wide, divisional, and departmental promotion. There is still one more vital promotional route utilized to help get the fashion story to the customer. The item promotion. The individual item, important enough and hot enough to merit attention on its own, might show up in a single department or embrace an entire division, maybe even more than one division. For example: the cape, city pants, the vest, boots. Any one of these items

Fashion Office Responsibility Sheet

Event: Sit-down Brunch and Fashion Show
For: Designer Shop Grand Opening
Date: Wednesday, September 3
Time: 11:00 A.M.
Place: Special Events Auditorium—Downtown Store

Name	Responsibility	Please Note
Special Events Director	Please reserve Special Events Auditorium for Sept. 3, plus day before for set-up.	
Special Events Director	Please book a combo or music group as background. Something light and easy, remember this is brunch, the fashion look will be elegant and casual.	Music needed from 10:30 A.M. to 1 P.M. For walk-in and walk-out music, plus the show.
Advertising Director	Copy for invitations on attached requisition. 1,000 needed.	Invitations must be printed and returned to fashion office for mailing not later than Monday, August 15.
Advertising Director	There will be no ad. This one is invitation only.	
Mrs. Buyer Designer Shop	Please have your special mailing list compiled and ready for addressing August 15.	
Mrs. Buyer Designer Shop	Please assign someone in your Dept. to accept reservations beginning August 21.	Invitations will be mailed August 19 and 20.
Mr. Director of Food Service	Menu attached, per our conversation. Brunch— serve at 11:00 A.M.	Reservations expected: Approx. 250–300. A final count will be provided by the designer shop. Contact Mrs. Buyer or her asst.

Name	Responsibility	Please Note
Supervisor of Porters	Tables and chairs for approx. 250–300 people.	Seat 4 at card tables, 6 at round tables. Final count will come to you from Mr. Director of Food Service.
Manager of Flower Shop	Centerpieces for approx. 30 tables of 4, and 30 tables of 6. Color scheme will be autumn orange, gold, and brown.	A final count will be provided by Mr. Director of Food Service.
Display Director	The ramp set up in T-shape as we discussed, will be fine. The set design you suggested will be great, but keep to soft earth tones. We need the colors of the clothes to project without competition.	If more reservations come in than expected, it may be necessary to take out one section of ramp to make room for more tables. Will advise.
Fashion Show Coordinator	Show time is 12 noon, immediately following brunch.	Please discuss with me which models to book, fitting dates, and rehearsal time.
	Show approx. 40 to 50 pieces.	
	Select from designer shop only. Use all designers.*	*For this show we are not interested in promoting specific collections but the total fashion picture of a new department.

may have enjoyed an easy-come-easy-go appearance on the fashion scene, but, nevertheless, when it was showing up big and strongly acceptable, an item promotion was in order.

A case in point—the cape. A revived interest in the cape or capelet has captured the imagination of designers in every area of fashion—coats, suits, jackets, dresses, blouses, women's, men's, children's. The average customer, looking for a coat might notice coats shown with detachable capes, a long cape for evening, or any number of other versions. However, she might not be aware of the cape trend in all the other fashion areas until it is all pulled together and illustrated for her. When she sees and hears that "capes are embracing all fashion," she may gain more confidence in selecting a coat with a cape. The strength of the promotion could very well whet her appetite, stir her interest, and awaken her acceptability.

The fashion director indicates to her management the growing importance of an item. "Everyone is cutting it," she reports, "It will be available in all price ranges and in great assortment of fabrics for juniors, women, children, and even men." The buyers, too, are seeing it in the market. It is checking out. Early sampling in a variety of departments indicates there is consumer interest. An item promotion is born.

How to Merchandise an Item Promotion. Management enlists the assistance of the fashion director to get the cape story together. First, she must learn what the target date is for the promotion.

Next, she checks with the buyers to be sure each department's stock includes the item or if it will be there in time for the target date. A department cannot be included in a promotion if it does not have the merchandise to back it up. Next comes selecting the over-all theme for signing, ads, and commercials. It is decided, after a meeting with the sales-promotion director, that simplicity is the strongest way to project this item. "The Cape." That is all.

The fashion director and her area coordinators pull sample pieces as illustrations for the newspaper ad. The buyers are most helpful in this connection. They will gladly assist in pointing out those examples of the cape they feel are most important, backed up with the best selection, that is, a range of styles available in a variety of colors and sizes. In making the final decision, however, the fashion director must be sure that the ad carries a diversified version of the cape, something choice from each department. Sometimes this necessitates taking pieces back and substituting with other pieces until the desired balance is reached. When all pieces have been accumulated, they are sent to advertising to be sketched. Alongside the cape illustrations, the copy of the item ad, in order to make a strong fashion statement, will boldly announce "The Cape." It is simple but strong.

When the ad is due to break in the newspaper (perhaps a television cape commercial is scheduled to run also), each department involved will be visually identified. A mannequin, showing how the new cape look is put together, will be evident with a simple sign stating "The Cape." In some departments capes will dangle from hangers or T-stands. If the promotion includes an accessory department as well as the ready-to-wear departments, and it mostly certainly could, then a counter sign and display should advise the customer that here, too, is the cape. If there is a fashion show coming up during this time, the fashion show coordinator would certainly include the cape look in a group or category within the show.

All put together (in displays, windows, ads, TV commercials), the customer can see the item expressed with effectiveness, with authority. It appears to her to be an important item. She is getting the message.

Division-Plus-Division Promotion.   Very often, one fashion trend can inspire the tie-in of one division with another. A splendid example of this was the Tweed fragrance promotion executed in 1968 and 1969. The fabric of tweed became a leading fashion look in ready-to-wear. Tweed, a fragrance of long standing, saw an ideal promotional tie-in. Tweed created an entire promotional package. All the leading fashion magazines carried ads of Tweed fragrance, illustrated with models in tweed fashions created by Country Set. The magazines carried editorial comment on the theme, adding impetus to the idea. Tweed proceeded with the plan by offering display material, buttons for salespeople, and fragrance samples for fashion shows.

The fashion office was totally responsible for "getting the word around," to the store personnel and to the customer. In this case, both the fragrance house and the ready-to-wear firm assisted in telling the fashion story. The tweed presentation, pointing up all types of tweed costumes, made a strong fashion statement. Ads, windows, interiors, television, radio, and shows all highlighted the idea—Tweed on tweed. With every fashion sales person and everyone in the fashion office wearing "This is Tweed Country" buttons in the store, the customer soon found herself thinking "Tweed on tweed" whenever she saw the fabric or the fragrance. Thus, the sportswear department and the fragrance department, two separate divisions, worked together for a special fashion promotion. It was a natural.

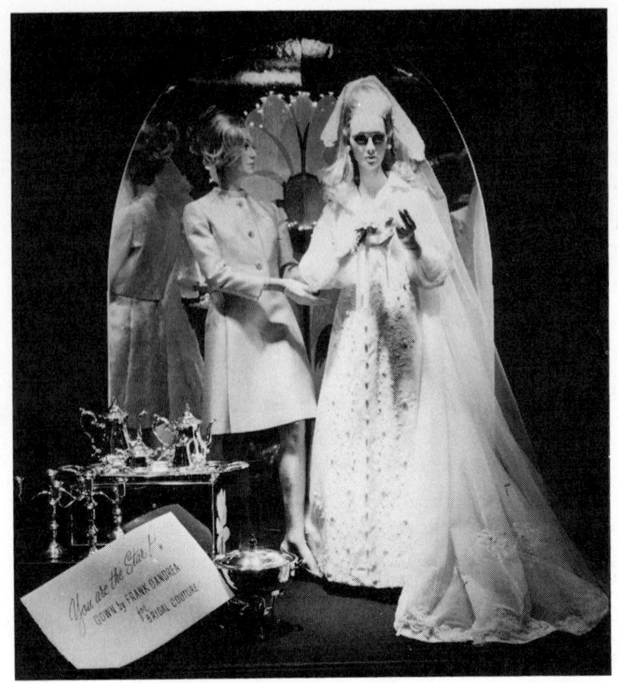

Left, the bridal promotion is a natural for division-plus-division involvement. This bridal window features the bridal shop, ready-to-wear, silver department. (Courtesy of Strawbridge & Clothier, Philadelphia.) Right, the bridal promotion, usually twice a year, summer and winter. Fashions, bridal registry, home furnishings, fine jewelry, services, etc., are all mentioned in copy. (Ad courtesy of Bullock's.)

Divisions lap over beautifully from time to time when an important designer lends his name and talent to a field other than his original one. For example, when fashion designers Yves Saint Laurent and Pierre Cardin created designer collections of linens and towels for Fieldcrest, stores who carried other Saint Laurent and Cardin merchandise could do a tie-in promotion. Displays could include their fragrances, their scarves, their couture fashions. Same would be true of Chanel fashions and Chanel fragrances. Chanel, by the way, was the first haute couture designer to come up with a personalized fragrance bearing her name. Before this, perfumes were available only from perfume houses. This innovation started a trend with big name designers everywhere. Now one can buy a fragrance, a scarf, a towel, a belt, a shoe, men's fashions, and women's fashions, all bearing the same designer's name. Thus division-plus-division promotional tie-ins are a constant possibility. The fashion office usually is assigned the task of coordinating such a tie-in. In fact, it would be the fashion office that would be most aware of tie-in merchandise throughout the store.

The Magazine Promotion. All of the leading fashion magazines are brimming over with magnificent ideas for promoting fashion. These

THE
BULLOCK
LOOK

A Bullock's bride is particularly lovely. No matter how big or small your wedding, Bullock's has the fashion know-how that can help you be the most perfect bride in Southern California. After all, we've been in the fashion business since 1907. In our collections you'll find the gown you've dreamed of wearing all your life. And elsewhere in the store, you'll find all the things that have made Bullock's a bride's favorite for so many years. Here you can choose your invitations, buy fine jewelry, arrange for a photographer, register with our Bridal Registry, order your wedding dinner from our catering service and plan your wedding trip at our travel bureau. Let Bullock's show you how perfect your wedding can be. Call your favorite Bullock's store for our schedule of bridal shows, where you'll see a romantic collection of new bridal gowns, and pretty things for your trousseau. The Bullock Look shown, $136 Bridal Shop at your favorite Bullock's Store except Westwood.

Bullock's

promotions, usually called tie-ins, are designed by very professional merchandising and promotion departments of the magazine. If the sales-promotion director or fashion director of a store is in need of a fashion promotion, the magazines graciously oblige.

The Early Promotions. *Mademoiselle Magazine* began promotional tie-ins with retailers with their first August college issue in 1935. *Mademoiselle* editors, recognizing that retail stores were faced with a doldrum month in hot, between-season August when business was slow, created a merchandising concept that would give stores an earlier ''kick-off'' for fall, back-to-college selling. At first, a small group of stores tied in with the magazine, and, as the word got around, more stores became involved. About 250 stores in each major trading area of America latched onto the August college issue tie-in.

Vogue Magazine, one of the first to tie with a major retailer outside New York, created a great deal of attention from merchants and consumers everywhere when they tied with Neiman-Marcus for a college promotion in 1937. Its success led to more, the *Vogue* 1937 Christmas issue, and in early 1938, a tie-in with Vogue's Americana issue, spotlighting the best of the American designers. In 1924 *Harper's Bazaar* began to furnish stores with information on editorial content and direction of the magazine.

The Monthly Promotions. Month after month, the national fashion magazines advise the retailer what is being featured in advance issues and propose a fashion tie-in for the store. The promotion is ''offered'' by the magazine, sometimes exclusively to one store in a community. The promotion may be accepted by the store if it is suitable to its program.

Accepting an offered magazine promotion carries certain requirements. The magazine is interested in assisting its advertisers and in promoting the fashion authority of its pages to the consumer through the retailer. The retailer, in turn, is interested in adding to its own fashion authority and stimulating consumer acceptance. A better reason, that is, to buy here and not there. The requirements that go along with a magazine's tie-in offer usually include:

1. Patronizing some of the resources featured editorially in the specific issue
2. Publicizing the promotion with newspaper ads, interiors, windows, signing, television, and radio

3. Presenting the fashion message of the promotion in a fashion show, fashion clinic, or some type of event to give significance to the effort
4. Documenting all efforts in connection with the promotion—pictures of the fashion show, windows, interiors, copies of ad tear sheets and newspaper publicity, duplicates of radio and television copy, and samples of invitations and programs used for an event or show

Since there is no charge involved in a magazine-offered promotion, and since it is usually offered exclusively to one store in each city, it is important to the magazine that some kind of effective identification is provided. Such as, "as seen in *Harper's Bazaar*," or *Vogue* says . . ." Visual credit plus documentation of everything that was done in connection with the promotion, is little enough to ask in return for the full treatment supplied by the magazine.

The Magazine Promotion Kit.   Well tuned in to the retailer's needs and manner of operation, the magazine provides the fashion director with most of the working tools necessary to get the show on the road. Once the promotion has been accepted by the store (usually handled by the fashion office), the magazine in turn sends out a promotion kit. Every magazine has its own technique, but in almost all cases, the kits are works of art.

Nothing is overlooked. Slick, color blow-ups of the cover of the issue involved . . . sketches of promotable fashion looks . . . resource lists of merchandise in the tie-in issue . . . suggested commentary for shows . . . suggested advertising copy or fashion slogans . . . [sig] cuts, mats for advertising reproduction . . . sketched ideas for windows or displays. In short, a completely designed promotion idea and how to produce, create, and exploit it. If a store fashion director needs help, the fashion books are prepared to graciously and effectively give it.

The Resource List.   The resource list is received from the magazine far in advance of a tie-in, often ahead of the promotion kit. This gives the buyers and the DMM time to check the list and order those pieces which will appear in the magazine issue that are suitable for the store. The idea is to have the merchandise in stock at the time the promotion breaks.

The Guest Editor.   In addition to all the help offered in the promotion kit, the magazine invites additional questions or offers necessary help by telephone. Some magazines have "field editors," that is, women assigned to various areas in the country to service the retailer. She is available to assist in any way requested. She knows the promotion thoroughly and undoubtedly has done it repeatedly in one city after another. This experience and knowledge she can bring to the store enlisting her assistance. This, too, is offered without charge.

However, many areas or cities not large enough to warrant a permanent "field editor," can request a "visiting editor." One of the reasons magazines require that promotions offered be accepted by a specific date is to schedule

Windows, featuring fashions from a specific issue, are part of a magazine promotion. Lord & Taylor window. (Courtesy of *Harper's Bazaar.*)

The magazine gets special treatment by the fashion store that has accepted the magazine's promotion. Swanson's of Kansas City, Missouri, newspaper ad. (Courtesy of *Harper's Bazaar*.)

personal appearances of guest editors. Another reason is to list the name of the store in the issue related to the tie-in.

A guest editor usually comes when a special event or fashion show is part of the promotion, and she may serve as guest commentator. In such a case, the magazine provides the store with glossy pictures and biographical material of the editor to add another facet of interest to the magazine's part in the effort. Again, this service is extended without charge.

The Home Furnishings Magazine Promotion. Not all fashion magazine promotions are devoted to ready-to-wear. Occasionally, a magazine like *Seventeen* will offer a beautifully laid-out fashion promotion dedicated to the home furnishings division. The promotion idea may include anything from "design your own room" to "fashions in table settings" to "how to entertain" or "party foods *he* will love." All geared to acquainting the young market with the home furnishings area and stir interest and recognition of home furnishing advertisers in the magazine.

The home furnishings magazine promotions (such as the types offered by *Seventeen* or those from specialized home magazines such as *Better Homes and Gardens* and *House Beautiful*) are usually regarded as divisional promotions. Almost all areas of the home division can get involved. If the home division has a fashion coordinator, he or she will handle all aspects of the promotion, relating to the fashion office where it applies. For example, if it is a youth-oriented promotion, then it undoubtedly would originate from the fashion office with the fashion director or youth coordinator.

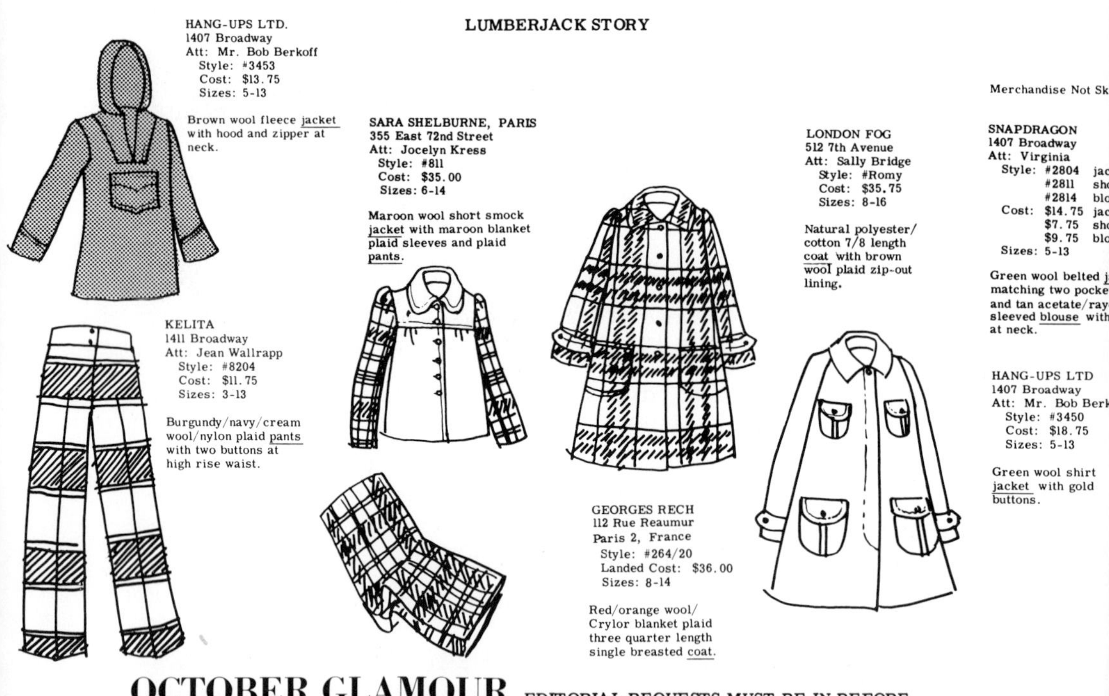

The Resource List. *Glamour* Magazine's list arrives in July for the October issue, complete with illustrations of the style numbers to be included.

Here it would get emphasis from the store's high school or college fashion board. If the promotion dealt with patio entertaining and patio cooking, the fashion office might lend an effective hand by presenting a show of patio fashions in the home furnishings area where model patios have been erected. All the proper documentation of what took place would apply here, too, as indicated earlier in this chapter.

The Accessory Magazine Promotion.   Another divisional opportunity to promote via the magazine is the accessory and cosmetic departments. Magazines are excellent sources on fashion coordination. *Glamour Magazine* would annually tie their September issue to "What to Wear with What." This could inspire an accessory fashion presentation, illustrating how to accessorize a series of costumes. All of the leading national fashion books are great inspiration for what's new in beauty care. Their interpretations of new cosmetic fashions and hair fashions can be beautifully tied to the corresponding departments with "as seen in *Vogue*" signing, displays, shows, and whatever lends itself to developing the idea. In areas such as this, the fashion director and her assistant or area coordinator can employ a world of originality.

The Magazine Ready-to-Wear Promotion. Ready-to-wear is the biggest area for magazine tie-ins. Such promotions can go either divisional or departmental. The editorial pages of the magazine usually dictate the promotion's direction. A high-fashion issue by *Harper's Bazaar* or *Vogue* would tend to pull a tie-in into the high fashion departments. It would be unthinkable to relate such an elegant issue, if it is that, to the entire division. This, then, becomes a departmental promotion only. On the other hand, the same magazines might use an entire issue to relate their fashion impact to a variety of departments and a variety of prices. All departments included would receive the same attention, publicity, and spotlight. All can claim (if their resource structure justifies it) fashion seen in *Vogue* or *Harper's Bazaar*.

The young departments have their own fashion leadership in national fashion books. The junior areas, catering to fashionable high school and college students, would put great faith in the fashion direction received in a promotion from *Seventeen*, for example. *Seventeen Magazine*, very sensitive to the interests and needs of its young readers, might propose a fashion idea not only on what's new, but also on where to wear it. Thus a

FASHION
EXTRAVAGANZA
OF THE YEAR . . .
a Fashion Week must

SEE FASHIONS STEP OUT
FROM THE PAGES OF

VOGUE
magazine

you are invited
to the

FASHION LUNCHEON
SHOWING

benefiting Subsidium—Memphis'
Parents School for the Deaf and Aphasic

TUESDAY, SEPT. 15
HOLIDAY HALL
RIVERMONT

MEET IN PERSON
RODRIGUES   famous designer
tor Peter Clements

BEVERLY PURCELL   Vogue
magazine editor

for Reservations and
further information
phone Goldsmith's 526-6633
DeSoto Room—Tickets 6.50 each

Vogue's **New York Collections fashion promotion. Twenty-six major fashion stores participated. At Goldsmith's of Memphis: above, the invitation; top right, the fashion show; bottom right, interior display.** (Courtesy of *Vogue* Magazine.)

VOGUE
$1.00 SEPT.
AMERICAN
FASHION
100
GREAT
NEW
LOOKS
THE
NEW
YORK
COLLECTIONS

A *Seventeen* back-to-school fashion show.

travel issue might evolve, based on the young generation's increased world travel, to encourage interest in selecting the most comfortable, most packable, and most fun clothes for whatever trip is being planned. *Seventeen*'s promotion kit for the travel issue will provide the details and suggestions for preparing and executing the tie-in.

Most magazine promotions would never happen without the sanction or urging of the fashion office. Such a promotion, after all, is not regarded as "immediate sell," nor is it necessarily the life line of a department or division. It is, nevertheless, a remarkably effective plus. In fact, the sum total of all promoting, a composite of many types and many approaches, is what helps a store send out its vibrations. If the customer is getting the right vibrations, if she is looking to the store for fashion leadership and spending her fashion dollar there, then it is the only testimonial the store needs.

Afterview

The routine used to coordinate an item promotion is applicable to almost any promotion, store-wide, divisional, or departmental. The work sheet or responsibility sheet used in a departmental promotion certainly is flexible enough to be utilized for any size promotion. The important point of any promotion is to have a plan, to be sure that all involved are informed of the plan, and, most important, to follow through. Many a well-laid promotion plan has gone up in smoke from lack of direction and failure to follow through on details.

Whatever it takes to get the fashion message to the customer can become part of the plan. A new season, a new trend, or a new item can inspire a whole new set of techniques or approaches. The first and uppermost thought to maintain as a guide line for any promotion is simply this: if the store does not see it as important, the customer will not.

It might also be well for the fashion director to realize that not all fashion promotions enjoy the dedicated interest and sympathy of the merchandising staff, selling staff, display, or advertising that she feels is deserved. However, if fashion leadership is what top management wants, she must stand unwavering in her enthusiasm for what must be done.

✻ *Chapter 9*

✻ *Fashion Projection through Advertising*

Everyone loves a good story, and the prime requisite for any good story is that it manages to hold your interest. It is the same with a good fashion story; it must hold your interest. In this case, the customer's interest. Newspaper advertising has long been the retailer's source of telling his story, complete with words and pictures.

Techniques change, of course, in storytelling as in anything else. People change, and life styles change. This is especially true with fashion advertising, because nothing is more closely related or more easily affected by new life styles and trends. Therefore, every year, every season (every item for that matter) dictates the texture or flavor of telling the fashion story.

How to Work with the Advertising Director

The advertising director in a retail organization is a remarkable machine. He or she runs a headful of gears at full speed at all times. He is programed for deadlines. With computerized precision he grinds out the routine materials.

185

He must also create new advertising ideas for a legion of buyers with a legion of different problems. While he is resting, he is supervising the advertising production department, copy department, and art department and approving, revising, or rewriting reams of layouts, copy, and illustrations.

The fashion director can identify with the advertising director. Neither ever puts on the brakes. There isn't time. However, when creative people meet, both operating in equal pressure chambers, it takes talent, finesse, and patience to accomplish their mutual objectives. An advertising director is a proud professional who would go an extra mile to turn a mediocre ad into a good one. He does not enjoy settling for less, and to do so is his greatest frustration. It is in this area that the kinship, or, better still, similarity between the advertising director and the fashion director is so prevalent.

On the basis of all this, it should not be difficult for the fashion director to identify with the feelings, problems, and goals of the advertising director. An excellent way to demonstrate such rapport is to respect the rules of the house—the advertising department's house.

Deadlines.   Deadlines must be met. A whole chain of complications can be created when deadlines are not honored. There are enough of the "unavoidables" around in the life of an advertising director keeping him well supplied with near-disasters, without the plaguing addition of the "avoidables." An unqualified respect for deadlines keeps the lines of good communication open. Copy, merchandise for sketching or photographing, and fashion information or direction, must be submitted at the prescribed "not later than. . . ."

Understandable Copy.   Speak clearly. Say what you mean. Do it briefly. These are top priority rules for good advertising copy. If a clear, effective fashion point is to be made in a proposed newspaper ad, the copy directions, too, should be succinct, to the point, and thoroughly indicative of the story line. Remember. Assume nothing. The fashion director may know what she means, but will the advertising department? Will the customer?

Merchandise for Illustration.   After merchandise for sketching is selected and taken to the advertising department, attach to each piece, in

A ready-to-wear fashion ad, completely accessorized with a specific accessory featured— the boot. The customer learns two things: what the fashion look is, and what goes with it. (Courtesy of Saks Fifth Avenue.)

writing, what the fashion message is. Very often, a personal appearance is in order, to verbally explain what is intended in the way of a fashion story. Again, assume nothing. The people in the advertising department are very perceptive, alert people, but they cannot be expected to know all the answers in regard to new fashion trends. They may not even know the questions. Even though they have attended the fashion director's educational sessions on new trends, there will still be blank spots in some areas.

When submitting merchandise for illustration (assuming it is women's ready-to-wear), the fashion office is also responsible for including what accessories should be used. Hats, shoes, bags, jewelry, scarves, and even hair fashions are part of the story. Accessorizing ready-to-wear illustrations is an excellent opportunity to show new looks from the accessory areas and clarify the new ways they should be used. The more often the customer sees a new fashion trend expressed correctly, the more quickly she is capable of accepting it. It is for this reason that the fashion director is involved with fashion ads (usually new-fashion ads only), to be sure the customer gets the fashion story in the most accurate and effective way.

Ad Preparation.   An understanding of the procedure of turning out an ad will aid the fashion office personnel tremendously in working efficiently and harmoniously with advertising personnel. Schedule the ad first, because space must be reserved. Advertising must have, in writing (usually on a form requisition), the size of the ad, the date it is to run, the nature of the ad, and information as to whether it is in black and white or color. If it is to be a fashion impact ad, coming out of the fashion office budget, then the fashion director is responsible for all aspects of the scheduling, preparing, and merchandising. If the ad is part of the advertising budget of the division with which she is working, all scheduling is done by the DMM. When deadline time rolls around, all copy, instructions, cuts or mats, and merchandise for illustrations, must be in the hands of the advertising department.

Followup is important. During the days of preparation, that is, while the advertising department is planning the layout, sketching, and writing copy for the ad, it is wise for the fashion director to visit the advertising offices and look over the shoulder of the artist to see if the interpretation of the fashion concept is correct. It is far better to correct an error at this stage of preparation than to discover mistakes after plates are made or after seeing a proof sheet. A major change at that point is almost too late. What's more, it is too expensive. Correction of a misspelled word in the copy or a mistake in price on some small thing can be fixed, but a major change, such as the wrong accessories on the wrong model, or the wrong piece of merchandise featured in the major spot, means the whole ad is

Right, sample advertising copy requisition. All information pertinent to the ad scheduled must be submitted to the advertising department in writing. (Courtesy of J. L. Brandeis, Omaha.)

BRANDEIS
ADVERTISING COPY REQUISITION

Fill out competely and send to Brandeis Advertising Dept. 18 days before ROP publication date, 10th floor downtown. Doubles, color ads, Roto, tabloids, special sections due earlier. Please ask for deadlines. Include merchandise, photos, tear sheets with copy requisition. No comparatives used unless shopped and all repeat items must be shopped again. Fill out comparative request.

DATE
AD RUNS_______________________

MEDIA_______________________

☐ ROP   ☐ COLOR

☐ ROTO   ☐ OTHER

☐ ENTERTAINMENT

BUYER_______________________ Dept._______________ Size of ad_______________
(number of inches)

EVENT_______________________ Item_______________ Price_______________

Art or Merchandise attached   ☐ Yes   ☐ No

MAIN THEME
What is most important idea to play up in ad? If omnibus ad, what is feature item?

Other important selling features

Sizes, colors, dimensions, fiber content, fabric, etc.

THIS ITEM AVAILABLE AT FOLLOWING STORES
NOTE: Write floor inside box

☐ DOWNTOWN   ☐ CROSSROADS   ☐ AMES   ☐ WESTGATE

☐ LINCOLN   ☐ GRAND ISLAND ☐ SOUTHROADS ☐ NORTHGATE

THIS AD ALSO RUNS

☐ World Herald   ☐ Blacker

☐ Star Journal   ☐ Other

☐ Grand Island

Date_______________
(if different from date above)

MAIL OR PHONE   ☐ Yes   ☐ No   COUPON   ☐ Yes   ☐ No

IMPORTANT: For the success of your ad, please fill this form out completely. Art or merchandise should accompany this requisition, this a buyer's responsibility. Incomplete forms will be returned and ad must be rescheduled.

down the drain. All major changes or adjustments should be made while the artist still has an eraser in his hand. It is the same with the copy writer; she also has an eraser. Once the layout is finalized, however, and the type is set, beware.

Other Printed Material. In addition to the newspaper ad, there are several other forms of print that come under the jurisdiction of the advertising director. The statement enclosure, booklets, pamphlets, and catalogues are all part of the advertising picture. The fashion director's involvement occurs only when fashion supervision is required. The procedure is much the same as with the newspaper ad. The same things to watch for apply in these cases. Deadlines are always hanging overhead, so timing is essential.

Invitations and Programs. The printed matter that relates more immediately to the fashion office is invitations and programs for fashion events. Invitations to fashion shows, for example, are the concern of the fashion office, because it is from the time that the customer is invited that the fashion image or fashion message begins. The color of the stock, the type of print or engraving, the theme and title of the event, are all part of what will be happening at the show, all part of the fashion statement.

A member of the fashion office staff could design and write a sample invitation to stimulate interest in the special fashion event. The format of the invitation might be "established." That is, just as the store's newspaper or magazine advertising carries a special look or signature, so invitations might remain a part of the over-all concept. Where the established format does not exist, each event presenting a different flavor or need might require or justify an original approach tailored to that event only.

Whatever format or theme the invitation requires, the pertinent information of what is happening where and when is most important. The guest receiving the invitation needs to know (in addition to the date, time, and place) whether there is any admission charge, if it is necessary to r.s.v.p., and, if so, the deadline for making reservations. The more understandable and appetizing the invitation, the better the response.

If a printed program is to be provided for guests at the show or fashion event, then this, too, should be drawn up with the theme in mind, perhaps relating to the look of the invitation to establish continuity and greater impact. If the program needs art work for the cover, this must be worked out with the advertising department. The fashion office needs to spell out the kind of art work. An elegant fashion show with a swinging cover on the program would be obviously a serious contradiction. The fashion office must guide the artist's brush, so to speak, to paint the best picture possible of what the show is all about.

If the content of the program is to include a line-up of those style numbers to be shown, fittings must be made early enough to get copy up to advertising before press time. If names of models are to be included, someone in the fashion office should be assigned to carefully proofread a copy of the program before it is run off. Nothing is more devastating, especially if the guest models are customers, than to have names misspelled. It is the alert, watchful eye that makes for a happy result when it comes to printed material. Once in print, mistakes are recorded for posterity.

Photographing Models.   When a piece of advertising requires photographing live models with merchandise from actual stock, the fashion director must be on hand to personally supervise the shooting. Usually, a shooting session must be done far in advance of the arrival of stock. It is up to the fashion office, therefore, to obtain the pieces that represent the looks they are trying to sell. The fashion office will also book the models for photography. The fashion director will request the model best suited to the type of garment, look, or theme. During the fitting session, the fashion director will advise the model on the type of hairdo, makeup, and attitude required for the photograph.

Attitude or fashion concept is the prime reason for the fashion director's presence during a shooting. The photographer, receiving instructions from the fashion director, will direct the shooting, but the fashion director must watch to see that the attitude does not become too sophisticated, too amusing, too elegant, anything, except what it is supposed to be. Attitude is what helps sell the idea. A good model is also a good actress and can interpret the mood of the garment when it is explained to her.

Checking out the model, helping her manipulate the costume correctly (belted right, draped right, tucked in right) is, of course, another important reason for the fashion director to be on hand for the shooting. It is her fashion opinion and, ultimately, that of the store, which is reflected in the photograph.

The set, backdrop, or location of the shooting is also part of the attitude.

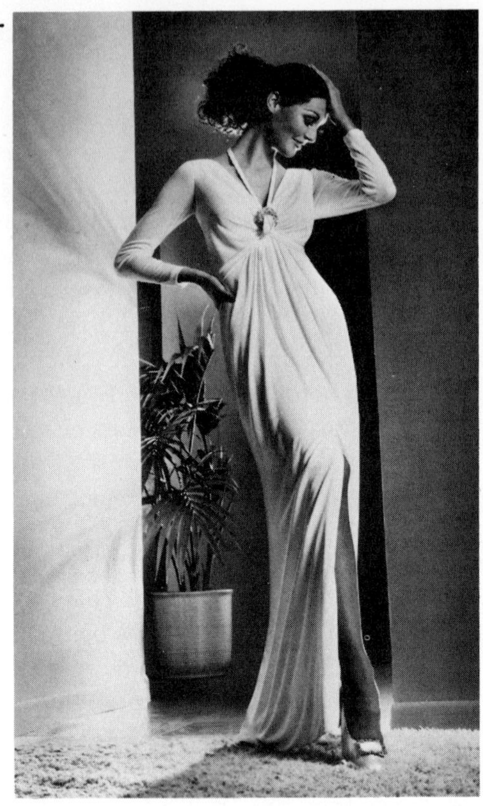

In photographing fashion, the background and lighting are set in keeping with the mood. (Courtesy of Helen Rose, Calif.)

The proper surroundings, either to enhance or dramatize the fashion, must be in keeping with the theme without upstaging the purpose of the photograph.

An example of improper or insufficient instructions from the fashion office to the advertising director and subsequently to the photographer, was the planned shooting of a new "antique look" for evening dressing. There was no way for the advertising director to know that the fashion office had not been explicit. He is not a mind reader. Whatever instructions for the setting he received, he passed on to the photographer. "An evening gown with an antique look." When the fashion director arrived in the studio she saw the model, dressed in the delicate antique gown with a Gibson Girl look, standing on the set beneath a huge, baroque chandelier. It was all wrong. It was entirely too massive, too presumptious. The chandelier completely upstaged the soft, delicate attitude of the dress.

Had the instructions been more explicit this would not have happened. At least it would not have gone as far afield. The chandelier was antique all right, but more of a European grand ball look. The gown was strictly after-the-turn-of-the-century American, a modest, feminine look. Very lovely for evening, but hardly suitable for a grand ball.

The props, the attitude of the model, setting, and lighting must contribute to the fashion look. At no time must they compete. If the costume in question should be a bold print city dress with five or six strong colors, it is important that the background not be too busy. It might be colorful, to help "pull out" one of the important colors, but still not busy. Simplicity of background is often effective in a photograph, in the same way that white space in a newspaper ad enhances the importance of an illustrated subject. It is not necessary for members of the fashion office to design sets for photographing fashion, but it is important to interpret the fashion for those who do build or design sets.

A general knowledge of what is possible and what is needed for fashion advertising is an invaluable asset to the fashion director. Even in stores where the fashion director does not get as completely involved with the fashion projection through advertising or in stores where they do little or no photography, it is still advantageous for the fashion director to have at least an awareness of what makes good ads and what does not. In one way or another, in a future job perhaps, the composite of her technical knowledge will put her in good stead when the challenge presents itself.

How to Merchandise Fashion Ads

The merchandising of the fashion ad starts with the promotion plan. Those "promotables," selected from the fashion director's presentation and then sanctioned by management, are those fashion stories included in the promotion or advertising plan.

On the advertising schedule, where all ads are noted daily, weekly, and monthly, newspaper space is reserved for whatever ads the fashion division has in mind. The leading fashion stories of the season would undoubtedly include new silhouettes, fabrics, colors, patterns, and accessory treatments. Each classification might merit a series or a single ad, but each one is merchandised to relate the message with impact.

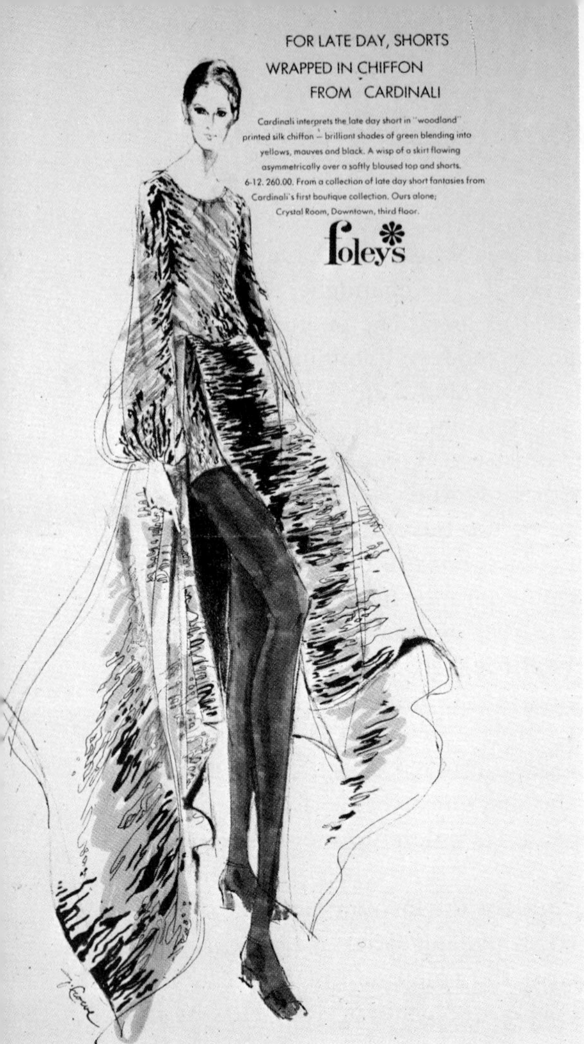

Foley's essential fashion ads appear in the newspaper's society section. To add emphasis to the ad's fashion importance, the art work is signed by the artist. (Courtesy of Foley's, Houston.)

The divisional merchandise manager, when consulting with the fashion director, might lay down a series of guide lines. "For this item we are looking for volume, so I would prefer moderately priced examples in the ad." The fashion director will then note that merchandise will be pulled from departments carrying the desired price lines. She will instruct her staff on what to look for. She will advise them about the purpose of the ad. The less they are in the dark, the better.

"This fashion ad, the new look in coats, I think is worthy of a full page. Mrs. Coat Buyer has selected about four or five pieces she is especially anxious to show. Look them over and see what you think." The fashion director makes a note to visit the coat department. When the fashion director and the buyer agree on which pieces would best do justice to the fashion impact they are after, the fashion director will instruct her staff to pull accessories for the pieces, making sure each one has an individual, effective look. Whenever possible, the fashion office uses actual accessories from stock to be sketched in ads. Very often a customer sees a hat in a coat ad or a piece of jewelry in a dress ad that she wants. If the accessory has merely been sketched from imagination it is frustrating to the customer; she cannot buy it. The real thing gives the ad that much more mileage.

Each ad is merchandised (pieces pulled from stock or flown in ahead of stock arrival) to publicize that which the store has for sale. Each ad must be illustrated with those pieces that best speak for the look, the fabric, and the color, whatever those trends are in which the store believes.

How Fashion Ads Differ.   If there was only one fashion story to tell per season, there would seem to be little need to create a ream of exciting, tantilizing, intriguing, and inspired ways to tell the story. "This is it, ladies!" would be enough. Not so. Even if there was but one fashion story or trend, the competitors would be in the same boat, all the more reason to get the fashion message to the consumer in such an irresistible way that you would be assured of her coming to your store instead of the competitor's.

However, there is never just one fashion story; there are many. And it is the differences in the trends and the differences in the customers that dictate the advertising techniques to be applied. The differences influence the frequency, style, size, and kind of space in the magazine section, society page, teen page, business section, etc. It is fashion for everyone, or a select few? It is strictly a here-today-gone-tomorrow fad? Is it fashion with such strong acceptability that it is destined to grow? Is it rehashed fashion, an updated look from last year destined to stick around this year and next year too? The advertising treatment is regulated by the answers to these questions.

Almost all fashion can be pigeonholed into these three areas:
Future fashion
Now fashion
Bread-and-butter fashion

Each of these, in its own way, is extremely powerful and vital to the total fashion picture. And in the area of advertising, each must be handled in a manner suitable to its characteristics.

Future Fashion. It doesn't take long for word to get around in these days of instant communication as regards coming fashion trends. Hardly is the idea off the designer's sketch page and into the cutting room when fashion forecasts reveal they have it on good authority that the fashion look will be so-and-so. It is not just the retailer who is hearing this prediction, it is the consumer, too. Therefore, to merchandise *ahead* of the consumer and to be a leader of fashion takes some doing. But, having done it, that is, having succeeded in sampling a coming trend ahead of the crowd, is top priority to tell about in advertising. This is the ad that appeals to the fashion customer interested in being first in her circle, her area, to appear in the new look. This is the ad on "future fashion."

Such a fashion ad, the one capable of giving the store its image as fashion leader, is the one the fashion director gives her personal attention. It is very possible that the sampling or testing of this item or trend was done at her urging or recommendation in the first place, and she is understand-

The two-figure ad, with a single fashion statement. A consistent format to underline the store's fashion image. (Courtesy of Filene's, Boston.)

ably anxious to see customer response to the merchandise and community response to the customer who buys it.

Future fashion is not yet a trend, but future fashion ads are capable of launching one. If the illustrations, copy, and banner lines or theme are provacative enough, a parade of curious, interested customers might drop in to see and try the new idea. Even for those who do not buy this particular piece of future fashion, two advantages are present: (1) the customer has been made aware of the store's leadership and may buy something else during her trip to the store, and (2) she may, through this early exposure of a new look, become one of the more prolific buyers a little later when selections are fuller and the trend is rolling. At any rate, the customer has found her way to the store; she knows where the escalators are and what floor sells her kind of fashion. Exposure is a vital beginning.

Consistency, of course, is one of the greatest boosters for selling future fashion. Ads on advanced fashion trends, appearing often enough, will create the desired dependency of the consumer on the store they now feel is on top of everything. Even when a future fashion ad is well done, sometimes the idea is so jolting that it is difficult for the customer to grasp it completely, immediately. She may call the fashion office for clarification.

"Can a woman my age wear the new look you advertised yesterday?"

"Would it be all right to wear my last-season's shoes with this new look?"

"Would you consider this new look too bold to wear to a dinner party at my husband's boss's home?"

A good fashion office is well informed about the newly advertised trend, the appropriate use, accessorizing and availability in which departments, sizes, etc. Questions come up most frequently at the introduction of a trend, and a knowledgeable fashion office staff, from beginners on up, can waylay a great many fears and doubts of the consumer.

A beginner in a fashion office will soon learn that many a customer feels like a beginner every time the fashion picture has a drastic change. Therefore, even a beginner in a fashion job can feel more confident about her fashion knowledge, limited as it may seem at the outset, because she is closer to the picture than the customer. Observing the kind of questions and reactions stimulated by the newly advertised fashion trends is an excellent teacher. The more perceptive the beginner is of just such small details, the more capable she will be in watching for details later when she has more responsibility.

Now Fashion. The very item or trend that once was projected in an ad as "future fashion" might very well be that which will eventually emerge as "now fashion." In other words, it is one that caught on. It is the trend that grew important and desirable through acceptance. No matter how great a fashion idea may seem to designers, manufacturers, merchandisers, fashion directors, or magazine editors, consumer acceptance is what puts a trend into motion. Now fashion is a trend in motion.

Unlike future fashion ads, which might be a total of one to announce a coming trend, the now fashion ads might evolve into a full-fledged advertising campaign. Included in the campaign might be ads of the now fashion in the high-fashion area, the moderate priced version, even a knock-off of the look from the budget area. And in addition to price levels, the campaign might present examples from the women's departments, juniors', children's, and men's. All of these ads on a specific fashion subject, if brought together under one umbrella, become an advertising campaign.

Now fashion, that which is currently acceptable and currently in stock, could start out important the first season and grow even more important in the next season. On the other side of the coin, now fashion could end up just that, great now, dead tomorrow. Its longevity is not the point; its acceptance "now" is. If it is not obsolete immediately, all the better, but its impact on the now fashion scene is the prime concern of the merchant. The fashion director's great concern is telling the fashion story.

The merchandising of now fashion ads is the most important advertising assignment concerning the fashion director. Here is the big story, the volume story. As a fashion director, everything the fashion division has to sell you must help to herald effectively, here and now, or forever hold your "piece"; the piece, of course, is the advertising copy that must tell the world what is going on.

Meeting with the members of the merchandising staff, the fashion director would learn exactly how many ads are to be devoted to this effort, what size they are, and when they are scheduled to run. The final advertising schedule would then be drawn up by the DMM and sales-promotion director. The fashion director, now fully aware of which ads are to cover which departments and which ads are to run on which dates, gets out a work schedule for her staff, to pull merchandise for the artists in advertising and to prepare fashion copy that might be helpful to the copywriter.

Bread-and-Butter Fashion.   Coming all the way down the pike, future fashion becomes now fashion, and now fashion (if it lives long enough and strong enough) might one day become a classic or a staple. Basically, that is what happens to trends that have endured the test of time.

Future fashion, the initial testing, to reach the forward-thinking con-

A ''now'' fashion ad: ''The Look

of Houston.)

sumer, is something of the appetizer. The now fashion is the entree, served up in a variety of inviting choices. But the classic old stand-bys or faithful regulars, no matter what else is on the fashion menu during a given season, are known as the "bread and butter." A future fashion might be ignored. A now fashion might bomb. But those classic staples, always dependable, always around, are a store's bread and butter. Whatever other tastes she may have, almost every customer requires some kind of bread-and-butter fashion from time to time.

In music, the new sounds are composed, sung, and flourish for a time. They come and go, but the old standards endure. However, just because a song has become a standard, is no reason to always play it with the same old arrangement. The arrangement, in fact, is the only part that becomes dated, the words and music seldom do. So it is with bread-and-butter fashion; only the arrangement is changed. A newer fabric, sleeve, color, or accent, but still the same song. Still bread and butter. But updated.

Bread-and-butter fashion ads never call attention to their past, nor are they ever called bread and butter in advertising copy. This is strictly an "inside" tag of the retail business. Unlike future fashion or now fashion, both of which are perfectly acceptable in advertising copy, bread-and-butter fashion, by any other name, is better. Call them "Updated Classics," "The Classic Look," "The New Standard," or anything that smacks of that which is "new." No woman cares to be associated with the old guard, even though she might recognize the concept as an old favorite. This is not deceiving; it is strictly psychological.

Fundamentally, this is exactly the way bread-and-butter ads are merchandised, with an updated approach, with the new language, new interpretation, new accessory treatment, the whole new thing. Take a sketch of an updated classic placed in an ad with a modern painting drawn in the background and the "suggestion" makes it new. Take another classic look and include it as part of a season's campaign, say, in an advertising handle such as "The New Spring." All spring fashion ads, upholding the continuity of the theme, would enjoy a fashion spot in "The New Spring" —future, now, bread and butter. Together they make up the campaign. Together they tell the entire fashion story for the season. And how well the fashion story is told—with clarity, enthusiasm, and authority—determines the happy ending.

Magazine Ads

A fashion ad in a national fashion magazine or special fashion magazine supplement in a newspaper, represents more than the specific garment being advertised. If it warrants the price of a full page (and the price is

A single figure in a magazine ad can handsomely promote a look, a designer, or a shop—all reflecting the store's fashion image. (Ad in *Harper's Bazaar,* courtesy of Bullock's, Calif.)

usually substantial), it must accomplish a great deal. The magazine ad, unlike the newspaper ad, is usually a showcase for a single item. One outstanding creation by an outstanding designer. One provocative look dramatizing a special fashion shop within the store. Something special, something that makes a vital fashion statement. The magazine ad, there-fore, can be a very important image-maker, for the store as fashion authority, for a department or shop "not to be missed when in town." The selection of the garment to be photographed or sketched and the theme or mood of the ad must reflect the desired image of the store.

The fashion director's approach to merchandising a national magazine ad, if requested by her management to do so, would be to first consider these things:

1. In which magazine is the ad scheduled?
2. Who is the reader of the magazine?
3. Which fashion look or department would appeal to this reader?
4. What type of fashion would accomplish the greatest impact?
5. In which issue will the ad appear, and what will be the editorial emphasis of that issue?

Answering these questions carefully will be the fashion director's starting place. The answers, as illustrated in the following two examples, will be her most reliable guide.

Example A	*Example B*
Q. In which magazine is the ad scheduled?	
A. *Harper's Bazaar*	A. *Mademoiselle*
Q. Who is the reader of the magazine?	
A. Affuent, young sophisticates, and mature fashion-alert women	A. College women, young career women
Q. Which fashion look or department would appeal to this reader?	
A. Elegant, spirited, (preferably from a French room, young designer, high-fashion contemporary department or fur salon)	A. Junior department, career shop, sportswear department, young contemporary shop
Q. What type of fashion would accomplish the greatest fashion impact?	
A. An exciting holiday gown from our most effective designer collection	A. A provocative example from our new young contemporary shop

Q. In which issue will the ad appear and what will be the editorial emphasis
of that issue?

    A. Holiday issue—   A. August college issue—
      holiday fashions   campus or sportswear fashions

Some retailers would not consider going into two magazines with such
entirely different readership, simply because their image would not permit
it. Other merchants, however, may desire appealing to a more diversified
audience. The fashion director who is consulted about what kind of magazine ad to buy, could easily guide her management into the correct path
by stating "we do not belong in this one," or "our customer is the reader
of this one." Also, for certain times of the year one magazine is more suitable
than another, such as the back-to-campus issues as illustrated above. It is
the fashion director's business to know.

Using this outline as a springboard, the fashion director is ready to take
the plunge and select or recommend which department should be represented in a particular issue of the magazine and which fashion item would
be most effective. Since most stores buy space in national magazines for
prestige only, deciding what will be the greatest image-builder must be
the prime factor.

After consulting with the DMM and the buyer of the department from
which the item will come, arrangements must be made to obtain a single
piece for illustrations or photographs. Also, arrangements must be made
to make sure the merchandise will be in the department when the ad runs.
This is best accomplished through consultation with the buyer.

Now it is time for the advertising director to get into the act. He must
be assured that the merchandise will be available in plenty of time for ad
preparation. The magazine's deadlines must be met. Also, the advertising
director must be filled in with explicit detail on the fashion story the ad is
expected to tell.

Magazine Ad Format. If magazine advertising is to be a regular thing,
that is, if a series of ads are planned, it is the underlining of the store's image
that will make for a more memorable fashion impact. In other words, all
the ads with fashion purpose should carry an identification, signature
motif, theme, or characteristic that will identify the store and its fashion
message. If such a format does not already exist, the fashion director may
be of some assistance to the advertising director in arriving at some treat-

ment that would be in keeping with the store's fashion image. It should also be remembered that the longevity of a magazine ad far exceeds the month in which it is issued. Months later that magazine might be reread at home or in a doctor's office or beauty shop. Continuity of format, therefore, helps the ad to stimulate stronger store identification.

All plans for the magazine ad must be submitted to the sales-promotion director for approval. If the ad and its entire conception originates with the sales-promotion director, he might submit the copy to the fashion director as a double check on proper fashion direction.

Regional Magazine Ads. A department store or specialty shop of national prominence and perhaps in an area attractive to the tourist trade and out-of-town shoppers, will be more interested in national advertising in the prestige or currently popular fashion books. A store not likely to benefit from such national exposure but nevertheless anxious to supplement or intensify its fashion leadership on its own home ground, would be more likely to take advantage of ad space in national magazines offered on a regional basis. That is, the ad would run only in those copies distributed in a number of states surrounding the advertiser's location. Thus, even though it does not appear nationally, the ad has the effectiveness of appearing in a highly regarded or much read national magazine. In this way, many stores, who might not otherwise be in a position to take advantage of such an association, can derive the benefit of advertising where the impact would be more immediately rewarding.

Magazine Credits. There is one way that all stores tying in with a national magazine can get national mention, whether they buy advertising space or not. That is the magazine credit, an excellent publicity plus from the fashion books.

In order to advise their readers of what store and in which city the editorially featured fashions can be found, "credits" are awarded by the national fashion magazines to retail stores at no cost. The credits might appear in the back of the magazine or as "on-page" credits. On-page credits are the most desirable. These choice bits of mention are located directly on the page with the editorial feature.

The on-page credit might come about in different ways.

1. Credit may be offered by the magazine to a store involved in a promotional tie-in with a specific issue.
2. Credit may be suggested by the manufacturer whose garment is being featured editorially. The manufacturer advises the magazine what stores are buying the style number involved. The magazine's merchandising department usually checks with the fashion director of each store for verification. "Do you accept this on-page credit?" If the store is buying the style number in question from the resource quoted, the answer is yes and the on-page credit is granted.
3. The last way to obtain on-page credit is store initiated. The buyer or fashion director requests credit mention from the magazine or from the resource being featured.

However it comes about, it is a form of publicity that provides good fashion identification and a share of fashion prestige.

How to Clear Magazine Credits.   When the fashion director receives notification from the fashion magazines that credits are available in a forthcoming issue, it is her responsibility to get "clearance" before accepting. A review of the resource list indicates to her which buyers might be involved. She would then send copies of the resource list to those buyers whose merchandise might deserve credit in the book.

Her communication might read:

> Dear Mrs. Buyer:
> Attached please find the resource list for *Seventeen's* August issue.
> Please check which resources you carry and note if the style numbers to be included in this issue will be in your stock for August selling.
> We would greatly appreciate your immediate answer, as we have a deadline to meet, requested by *Seventeen*. They must have have immediate clearance to make the issue.
>
> Miss Fashion Director

When the replies from all the buyers concerned have been returned to her desk, the fashion director sends one copy, with all style numbers and

BAZAAR

Harper's

717 FIFTH AVENUE, NEW YORK 22 • 935-5900

EDITORIAL CREDIT SLIP

Harper's Bazaar plans to show editorially the merchandise described below.
PLEASE HELP US WITH THE ACCURACY OF THE DESCRIPTION!

CHECK YOUR STOCKS TO BE SURE THAT THE MERCHANDISE LISTED
BELOW WILL BE IN STORES WHEN HARPER'S BAZAAR IS ON THE STANDS.

IMPORTANT { TELEPHONE NECESSARY
CORRECTIONS IMMEDIATELY
935-4026, 935-4027

PLEASE CHECK, CORRECT, SIGN AND RETURN ONE SLIP IMMEDIATELY

Date of Issue: February

Space: Full pg. col.

Resource: Boutique Donald Brooks

Fabric: Avisco rayon crepe by Maxwell

Style: #764, 765

Sizes:

Wholesale Price:

Retail Price:

Approximate Editorial Description:

#764: Midriff top with long bloused sleeves and scoope
neck, ankle length wrap skirt.
#765: Long dress to the ankle with tie belt and halter
neckline and sleeveless.

Credits to Appear:
Manufacturer:
Retail Stores:

Boutique Donald Brooks
Saks Fifth Avenue
Sakowitz
Goldwater's
Brandeis
H. and S. Pogue
Swanson's

Approved by:
Date:

H-76-10M-E00098

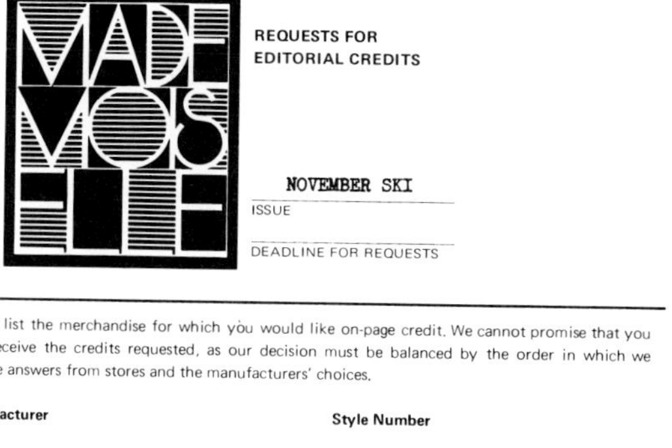

Magazine editorial credits: *Mademoiselle* Magazine request form for editorial credits, and *Harper's Bazaar* confirmation slip of editorial credit granted.

resources to be carried in the store from that issue, back to the magazine. Only those numbers that have been "cleared" can be included. When a customer reads the magazine and sees the store in her city listed on a page with a dress she wants, she expects to find that dress available. Some customers, [far from the city in which a retailer is listed as a *Seventeen* store,] may write and order the clothes they see illustrated. "Please send me a size 9 of the dress on page 56 of the August issue of *Seventeen*. Please charge to my account."

How Credits Began. *Haper's Bazaar, Vogue and Mademoiselle* were among the innovators of the magazine credit. At first, only fashion stores in New York were given the nod. Later, in the mid-thirties, major retailers throughout the country were receiving back-of-the-book or on-page credits from the leading national fashion magazines.

In her autobiography, *The World of Carmel Snow*, Mrs. Snow (one of the first great editors of *Harper's Bazaar*) said, ". . . when we were the first to publish out-of-town credits, telling our readers where they might buy the clothes we featured in Chicago and St. Louis and Los Angeles and San Francisco, we were threatened with a boycott from New York stores until Andy Goodman of Bergdorf Goodman brought them back in line."

Afterview

"Assume nothing" is a favorite phrase. It has appeared often enough thus far to have made a noticeable point. The point is, wasted time and motion, errors and misstatements, hurt feelings and misunderstandings occur all too often when it has been "assumed" that someone at the other end knows all the answers. Especially in the area of advertising, to "assume they know" or "assume they have been told" is suicide. It is far safer, and wiser, to repeat a direction than to omit it. To assume is the mark of an amateur. A pro seldom does.

Advertising is a remarkable area for learning how to project fashion. The beginner who is watchful, even if her job is only to run the fashion merchandise from the fashion office to the advertising department, can translate every little bit of information she picks up into valuable knowledge. The beginner can almost play a game of skill with her meager tasks, such as being a messenger for the fashion office. Why did they select this particular dress to sketch? How will it look with these accessories? What is the point of the ad?

When she sees the finished product, that dress she carried up for the artist to sketch and those accessories she bagged up and transported, there it is, a huge, beautiful figure in the middle of a full-page fashion ad. The look and the theme begin to have a special meaning for her and even the department from which it came. "Did it sell? That dress I took up for Sunday's ad?" she might find herself asking the buyer.

"Did it! Over half the pieces we had in that number walked out the next day!"

"Really? Wow! That's great!"

Yes, it's great. This beginner shows promise. She is involved. She has identified with the whole picture. To empathize with a fashion effort is a mighty strong indication that she could be good fashion coordinator material.

Chapter 10

Fashion Projection through Display

In projecting the fashion image of the store, the fashion director will find that display, very strongly and quite immediately, will help her to do a most impressive job of telling a fashion story.

Through display, a perceptive merchandiser can look at any store and notice immediately that stores merchandising position. He can see when it is not just handsomely decorated but is also the last word in fashion leadership. He knows at once whether it is a promotional store or a fashion store. He knows if it is a leader or a follower. The customer, too, although not as analytical as a professional retailer, knows by what she sees, what the store is all about.

Making a Fashion Statement—Visually

The visual fashion statement made by a retail institution, modest or magnanimous, speaks loud and clear to every customer who walks in the door. Through imaginative presentations, the customer is made aware immediately and easily of many things about the store. Three of these are most important:

211

1. The personality of the store.   Display should reveal how the store sees itself—elegant, contemporary, avant-garde, conservative, entirely one or the other, or perhaps a bit of each assigned to specific areas in an attempt to be all things to all people.
2. What is new.   If fashion leadership is the goal of the store, this category is most important. Display is the all-time "must" for presenting the newest looks in the newest way.
3. Projection of peak trends.   The customer who is well informed and knowledgeable about what is going on in current fashion, still must be reassured that the store is equally knowledgeable and right on top of peak trends. By underlining and underscoring visually, the retailer indicates how strongly it believes in what it has for sale.

The Windows

Outside the store, before the customer takes the spin through the revolving door, she knows something of what is going on inside, but, more important, her appetite has been intensified or she has been given a bright new idea. The customer has learned a great deal more. If the windows are well done, she has learned about:

1. An important new fashion color
2. A new fashion silhouette
3. What fabric is leading in importance
4. The personal appearance of a fashion celebrity in the store
5. A special event of store-wide caliber, such as an import fair
6. The forthcoming season (How else in July would a woman know it is time to buy a winter coat?)

And so it goes. In stores' efforts to instruct and sell, retail windows have been dramatized throughout retail history with such inspiration and excitment that they have become famous as entertainment.

Out-of-towners take special joy in going window shopping. During a special event or holiday season, people will travel far from surrounding communities to a large city to see, for example, the Christmas windows. Therefore, with the dual responsibility of retail windows (1) to inform and (2) to entertain, the planning must be thorough and inspired.

Continuity of Display.   It is wonderful, of course, to present exciting exterior displays, but if it comes off as "just so much window dressing," all is lost. The continuity of display within the store and the merchandise to back it up, must be there.

A dramatic window can be a testimonial to the importance of a new fashion look. Photo by Malan Studio, New York. (Courtesy of Bloomingdale's, New York.)

Interior Displays

Although windows are depended upon to make good first impressions (after all, they do make a store look inviting and appetizing) interior displays are first in importance today. It stands to reason. Here, inside, in the department, at the point of sale, is where the most stimulation is needed to invite and entice the consumer.

There was a time when displays were jazzed up with a lot of goop and gobs of flowers and tinsel and an overhelming amount of props. Too many mannequins, crowded into a display area, upstaged everything else in the department. Everything was getting a lot of attention—except the merchandise. Today, with expanded classifications and the rush of changing trends and stepped-up seasons, it has been realized that the merchandise itself can come front and center. The merchandise itself is exciting, or at least it should be.

Adopting a more contemporary look, perhaps with the clean-cut looks of glass, plastics, chrome, and steel, merchandise can come forward in displays with a genuine, understandable sell. There are times when the absence of mannequins is more desirable in displays of ready-to-wear,

Beautiful fashion windows underscore the store's fashion excellence, and its interest in the consumer's needs. (Courtesy of Lazarus, Columbus, Ohio.)

Stores where ''window shopping'' is important. One fashion piece
presented simply and changed often tells an up-to-the-minute
fashion story: Left, with an attention-getting backdrop; Right, with a
single prop, for drama. (Courtesy of Bonwit Teller, New York.)

and there are other times when mannequins are a must to show the hem
length and total leg accessories of a specific look. There is a right time for
everything, but in moderation. This adage has become extremely applicable
to many areas of in-store displays.

Boutiques and Shops

Perhaps the most beautiful example of how the merchandise itself is the
feature, is found in special boutiques and shops, either those within
the store, free-standing specialty shops, or independent twigs within a
shopping center. All of these, come alive and speak their piece much
better when the merchandise is the stand-out. After all, the greatest
advantage of the boutique is to spotlight, to feature, and to pull out
specific merchandise.

Above, the college shop. Young mannequins outside announce what's inside. (Courtesy of Abraham & Strauss, Brooklyn.)

Below, in a boutique, the individuality of the merchandise projects. The Maisonette Boutique. (Courtesy of Neiman Marcus, Dallas.)

Fixtures more than props, architectural background more than decor, make this kind of uncluttered display possible. Panels and frames that move and adjust on which hooks and clear plastic chains, or rods and tubes, or ropes can be attached or detached as needed have been utilized with great success. For hanging merchandise such display equipment provides built-in flexibility and numerous change possibilities. Units that nest, fold, or pull apart might be just the ticket for a certain look. Whatever the choice of atmosphere selected for any display area (windows, departments, boutiques, shops) the display material must be in keeping with the mood of the merchandise, and it must reflect the quality of the merchandise.

How to Work with the Display Director

All of this philosophy about display is not included here for the fashion director to tell the display director how to run his department. It is, in truth, for the other side of the coin, to help her run her own department.

When working with the display director, as with every other executive to whom she must relate, the fashion director needs to have a basic knowledge of the function of that executive. She needs to relate to his objectives. In short, she must know how to speak his language.

Change—The Magic of Display. If departments are to benefit from turning their stocks often, the displays, interiors, and exteriors should also change often. The racks and back room could be filled with newly arrived merchandise, but unless the display areas are changed regularly no one would know it. A customer shopping in the store every week could enjoy the surprise of a new look in the departments she frequents almost every time she stops by. In fact, that is primarily why she does stop by. Something new has arrived. Without asking anyone or being told, she can see it.

The change may be just a simple thing, a new color grouping on a T-stand or a clothes tree, or a new fabric look expressed in variety of ways but displayed together for emphasis. It may be a new designer sampled on a mannequin, just one, but changed so often it seems that there is a endless stream of new ideas by this or another prolific designer.

Display, hour after hour, day after day, makes fashion statements more continuously than any other means. Its immediate relationship to the merchandise is, therefore, the primary factor. The use of merchandise as display or rather the central feature of display is what it is all about.

Fashion Meetings with the Display Staff.   If changes must be made so often and if those changes must represent the fashion merchandise in an effective, refreshing manner every time out, an endless stream of fashion ideas and imaginative approaches are needed. No display department, no matter how well informed and creative, can do this continuously without a little help from its friends. The fashion director, on the other hand, knows full well that one of the most important friends of fashion is the display director.

Everyone profits from inspiration. An exchange of ideas in the area of fashion and display helps eliminate the mystery of how current fashion trends should be handled. Many stores report that their creative areas, fashion, advertising, and display, meet on a regular basis to clear the air. "Just what do you mean when you say 'soft?'" a member of the display department might ask the fashion director in one of their meetings. A good question. To her it might mean one thing, to him something entirely different.

Not only is a verbal explanation important at such a session, but here is a golden opportunity to demonstrate with actual merchandise and to clarify. "This is soft," she could explain, holding up a garment. Or, she may show two, three, or half a dozen examples that come under the heading of "soft." The display department, having seen some bona fide examples of whatever is in question, now has a clearer picture of what it has to work with and what must be accomplished.

If the display coordinators work out of the fashion office the problem is less complicated, because they are educated by the fashion director as to what each and every look or trend is like. If the display coordinators report to the display director, fashion meetings are more of a necessity to continually update and explain what's new or the new way of handling a standard or classic look.

"We have never put jewelry on this type of garment before," a display person may protest.

"Well, we do now," the fashion director explains, "It has all changed."

How Fashion Change Affects Display.   Change is the one thing most dependable in the world of fashion, and rapid change. Here is a fact that makes it impossible to rely on last season's thinking, sometimes even last month's.

For example, the display director usually goes into his market many months ahead of a season, and he must know at that time what his basic needs will be to tie in with anticipated fashion trends. Let us assume that with the indication he had from the fashion director, the mannequins he had in stock were sufficient for what would be coming up. Suddenly, quite unexpectedly, a trend pops up strong, and the silhouette or line

An untraditional wedding look is an inspiration for a stylized window treatment. Photo by Malan Studio, New York. (Courtesy of Bloomingdale's, New York.)

of the trend hangs like a wet dishrag on most of the mannequins available around the store. Or, a leg fashion appears, such as the "hotpants" or city shorts of '71, and mannequins with the correct length of leg for this look are needed. In such cases, rather than display these new looks incorrectly, having the hemline hit the leg in the wrong place or fall in clumsy lines on the body, a better choice would be to hang the merchandise in a unique manner "sans" mannequin.

On the other hand, if a new body look is emerging making most of those on hand obsolete, new bodies in mannequins may be a necessity. The fashion director working closely with the display director can tip him off if he has not already heard the word. "The way these new things fit, the mannequins we have are too busty. It's a long and lean look. The hair fashions are wrong, too. Think we could get some new 'bodies' for the fashion area?" Walking through the store, the display director can see that newer bodies with longer legs would be better. The idea goes into his budget for his new season purchases. It will not be necessary for him to throw away the mannequins he owns. Many can be utilized for certain classic looks, and some can be sprayed a bright pink or orange and used as a display piece on which to hang accessories.

Display and the Color Story.   Even though the display director attends the predictive presentations of the fashion director and his people attend the orientation meetings that follow, he needs constant communication with the fashion director. The range of colors that are leaders or those that turn up most popular, is no indication to the display director of what the lead color story will be, if there is one. If the fashion director and management decide there is indeed one color which is so smashing that a total store color promotion is in order, the display director is the absolute focus for making it happen. He needs to know exactly what color is under consideration. Just saying orange, red, green, or brown tells him nothing. He needs an exact color chip or fabric swatch of the color in question. The new season's orange may look like none other. With the exact and unmistakable color in hand, the display director can buy all the necessary props and trim in his market to add exciting emphasis to the story.

Display needs direction from the fashion director to create magazine tie-in windows and displays. A Lord & Taylor window. (Courtesy of *Harper's Bazaar*.)

HARPERS
BAZAAR
Flower-power put-on
from Traina Boutique
right out of the pages of Harper's Bazaar
and into Designer Boutique, Third Floor
BAZAAR
FLA 50 Pages Of Great Fashion Looks
WOW! HOW TO FEEL BETTER ALL OVER
POW!
GO! TO THE

One store decided to do all their young departments for fall in "athletic colors," the bright, bold looks of football uniforms from surrounding universities and those throughout the country whose colors lent themselves to fashion identification. The fashion director had picked up the idea from a fabric presentation and expanded it in her store, because their community was highly college-football minded and she knew their customers would be very receptive to such an atmosphere. The display director knew exactly what to do. The junior area was converted into "the stadium," where all well-dressed football fans could find their sport clothes for the big games, for parties after the games, and for traveling to and from the games. It was a young, spirited idea for people of all ages, and the display director made sure that spirit reflected all over the fashion area; he even expanded it to other parts of the store where suitable.

Display and the Magazine Promotion. Documentation of how the store participated in a promotion in connection with a fashion magazine tie-in (see Chapter 8) comes strongly from display.

The fashion director who has accepted a magazine tie-in and committed the store to windows and interior displays, must consult with the display director to schedule, reserve, plan, and coordinate such display areas. The display director needs complete information (there is usually a packet within the magazine promotion kit designed especially for his use) on what is expected. If the fashion director prefers to use an approach different from that provided in the promotion kit, she must send a directive to display, covering all the facts on what she has in mind.

At the outset of the planning there are certain areas of information in which the display department and the fashion office should consult. These might include:

Number of windows needed
Location of windows
Dates devoted to this project in designated windows
Merchandise to be featured
    From which departments
    Number of pieces
Theme of the promotion
Identification required on signing
    Name of magazine

Issue involved
Glossy pictures of visiting editor
Announcement of any special event related to the tie-in

Magazines send blowups of magazine covers, enlargements of fashion illustrations, or sketches of fashion looks to be featured. They supply the glossy photographs of a guest editor who is to make a personal appearance. Sometimes travel posters and other printed material is supplied in connection with the tie-in. All of this material can be utilized by display in windows and departments, on escalator and elevator cards, and on in-store posters. If not enough copies are supplied, additional ones may be obtained on request or will be supplied by the magazine for nominal charge.

If such visual material is to be relayed to the display department, the fashion office would advise the display director of what he could count on for his use and when to expect it. Most magazines are very good about respecting deadlines and have material shipped in plenty of time for display installations.

Display and the Area Coordinator. If a store is large enough to warrant a staff of area fashion coordinators working out of a central fashion office (see Chapter 3), the display department works much closer with area coordinators, especially in the instances of individual area changes.

Each area must have a "look" indicative of its merchandise. A good area fashion coordinator will make sure that the department or departments under her jurisdiction reflect the last word in fashion accuracy. Accuracy, of course, means the best or truest interpretation of the current fashion message. For example, the area coordinator of the junior departments would be correct in objecting to the use of highly sophisticated mannequins in her area. These belong where high-fashion clothes are sold. The junior area would be best served with young, realistic mannequins, who stand, lunge, stretch, lie, or sit the way girls who buy clothes in that area normally would. Their faces, too, and hair fashions should relate to the costumes they model. In short, a department is best served with interior displays that make their clothes come alive.

An area coordinator is the one who is best qualified to know immediately which mannequin looks are best for her area. She will also know that bold, abstract, stylized display treatments are excellent for some fashion concepts, disaster for others. By thoroughly knowing her merchandise

Display Mannequins: Above, mannequins' hair fashions should be current and coordinated with ready-to-wear. Also a variety of ethnic types brings realism and camaraderie into the display. (Courtesy of Burdine's, Miami.) Lower Left, stylized mannequins are compatible with young, sleek fashion. (Interior display, courtesy of Burdine's, Miami.) Lower Right, young fashions belong on young-looking mannequins. (Interior display, courtesy of Foley's Houston.)

and the type of customer who buys it, she can help make the entire atmosphere more appealing.

It is also important for her to know when the look must change. Even in an area where very modern, impressionistic display treatment existed because the existing fashion trend justified such a look, if a whole new flux of romantic, feminine merchandise arrives into this department, the display look is jarring. Of course, the area coordinator is in close touch with her fashion office and the buyers in her area to know when such a change of merchandise will take place. She can, therefore, anticipate and plan for a visual presentation change to match.

It is in this connection that she works closely with the display department, advising them of what will be happening far enough in advance. Display material must be ordered far in advance, so there should not be too many surprises tossed into the lap of the display director. He is a genius of improvisation, and he has had to prove it over and over again, but it is not his favorite way to live, and a well-organized area fashion coordinator will exercise the wisdom of anticipation. If her department had headless, faceless, stylized mannequins for a very new young look last season, she demonstrates her worth when she knows that romantic, feminine fashions cannot be effectively displayed on headless figures. These need lovely "whole" figures with soft faces and hair styles appropriate to the gentle feel of the costume.

The area coordinator must "understand" the merchandise with which she works, and it is her responsibility to help the display people understand too. "This would lend itself perfectly to an outer-space look," she might suggest. And the display department would know which way to go. "This is a fashion idea that must not be taken too seriously. We should not play it too straight—a gag treatment would be fun." There are one hundred ways to go, but only a few that are correct. In display, as related to fashion, the more accurate the interpretation, the more attractive the result. Women tend to identify with the physical structure of a mannequin; a junior figure used in a mature woman's department might make the customer angry.

Display for the Male Customer.   Men, on the other hand, do not identify with mannequins as readily as women. A handsome face on a male mannequin doesn't do anything to the male customer. He would be more likely to identify with the mannequin (depending on the man, of course) if it were standing in a window or an area with a female mannequin. A male lifeguard with a window full of bathing beauties, the bridegroom in a bridal scene, a father image with mother and child mannequins for an Easter or Christmas display, or a Beau Brummell, elegantly featured with a beautifully-gowned woman on his arm. In most cases, men are more easily content with seeing a half mannequin, that is, the body of a suit with no legs and no head. He likes to see the cut of the coat, the drape of the line, the fit of the collar, and the new width or knot of the tie. The rest be hanged.

After all is said and done, the area coordinator and the display people should consider the customer first. His or her feelings concerning the merchandise must not be jarred or offended. They must be, instead, inspired, intrigued, tempted, or entertained. All of these reactions stimulate a favorable response, namely, the desire to buy.

Display—the Stage

Mannequins are only one aspect of displaying fashion. The area coordinator can join members of the display staff as coauthors of exciting display productions with an all-star cast of new fashions. Even though not a word is said, the technique of display would announce to the customer "the new hit"—"for the leading lady"—"the award winners." Whether it's an elaborate display, a small vignette, or a glorified T-stand, it matters not. What does matter is that the customer gets the message of what the department is all about through the interesting, tasteful, clever, or just plain easy manner of a single, simple display piece. If the store has succeeded in "pulling out" into a position of easy accessibility the piece or pieces of merchandise which represent the area, the customer could very well be more than half sold before she tried on anything. The area coordinator, working closely with display, has this great responsibility, here in the department, at the point of sale.

How to Schedule Window Themes.   We have established the need for frequent change of display areas. Now we deal with how those changes come about and how it is decided what the changes should be. The scheduling of windows, for example, usually results from the promotion schedule drawn up earlier by the sales-promotion director, divisional merchandise managers, and the fashion director. The names on the planning team vary from store to store, but these are typical of most. The fashion director, during the meeting for window planning, submits a list of leading fashion items and looks that she feels are ready for the spotlight through window displays. This list is based, not just on her research of important trends, but on what the buyers have actually purchased. The divisional merchandise manager, if he is in accord, verifies when merchandise will be in stock to cover what is to be shown in the windows. Then it is most likely that the fashion director's list will be examined for final decisions on the order of importance or best timing for scheduling. If the store plans to change a bank of fashion windows every week, it may schedule what goes into those windows four to six weeks in advance, always permitting, of course, the possibility of change. The fashion director's suggested list, with the approval of the divisional merchandise managers, might include:

First Week: Bridal gowns
Second Week: Color story
Third Week: New dress look
Fourth Week: Coats

If the display director is present at the meeting (he should be), some plans can be made on the spot as to what slant should be taken in each case—bold, contemporary, understated, stark, quiet, dramatic. These moods take their inspiration from the merchandise to be used. The merchandiser usually decides from which departments he wishes the merchandise taken. For example, in the case of a color story any or all fashion departments could be included. In some stores certain windows are devoted exclusively to special departments, and the changes must all come from that area.

If the display director is not on hand for the meeting, it is likely to fall to the fashion director to send him a run-down on the fashion plan for the windows. The display director, in turn, advises the display coordinator for windows what is coming up, and the window coordinator will communicate from that point on with the fashion director. When it is time to pull the fashion merchandise for the windows, or if there are any questions as to which items best fit the theme or how they should be accessorized, the fashion office is his advisor.

Again, teamwork. It is the fashion director's responsibility to see that the fashion story is expressed *correctly* in the windows, in the concept of the current trend, and it is the display director's responsibility to interpret the fashion story *effectively*.

Sign Here, Please.   Signs in windows or in interior display areas should

Good fashion window display and succinct signing tells the story effectively and clearly. (Courtesy of Neiman-Marcus, Dallas.)

speak the language of fashion, succinctly, effectively, and clearly. The fashion director, of course, speaks this language well, and often; in the case of signs, she serves as interpreter of the language. The display director may ask her, "How do you want us to banner this color story?" "What would you prefer we call this new look?" These and more detailed questions may come the fashion director's way when signs are being planned, so a more efficient way to fortify display and the sign shop with clear, hard facts is to submit a fact sheet to the display director on each look scheduled for windows.

The fact sheet might include:

Windows #19, #20, #21, #22
Item: COATS
Description: These should all be fur trims
Include designers: Cuddlecoat, Originala.
Signs: For the Woman Who Loves Fur . . . a Little.
(This is a top trend—important is the new placement of the fur)

The sign requisition may be issued by the display department, but the words may have been suggested, upon request from the display director, by the fashion office.

How to Pull Fashion Merchandise for Display.   Merchandise cannot be taken out of stock for display purposes without authorization. Even though the systems used by stores differ, the routine is still a matter of checking out and checking in. To avoid confusion with merchandise checked out by the fashion office for fashion shows and television commercials, merchandise pulled for display is noted on a printed form or record book that clearly states the difference. Merchandise that has not been checked back into the department or not properly cancelled in the merchandise transfer records, will be considered a shortage and charged to display or the fashion office. The record also serves as a "tracer" for merchandise that might be needed for some other purpose. If the entry shows that display has it or that the merchandise was checked out on such-and-such a date by the area coordinator of junior fashions, tracing is less of a problem.

What to Pull.   The business of knowing exactly which pieces to select is the result of good fashion direction. The following routine is applicable to both windows and interior displays.

Let us assume there is a great interest in plaids and the store's fashion departments are well stocked with the new expressions of this pattern in coats, suits, dresses, sportswear, and accessories. "We're Mad about Plaids" may be the banner of the promotion, and the displays have to prove it. The fashion director sends a directive to all concerned that plaids are to be expressed differently in each department to show its many new looks.

1. Coat department—a display of blanket plaid coats and capes (REDS)
2. Sportswear—pleated skirts, kilts, ponchos (YELLOWS)
3. Junior area—plaid suits, pant suits, dresses (GREENS)
4. Designer shop—plaid ensembles (BROWNS)
5. French room—plaids for after dark (BLACK AND WHITE)

The fashion director's decision to go this way is based on seeing the displays through the eyes of the customer. A store full of plaid could be overwhelming, and all kinds of plaids displayed in every area at random would not only be a hodgepodge, but also monotonous. However, developing the great new expressions of plaid in separate color stories makes each group look entirely different, more exciting. Next, if each of these different color stories in plaid are accessorized differently, devoting special attention to urging forth the most dominant color or highlighting the fabric's texture (plaids might show up on wool, velvet, taffeta, chiffon), something wonderful happens to what might have seemed an ordinary plaid at the outset.

How to Pull.   The area coordinator responsible for the designer shop is ready to assemble her display pieces for the plaid promotion. Her assignment is "Plaid ensembles (BROWNS)." She selects two outfits, one dress with plaid jacket and one dress with plaid coat. These are to be draped on mannequins in the designer shop and each must be completely accessorized. One ensemble appears easy to put together; it needs only the simplest of touches, browntone hose, brown alligator shoes, beige hat (suit type), and beige gloves.

The other ensemble needs more attention. The plaid includes several earthtones that might be more difficult to coordinate with accessories. The coordinator decides to take it along with her to pull accessories.

She stops first at the scarf counter. The neckline of the ensemble is empty. A scarf would soften the line. Orange. That would brighten it. She tries a few, decides on one that has just the right shade and shape, and records her choice in the display merchandise transfer book. Next, she stops at the handbag department. She holds up a few against the fabric and finally decides on the size and shape that fits the silhouette. Another stop takes her to the glove counter where she selects two pair (one for the other model while she's at it) and signs out her selection. There is one more stop, the jewelry department. Something simple in some new polished wooden jewelry seems perfect as a final touch. She checks these pieces out, too, in the same way she did the other accessories. Each department, with a separate book, has a separate record of what has been taken, for what use, and by whom.

The shoes are not pulled from stock as are the other accessories. Display and the fashion office very often have a season's supply of current looks in basic colors (brown, black, navy, beige), suitable for a variety of looks. The coordinator selects two pair from this stock which she feels will be suitable.

Assembling the Display. Everything is pulled and it all goes back to the designer shop to be assembled. When the mannequins are dressed, the area coordinator arranges the accessories on the ensembles as she visualizes they should be. The effect may be exactly right. On the other hand, the coordinator may step back and decide, "that handbag is too heavy." "Maybe a smaller one would be better," she considers. "Maybe none at all would be better." This is how it is decided, and if there is serious indecision about what to do in any display problem, the coordinator might call the fashion director to take a look.

Display and Fashion Shows. Behind the scenes of every important fashion show are the talents and efforts of many unsung heroes. One of these is the display department, without which the fashion office could not raise the curtain.

Many in-department fashion shows require little more than a ramp, a few chairs for guests, and a microphone. The display department can rig these up a few moments before show time, with little more planning than the notice they have had on the fashion show schedule (a copy of which goes to everyone in the store involved in or affected by the event). Very often, in such cases of shows held "on the floor," little or no decor is

**For major fashion productions, display helps the fashion director
with sets, lighting, and runways. J. L. Brandeis, Omaha, Career
Girls' Night.** (Courtesy of J. L. Brandeis, Omaha.)

required. Perhaps it would only be an appropriate sign nearby or on the
ramp, identifying the show and announcing the time of presentation and
name of guest commentator.

When it comes to the big shows, those for which a large audience is
expected, the physical setup requires a great deal more attention. Since
staging is a major contributor to the effectiveness of a production, the
talents of the display department are indispensable. Most stores do not
wish to go beyond their own staffs for the majority of their fashion productions, therefore, an imaginative and cooperative display director is a
blessing to the fashion office.

If the fashion show coordinator is anxious to give a new show with new twist, something different in staging, lighting, or production, she needs to create or enlist the creativity of the display people to come up with good ideas time after time after time.

After the show has been booked, the fashion office must decide where it will be held. The physical setup dictates to some degree what the possibilities of production might be.

Ramps.   If a stage is available the display director will need to know the theme of the show, how the stage is to be utilized, decorated, and lighted, and if a ramp will project from that stage. If so, he must know what size ramp and what shape.

Most stores have stock ramp sections that can be joined together to make a variety of lengths, widths, and shapes. The fashion office needs only to advise display, "we will need a conventional straight ramp, projecting three sections from the stage," and the directions are easy to follow. If a t-shape ramp is required, a u-shape, a horseshoe, or a zigzag arrangement, the directions should be clearly stated in writing.

If, on the other hand, the standard equipment available is unsuitable for a special treatment, the display department must know the wishes of the fashion office much earlier in the planning stage so that a design may be drawn up and demensions planned. This will then be submitted to the carpenter shop for construction.

If the size or shape of the ramp requires special covering, that information must also be passed along to display. Perhaps a special color scheme is part of the plan and skirting material for draping around ramps will need to be ordered.

If the lighting plan is something other than that which the display department has on hand, spots and scoops, or color lenses will need to be obtained to create the desired effect. It is a good idea, therefore, for the fashion office to learn something about the kind of equipment the display department has available. It will make some of the general planning easier for both departments.

The average show cannot require a major production every time, but a few imaginative touches can certainly create the illusion of extensive planning. If the fashion office personnel find they are not "show biz" oriented from a staging point of view, the display director is a good strong shoulder to lean on. Usually a few well-written words regarding the theme

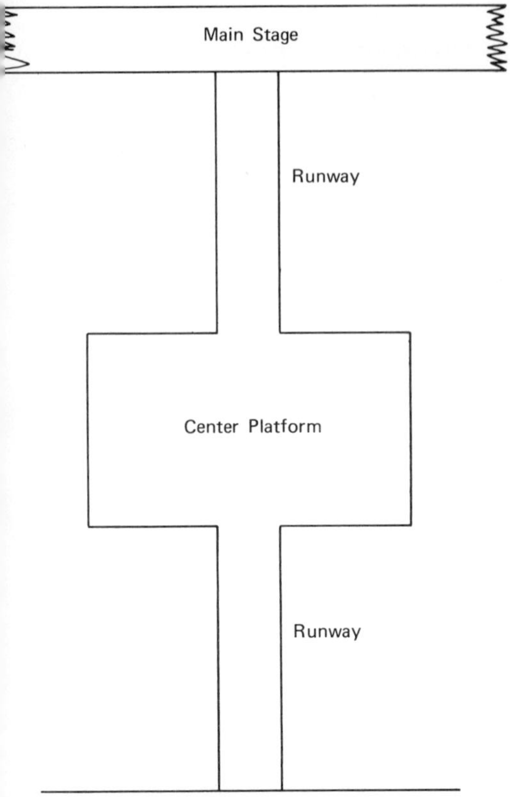

Main Stage
Runway
Center Platform
Runway

of the show, size of audience, and purpose of the event, will inspire display to come up with exactly what is needed.

Props.   In addition to ramps and lighting, props and sets very often need to be collected or built to embellish a show. A prop list, if many props are needed, should be drawn up, explaining how each prop will be used. This will clarify the size of each prop and its proportion to other props, how it is to be "set" on stage, and what arrangement will be necessary to "strike" the prop. Will it be carried on and off the stage by a model? Will it be set and removed by a stage hand? The display department must know these details in regard to all props or stage settings ordered by the fashion office.

Display and the Major Production.   Although a fashion office may book and conduct a staggering number of fashion shows per year, perhaps only one or two of these will fall into the category of a major production. The kind of major production referred to requires a major effort on the part of the display department.

For example, the fashion director, presumably the author of the show, has been engaged to produce a fashion extravaganza as a city-wide benefit. It is one in which the audience expects nothing short of a Broadway review, with fashions subtly woven in here and there. It's a big undertaking, and staging is the basic secret of making the whole thing come off as a "first."

The Sets.   The display director and author (fashion director) consult. The author has decided that this year's production should be done in three exciting scenes, each requiring a separate set change. She has designed these sets as she sees them and submitted her three ideas to him for refining. Before the display director can interpret the suggested sets, he must know exactly what she intends to happen in each case.

"I will need motion in scene three," she might explain, "so a turntable at stage right will have to been rigged to go into motion on cue."

The display director considers that an easy order. The turntable will be electrically operated by a switch backstage which will be turned on by

To help make a fashion show a standout: (a) shape of ramp, (b) use of hand props, (c) use of animals. Benefit show at Fountainbleau Hotel, staged by Jordan Marsh, Miami. (Courtesy of the Israel Bond Organization.)

the stage manager at the precise moment necessary. In fact, the display director, most familiar with the workings of the entire production, may very well be called upon to serve as stage manager.

Before building begins on the sets, the display director will undoubtedly submit blueprints or sketches of the sets and explain how he feels they would work best. The fashion director will review these plans with the display director, perhaps moving a set of stairs more stage left, taking out an entrance upstage center, on substituting a new idea they both find more intriguing than the original plan. Finally, the plans are passed along to the construction department for execution under the guidance of the display director.

Ramps, sets, props, lighting, and sound are usually the responsibility of the display department, unless special outside technicians are hired and outside equipment rented. Many stores, however, prefer to utilize the talents "in the family." When something can be done with its own staff, all the better. Actually, this is an advantage for the fashion director. Under this arrangement she can create with less restrictions. Sets and props, for example, made with loving hands at home are easier on the store's budget; they can be broken down or adjusted for re-use in other shows, display areas, exhibits, and any number of things for which display is called upon to contribute material.

Applause, Please.   For all this splendid cooperation and creative talent on a major production, when giving credit on a printed program, the dis-display director's name should be very much in evidence along with any other members of his staff he may wish to have included. If there is no printed program, then it behooves the fashion director or commentator of the show to acknowledge orally the display director or members of his staff who have made an outstanding contribution. A little applause is the least the fashion office can do to thank the display department for literally standing on their heads to deliver the special effects requested.

Afterview

A store cannot compete today using techniques of yesterday. New merchandise cannot be housed effectively with old hat surroundings. Department stores cannot completely renovate or rebuild giant stores, but with fashion-oriented displays (windows, interiors, and shops) they can create the illusion of a "new department," even within those hallowed old walls.

Many stores, whose customers do not stroll by in droves (such as in New York, where pedestrian traffic is tremendous all day long) regard their windows second in importance to their interiors. It is in the department, at the point of sale, they feel, where the action is. Here the customers can get more involved with the display—she can examine, touch, feel, ask for her size.

Whatever the focus of display, the important fashion story must be present. That comes first. Too many departments are arranged for the convenience of the clerk, not the customer. This is a trend that needs changing, and astute merchants are making valiant efforts. The fashion director's role in this entire matter is to keep a watchful eye. While everyone else is busy drawing up floor plans, picking the wallpaper and carpeting, and selecting the fixtures, someone must be sure that the fashion image does not get buried in the rubble.

Chapter 11

Fashion Projection through Broadcasting

There once was a time when the retailer and the electronic media (radio and television) seemed destined never to get together. Radio and television were fine for selling soap, refrigerators, automobiles, and cough medicines, but fashion? Not likely. Besides, how?

Advertising to the retailer meant newsprint. Run an ad. See the ad in the newspaper today, and see the people pour in tomorrow. Advertising successes were judged primarily on immediate reaction. Radio and television, seemingly so expensive for the brief moment the commercial was on, appeared too intangible. If a crowd of people was not waiting outside the store when the doors opened on the morning after a commercial, the merchant doubted the effectiveness of the effort. Time salesmen for broadcasting stations found it difficult to waylay the merchants' fears that their messages would be heard and would eventually bring results.

That was the state of affairs of retail advertising on the air several years ago. Even though a great number of products and industries had experienced tremendous success with the broadcasting media almost from its inception, the retailer was the most stubborn, the most skeptical.

239

How the Retailer and Broadcasting Got Together

Before the American listening and viewing public's interests became jaded, radio and television overshadowed most everything else in the area of entertainment. Motion pictures felt the pinch created by television. Rock-music radio stations claimed the teen world. There was reason to doubt that teens did much newspaper reading, and the greater number of cars on the streets and highways, with more car radios, guaranteed a captive audience during regular driving hours.

Retailers began to listen. Broadcasting might have a place in their advertising plan after all. The serious problem facing them now was how to use broadcasting. The used-car dealer and the hard-sell pitch came off lucky, but how in the world, asked the fashion merchant, can we sell fashion? The networks and advertising service agencies, such as TvB (Television Bureau of Advertising, Inc.), made studies, surveys, and presentations for its members' advertisers or potential advertisers, trying to instill confidence and know-how in the retailers' approach to advertising in the broadcast media.

When the word got around (from the brave, progressive independents and chain stores who recorded successes) that learning the correct techniques and using persistent exposure did the job, things began to happen. Retailers took the plunge, stubbed a few toes on the way, but finally turned out to be one of the largest advertisers in the local broadcasting media. According to a survey of eleven major markets (big cities) by TvB, department stores were in third place in frequency use of local TV as early as 1958. The smaller markets (smaller cities) eventually followed.

Radio Came First.   Still regimented by their past experience (the run-an-ad-today-see-immediate-results-tomorrow approach), radio advertising was expected to produce in the same way. It would and it could. However, there was one catch. It was impossible to squeeze the same amount of copy into a minute commercial as that which appeared on the page of a newspaper. To tell all the facts about a number of items, or to go into windy detail about one item in a radio commercial with newspaper copy technique, was a disaster. How to use the medium was the big hangup.

There was a time when retail newspaper ads were cluttered with reams of copy and overcrowded with everything, descriptions, illustrations, prices, headlines, floor lines, and store locations. But eventually, even such "dirty" pages were replaced with "clean" makeup. Retailers learned that white space has sales power. This was the lesson that had to be learned in radio and later in television.

How to Use Radio.   The retailer was not quick to learn that cramming a volume of words into the alloted time slot was not the way to hold the listener. In the days when almost all commercials were at least a minute long, (and sometimes ad-libbed for five minutes, before FCC regulations), the message seemed endless. The announcer rambled on with more facts than the average listener was able to retain. The loaded commercial was not entirely ineffective, but the power of radio, when more of its charms were uncovered, was yet to come.

The merchant learned about hard sell and soft sell. The hard sell, ideal for big sales, close-outs, special purchases, big savings, and hurry, hurry, hurry, was fine in its place, but certainly no way to sell fashion. The soft sell, easy pacing, gentle language, more difficult to write, and more difficult to deliver, was hard for the retailer to utilize.

To begin with, store managements had no one to advise them. The radio stations themselves had much to learn about the problems and needs of retail selling, especially fashion. This was a long time coming.

The designation of advertising dollars into broadcasting met with great resistance even when management sanctioned such a plan. Merchandisers and buyers, responsible for making figures, strongly protested. "Not with my advertising money you don't experiment," was a cry heard regularly from fashion departments. It was understandable. New advertising budget structures helped get the show on the road.

In their use of broadcasting, there was much for the retailer to consider.

1. What merchandise is to be advertised?
2. Who is the customer for this merchandise?
3. Which station has this customer for a listener?
4. At what time during the broadcast day is this customer tuned in?

Buying Radio Time.   The careful buying of radio time requires the guidance of the previously mentioned questions. Is it a teen audience to be reached? Then a rock music station is the best choice. Is the merchandise for the working man or woman? Then driving times, to and from work, are ideal slots for reaching employed people. The housewife? This is more complicated. Ratings must be checked to get some kind of clue as to the share of audience claimed by each station, most desirable listening hours according to programing, and even a survey study of the listening habits of the homemakers of the community.

When the most desirable station or stations have been selected and the best time slots specified, the advertiser has to decide on the kind of schedule he will buy. Will it be a regular schedule, day after day, week after week? Will it be just a special purchase of time for special sales, special promotion, or peak periods such as Christmas, back-to-school, Mother's Day, etc.? Will the store run "saturation" campaigns on the air? The saturation campaign (large numbers of spots, continually repeating and hitting hard on a specific item or event) is ideal for sales events but not the most desirable choice for selling fashion. This is not to indicate that large numbers of spots repeated often on a fashion subject are not desirable. The more the better, but fashion commercials are likely to show up on a regular schedule in a compatible time slot so that the correct audience receives the message. By contrast, the sale commercials or those projected in a saturation campaign, might fall anywhere on a schedule, some in prime time and some in less expensive time slots. This is usually wrapped up in a "package," an assorted time schedule for a specific number of spots.

The fashion director does not buy radio time. Nevertheless, it is important for her to know what guides the store's purchase of air time and how and where it will be placed. She is in a better position, therefore, to approach her sales-promotion director and request advertising assistance for her fashion promotions or events.

"We will need some help to publicize our big teen show in August. Could you allot a number of spots on the rock stations for this event?" "We will be selling tickets to a luncheon fashion show in September and need all the exposure we can get. We need to reach the career girl and young homemaker. How about reserving some of the radio time we own so that we can reach these women?"

The fashion director may even be aware of a particular show or time slot when she knows her customer is most likely to be listening. This, too, she should specify. If she is not aware of which area of advertising would get her the best results, she may be asking for the wrong kind of help. And, ask she must. It is not always possible that air time (or any kind of advertising assistance) will be offered unless it is requested. The fashion office soon learns—"them that asks gets."

The Advertising Agency and Radio.   The actual purchasing of radio time is usually done by the sales-promotion director, in some stores by the advertising director, and sometimes by an outside advertising agency retained by the store. In most cases, the advertising agency is in a better position to survey the market and evaluate the time slots best suited to the store's needs. Also, as a buyer of other air time for other accounts, they are able to take advantage of frequency rates. Through this kind of service, the advertising agency is best equipped to select the most effective time schedule at the best price.

How to Sell Fashion on Radio.   The difficult part of selling fashion on radio is deciding what works and what does not. Better still, what works *where*.

The most difficult kind of fashion selling on radio is anything in the prestigous area. The total image of the station must be thoroughly considered, not only the lack of visual illustration, but also the "atmosphere" in which the message is nestled. If a totally prestigous station is not available (such as an FM or classical station), then at least a more elegant time segment, such as the broadcasting of symphonic music, or some type of lofty-purpose programing would be suitable. Even if the programing were of a lighter nature, and there is no reason why it should not be, it is best if it does not attract the element of hard sell. A personality program, such as one hosted by Arlene Francis on WOR, would be a possibility for selling fashion. In areas where such programing is available, it is important that the program's personality and the store's image are compatible.

In this category, designer fashions, furs, fine jewelry, silver, interior design, or any fashion home furnishings area would be considered possibilities for prestige handling. All of these come under the heading of image-makers. However, many retailers feel that image, per se, is best obtained in other ways. By assigning prestige selling to other facets of advertising they can reserve radio budgets for the places it does the most good.

Regarding the most effective use of radio, more retailers are inclined to include sales and promotions at the top of the list. As regards fashion, the line-up of importance might look something like this:

1. Teen fashions
2. Peak items of new fashion
3. Opening of a new shop

4. Announcement of a celebrity or fashion notable's personal appearance
5. Fashion shows and special events

When the minute-long radio commercial became less frequently used (giving way to the thirty-second spot, or less) the selling of fashion by radio improved. Thirty seconds is plenty of time to tell most of the pertinent facts about a specific item or idea.

Teen Fashions on Radio.   Naturally, the available listening audience is what draws the advertiser. Young music lovers, with transistors at their ears wherever they go, car radios, bedroom radios, and clock radios turned on at every possible moment, listen constantly to the beat and the sound of their contemporaries. The disk jockeys blurt their language, and report on their interests. They communicate. The advertiser, too, has that very thing in mind—communication.

Copy for the youth market must be written, if not in their jargon, certainly to their interest. The image of the merchandise and the copy for the commercial must be compatible. The delivery, too, must communicate. Undoubtedly this is why so many personalities on rock stations deliver the commercial within the contents of their music segment. The listening teen customer relates to the total sound. A contemporary station, with contemporary music with commercials from a contemporary store makes it all ring true.

The fashion director, aware of the hottest in fashion for the youth market, makes sure that it gets its share of attention and that the departments have the merchandise. "If we are going to capture the young market, we certainly want them to know, early and repeatedly, that we have the new look in jeans," she might urge. "This item should get top priority in your radio budget."

When the advertising agency begins to write copy on "the new look in jeans," they will need to know what that means. A member of the fashion office pulls out samples, explains the way the garment can be used (with what coordinates, accessories, or new treatments) and what fashion terminology fits the sales pitch.

Peak Items of New Fashion.   As indicated earlier, there are limitations to selling fashion on radio. However, with the correct items selected and properly handled, radio can be an important plus in areas outside the youth market.

Future fashion, an early projection of a possible fashion trend (see Chapter 9), has no place in radio. On the other hand, now fashion, with items at their peak, deserves all the attention it can get. In such cases, descriptions are not necessary. Just the mention of the item, letting the world know, "we got 'em, all sizes, all colors, and all departments," can be the radio approach. The copy will be written and delivered in keeping with the store's fashion image. This time the young disk jockey is not involved nor is the rock station. This time the time slot, station, and delivery is determined by deciding who would be the most likely customer for that item. A new hot trend in shirt dressing, a new boot, a new look in metal jewelry, leg fashions, and hundreds of other possibilities. If certain items already enjoy customer acceptance, then additional push on radio, perhaps for specific brands, is a possibility.

With new fashion, the fashion office's services would be enlisted to provide the copywriter with exactly what is meant by that special kind of shirt dressing, that new boot, or new leg fashion. Since the item cannot be seen, the oral facts must be clear, to the point, and absolutely accurate.

Opening of a New Shop.   Radio comes up smelling like a rose in this instance. A saturation schedule can be purchased on radio to announce the opening of a new shop in the store. Short, concise commercials presented in the form of an invitation urges listeners to "drop in tomorrow, the opening day of our new shop."

The fashion office needs to be sure that the advertising agency thoroughly understands the fashion image desired for the shop. It is at this time, the beginning and the opening, that the image can be established. So, if it is to have an elegant flavor, a bizarre atmosphere, or a romantic or mystic environment, this message must be carefully carried within the lines of the copy. It is at the outset that the tempo of the shop is established. Careful coordination should be exercised between the fashion department and the advertising agency. A directive, written by the fashion office and submitted to the Advertising Agency in advance of copy preparation, would be extremely helpful for everyone concerned. Even if it is just a few words describing the intention of the shop or the kind of merchandise carried there, there is less chance for misunderstanding. The fashion office soon learns that to "put it in writing" saves a lot of grief. Better still, in addition to the written directive, a tour through the shop with the agency representative or copywriter would be ideal. A member of the fashion office, acting as guide, can further explain the written description.

Personal Appearances.   The immediacy of radio is very often a blessing. Occasionally when something unexpected or unplanned turns up which is too good for the store to pass up, getting out publicity may be a problem. For example, there is an unscheduled celebrity, suddenly available for a personal appearance at the store. A great drawing card, but how to get the word out at such a late date is a problem. It is too late to schedule an ad in the newspaper. Maybe too late for production, or getting enough time on television. However, radio spots, easier to squeeze in and easier production-wise, can get a hurry-up job done. Perhaps a recording of the familiar sound of the celebrity's voice can give the announcement the punch it needs.

Even when the need of exposure is not urgent, the announcement of visiting dignitaries or celebrities is ideal fare for radio. The invitation form of announcement, expressed with the personal touch of the human voice, has a great deal going for it. The fashion office, often responsible for the care and feeding of a visiting personality, primarily in the fashion division, may also be responsible for the celebrity's whereabouts during the visit, and any biographical material necessary for publicity. Where there is a special events director, he or she might take on this responsibility, but if the guest has a fashion identification, the fashion office is usually involved.

Fashion Shows.   All channels of advertising can be enlisted to publicize a fashion show, depending how big and important it is. Radio, already saluted as an ideal "announcement" or "invitation" media, certainly can lend its usual effectiveness in this way for fashion shows.

Naturally, of all the announcement-invitation-type spots destined for radio exposure, the fashion show announcement is the one most strongly associated with the fashion office. In this case, all pertinent information regarding the show must be supplied, in writing, well in advance of the show to permit the advertising agency or advertising department time to reserve air time, schedule appropriate time slots, write the copy, and produce the spot. In thirty seconds, the announcer can tell the listener everything she needs to know about the show—where it will be, when, what time, admission fee, where to r.s.v.p. (if necessary), who will be there, and what will be shown. If a guest commentator or special attraction is planned, this, too, should be incorporated in the radio spot.

Hard Sell—Soft Sell.   All of the foregoing examples of selling fashion on radio are primarily soft sell. If there is any "punching" done at all, it might come under the heading of "enthusiasm, excitement, elation." One does not need to strongly bend the listener's ear to sell fashion. What is needed is the true flavor of its intent and purpose. The listener does not have to be hit over the head, so to speak, with a fashion story; she only needs to be informed. The technique used to impart the information would follow, of course, the image of the store.

Hard sell, on the other hand, belongs completely out of the fashion area, into the promotion area. Sale events can stand hard sell. Beating the drums, to stir up excitement, to transmit electric urgency about the event (great savings, great buys, great values) is necessary when crowds of shoppers are to be attracted or the sale event is "for a limited time only."

Both approaches have their place. They will appear in one way or another in all areas of the media-mix. Understanding how, when, and where is the way to successful retail selling through broadcasting.

Television and the Retailer

From the early days of television, the paradise for the used-car dealer, the cigarette maker, the breakfast food giants, the retailer saw little or no future in this medium for himself.

He tried, but nothing seemed to work. Television was ineffective, he felt, no matter how cooperative the station seemed to be, offering assistance in production, writing copy, casting, and recommending most suitable air time. The results seemed spotty, sometimes pretty good, most of the time not good. What with all the added headaches of working and planning a TV commercial (a world they found too difficult to understand and for which they could not always draw on their own shop for help or execution), it just wasn't worth the trip. If a store wanted to throw a big sale, an impressive ad in the paper and some hard sell on radio usually did the trick. Why struggle with television when there were other avenues to choose?

Video Tape.   Before the days of video tape, live commercials were a tremendous chore for the retailer. He had to transport stacks of merchandise to the TV studio every time a spot or program was to be aired. In the case of hard goods, truck loads of furniture and appliances had to be transported. If the commercial was to be repeated, the merchandise had to be stored at the TV station and reset every time the advertiser hit the air. For one or two spots this may not sound like too much of a problem, but if any volume of advertising was considered, such as exposing many items from many departments, this became an obviously troublesome chore.

When video tape came into general use (about 1959) the use of television became less complicated. Eventually, one commercial could not only be taped for repeated use on a station, but when equipment on all stations became synchronized, a dub of the same commercial could appear on several stations at the same time. Another virtue of video tape was the instant playback. One could tape a commercial and play it back immediately for approval. If approved, it could be edited, dubbed, and used as often as the advertiser desired. If it was not approved, a simple roll of the tape and it could all be cut over. Not only could errors be eliminated, but many a commercial could be improved or changed before being aired to the world. Now there was just one last issue bugging the retailer.

Color vs. Black and White. Retailers protested strongly that fashion was not getting a fair shake on television because black and white made most clothes look dull. Contrasts were lost. Unless the costume had a definite light/dark contrast, photographing fashion for TV left much to be desired.

The really big boom in fashion selling on television came when local stations acquired color equipment to transmit color, either from the station or remote (perhaps directly from the store or some outside fashion event). Color strengthened the fashion story, made it come alive, and whetted the viewer's appetite for that marvelous red coat . . . that brilliant green dress. Even though many viewers might be seeing the same program on a black-and-white set, the retailer felt encouraged to trust television with his fashion-advertising dollars.

Selecting Television Time. *Program* selection in television is as important as *station* selection is in radio. A television station is not as susceptible to "image" as is a radio station. An advertiser is more likely to suffer or enjoy audience reaction from program association. For example, sponsorship of a regular newscast could reach one kind of audience, sponsorship of a golf tournament another kind, and a cooking show, kiddie show, or horror movie would reach still different audiences. Sponsorship depends on the product being sold, the viewer the retailer is trying to reach, and the image the store is trying to maintain or gain. All these factors guide the purchase of television air time.

The selling of fashion needs special attention. One does not schedule a commercial about formal ball gowns during a golf tournament. However, what better place to promote the pro shop or sportswear departments of both men and women? For a more sophisticated approach to television program selections, the retailer considers the viewing habits of various age groups, income groups, and ethnic groups. This is especially important in radio but is also applicable to television.

The Power of Repetition.   If a merchant were using newspaper to make a sales impact, he might buy a bigger space, a full page, a double truck, or even an entire section to add emphasis to the importance of the event or items on sale. In television, he certainly would not expand the length of his commercial message. He would, instead, use a saturation campaign, repeating the message many times, in many different time segments, or over and over again in the same time slots each day. The advertiser gains two things with this kind of impact: (1) the established audience catches the commercial at the same viewing time each day and gets a repeated exposure to the sales pitch, and (2) the advertiser reaches new viewers that didn't catch the message earlier that day or the day before. In other words, the advertiser gets two cracks at the audience—the regular listener and the newly tuned-in listener.

The power of repetition is most commendable in selling fashion on television. The first time a fashion idea is seen on the screen, the viewer is introduced to the look. The next time the viewer sees the same commercial she considers its merit, identifies with it, and toys with the idea of maybe looking at the garment in the store. The third time she sees it, it reminds her of her former impression and prompts her to action. Hopefully, that is what happens to the viewer observing a fashion commercial. If it is well done, related accurately to the type of viewer known to be there, the chances are very good.

This is not to say that the viewer cannot be moved to response or action after one exposure to a commercial, but where apathy or distraction sets in, the power of repetition insures instant recall of the product and the store. Repetition and continuity of scheduling is the secret to the intelligent use of television advertising.

How to Work with the Advertising Agency

The sales-promotion director and DMM may allot the necessary budget for TV advertising, and buyers may decide what fashion items they would like to expose on TV, but someone has to put it all together. This is where the specialized know-how of an advertising agency is a must. The agency,

Sample television copy for a 30-second spot. Video instructions are always on the left; audio copy is always on the right.

J. LIPSEY AND ASSOCIATES   311 SOUTH 15TH STREET • OMAHA, NEBRASKA 68102 (402)

ADVERTISING AND PUBLIC RELATIONS

TV COPY

ACCOUNT BRANDEIS - DE MARANVILLE - Ball Gowns

DATE   9/7, 20-22   DeM-71-19

STATION   KMTV, WOW-TV, KETV

VIDEO

AUDIO

VTR

1: Brandeis (TRILL) better for fashion.
    SOME VERY LUSH MUSIC

VERY SOFT FOCUS--   2: Enchanted evenings are waiting for you
GIRLS MOVING EITHER   this season in a gown from Brandeis.
AGAINST UP OR   Be utterly feminine in the softness
BETWEEN PILLARS--   of swirling chiffon . . .
USE AIR TO BLOW
DRESSES, ETC--   Or elegant and mysterious in the
                             lushness of velvet . . .

                             Be ready for adventure . . . for
END WITH 3 GIRLS   romance . . . in a gown from
DRESSES MOVING, ETC   Brandeis . . . French Room . . .
DISS TO CARD   Omaha, downtown and at the Crossroads.

usually working directly with the store's sales-promotion director, is equipped to advise on the best time segments to buy, which stations, and which programs. The agency can report on the availabilities, the ratings, and costs, and can recommend the best way to go.

An important part of an advertising agency's service is its knowledge of television production techniques. An agency is also an idea factory. It is their job to translate the store's fashion or quality image or its promotion message into audio-video effectiveness.

Because television is more than a radio with pictures or a newspaper that moves, the presentation of the store's message has special requirements. Television requires:

Video production
Audio production
Product animation

Within the framework of these requirements, copy must be written, settings planned, action planned, special effects planned, talent selected, and models booked, fitted, and directed. With so much time-consuming detail involved, the agency takes a great deal of the pressure and responsibility off the store's personnel. However, when it comes to fashion projection on TV, the agency works with the fashion office.

Fashion Guidance for the Agency.   The store's fashion authority is the fashion director. To guarantee continuity of its fashion philosophy in this advertising medium, as in all the others, her guidance is essential.

What is meant by poster-blue? Is it this one or that one?
What accessories go with the new coat look?
What is meant by figurative prints?
How should the new African jewelry be dramatized?

The questions are endless because the change of trends is endless. Only someone who is close to the changes, aware of what they are and what they mean, can direct the honesty of the message.

As noted earlier, the staff members of the advertising agency are also invited to the fashion director's fashion presentations to be sure they are informed of what each season's story will include. But since they are not working with the trends on a day-to-day basis, it is important to specify as each commercial attempt comes up, what is meant and what is needed.

Merchandise Selection.   The fashion office figures strongly in the area of merchandise selection. Not only do the fashion coordinators pull fashion merchandise to truly reflect the trend or item in question, but they must also consider the advantages and pitfalls of this intimate medium of communication, television.

The greatest features of fashion, color, texture, and head-to-toe coordination, could only be imagined before color. Tweeds, plaids, and prints, plus the color and contrast of accessories, were difficult to dramatize. Color made it all happen. A tight close-up on a great woven wool tweed, for example, tells the viewer immediately all about the texture, color, and character of the fabric.

Color.   However, even with color, some things do not come across effectively. Solid black and dark colors conceal detail, unless the silhouette is all that matters. Stark white, too, although dramatic for a certain type gown, is usually best replaced with color, even if it is delicate or pastel.

All this the fashion office keeps in mind when the buyer hands her a few pieces for a fashion commercial. "Every piece black, with beige?" If the pieces did not represent a color trend, and they were also available in other colors, the fashion office would be wise to color coordinate the group with more photogenic choices.

Motion.   Movement, too, is an exciting advantage that can only be found in television. Wherever possible, this factor should be considered. The fluid, floating feeling of a soft fabric, the swish, flare, and dash of a bold fabric, be it a gentle, understated look or flamboyant avant-garde treatment, if it's the character of the look that carries the message, there is no place it can come more alive than on television.

The Magic of Television.   Television is a personal, intimate medium. People come to TV for an emotional experience. They want to be entertained, to be informed, to feel, to relate. Thus, an exciting message, a personable message, an enchanting, glamorous, or amusing message related to fashion, can very well jar that viewer out of her apathy or resistance to a particular store. For example, many customers who would not look at the store's newspaper ad because, let us say, they do not look to that store for fashion, are exposed and captured (at least in the beginning) by a message on television.

Through this personal medium, a store's fashion image can best come alive. It can talk, move, smile and entertain. These are not necessarily the virtues that make a strong sales pitch on television successful. If the price is right, and the goods desirable, chances are it will sell. But fashion is different. It depends on image, charm, beauty and excitement. These and many other emotional ingredients make the fashion message on television sell merchandise, make friends and draw customers to come see.

The selection of fashion merchandise, therefore, carries responsibility to entertain, to inform, and to stimulate desire. All of this and more. A series of well-done fashion commercials by a store could very possibly enhance its fashion image, fashion authority, and fashion leadership, not a small load by any measurement.

How Will It Televise? When detail is necessary in a newspaper ad, the artist or illustrator can very easily draw every seam, tuck, stitching, pocket, and button. But on television all of this could be lost unless colors of the detail are in strong contrast to their background. A gown of pink lace with appliqued pink lace petals might be the most divine creation around, but is very likely that most of the precious detail would be completely lost on television. If the petals were in a contrasting color, considerably more detail would come through. Commentary helps, of course, but television is a visual medium. The viewer should be able to see what is shown, not just be told. Television should not be treated as a radio with pictures.

Television is an X-ray machine at times. Every wrinkle, every ill-fitted undergarment, and every crooked line can show and break up the mood. The sensitive television camera, while failing to pick up pale or subtle detail, has an uncanny talent for picking up unexpected flaws. The fashion office must watch carefully for those pieces that will fail to come across or will make the wrong kind of impression.

Guide Lines for Choice. A good way to avoid mistakes, especially for the beginner, is to follow a simple check list on what the merchandise is expected to represent.

1. What will the merchandise be selling?
    A department or shop
    A color
    A fabric or fiber
    An item
    A trend
    A length
    A designer or manufacturer

If the TV commercial is to be on a department or shop, a representation of pieces indicative of that area must be pulled. If it is to be a color, smashing examples from several fashion departments might be included. It is the same with a trend, an item, or a length. When it comes to a fabric or fiber, the garments must be honest representatives of the ingredients advertised. If it is a commercial to herald a designer or manufacturer, the task is much simpler; one must simply select those pieces best suited for television from the named collection. Whether it is Christian Dior or Jonathan Logan, the pieces in stock are the pieces used.

2. How many pieces and how many models have been ordered by the agency? This is important to know before pulling. It is entirely possible that three garments shown will require three models, but is is also possible (through the magic of television editing) for the same model to wear all three pieces. Knowing this in advance, the coordinator responsible will pull the specified merchandise in sizes corresponding to the need.

3. What production facts about the commercial might influence the choice of merchandise? Actually, it should be the other way around—merchandise gets first consideration. Production and format and copy should be drawn up to express the clothes. However, there are occasions when certain special effects or production plans influence a selection.

For example, if a model is going to be "keyed" into a set or prop, the the costume cannot be blue. If blue is the key color, her dress would completely disappear. The special effect would not work. Undoubtedly you have seen "keyed" production, a model made to look very tiny, sitting on the brim of a hat, or climbing out of an oversized object.

On the other hand, if the agency advises the fashion office, "We are going to open up on a silhouette shot," it would be understood that the models and the garments will need to be receptive to silhouette lighting.

Line and movement are very important in such a shot. If the models are not required to pose in a "freeze," the important action of the fabric must be considered, chiffon that floats and can be blown for motion, action-cut crepe can swirl, sleeves can billow . . . tiers can show dimension. A magnificent brocade gown with straight lines may look devastating with the lights on, but in silhouette it might look as though it were as stiff as a board.

The possibilities of production requirements are legion. What's more, they change every season, every year. The important issue is that whoever is responsible for merchandising or selecting fashions for television commercials must be up to date on what is happening.

4. In coordinating a commercial where more than one garment is shown, what is the best way to insure against similarity? It is very possible to select three different garments, a yellow shirt dress, a yellow suit, and a yellow shirt and skirt, and have all three photograph almost exactly alike. If there is little difference in the line, no difference in trim or detail, and no difference in color, it is very possible for all three to come off enough alike to be alike.

If color is a factor in a commercial, then the example of a dress, a coordinate, a suit, or a coat must be different in almost every detail. Besides watching a more exciting commercial, the viewer can enjoy a thirty second fashion show and come away with the feeling that the store has a great selection of everything. Accessories, too, help to enhance, dramatize, or punctuate the various looks. Individuality is what each garment should enjoy. Without it, there is no point in its being there, soaking up expensive air time.

Models Make the Clothes.   A dress on a hanger is a dress on a hanger. A dress on a bad model would be better left on the hanger. Even an ordinary dress on a good model can stimulate the imagination. Selecting models for television differs in several ways from selecting "ramp" models or "showroom" models. A fashion show model can be almost any height or size, depending on the clothes being shown and the audience they are facing. Television cameras make a skinny girl look slim and a plump girl look fat. Approximately ten to fifteen pounds can be added by the camera. Height is not as important on television as are body measurements. It is usually difficult to tell how tall someone is unless they are standing next to someone whose height is a known fact. Tall, thin girls, however, usually come off best.

In addition to size and more important than size are a model's photogenic qualities. Sometimes the most sophisticated and colorful ramp model will have the wrong kind of personality for TV. Another model, seemingly plain, might photograph like a dream and come across on the screen with everything the viewer likes to see. This is not to say that a ramp or fashion show model cannot also be a good TV model; it does mean, however, that it does not necessarily follow.

A model or personality who is photogenic does not necessarily have to be a beauty. A certain something—a soft look, a pixy look, a dramatic look. Whatever that something is, if it works, it is what it takes.

Movement, too, makes an interesting difference. Many of the movements and gestures or techniques employed by the model may come off quite well in person, but for some reason, on television where everything seems exaggerated, those same movements are too much, not enough, unattractive, or unappealing. This is not at all unlike some motion picture stars who react to a camera in a way they react to nothing else. The model who has great rapport with the camera can do wonders for a fashion commercial.

How to Find TV Models.   A fashion office might be able to pull all it needs for TV right out of its "stable" of fashion models. If the regular crew works out, fine. But if they do not, it is wise to hold auditions specifically for TV modeling. These are best held right in the studio on closed circuit camera. This way it is possible to see the model's photogenic qualities, and scrutinize how she moves, how well she takes direction, and how flexible her effectiveness might be in various moods on camera. Some excellent models, who thrive on a live audience, freeze on camera. Others, not too fond of the live audience, come alive for the intimacy of the camera.

Personality Identification.   Just as a store would prefer to have an announcer or commentator whose voice is associated only with them, the models the fashion office engages for television exposure would best serve the store's image or personality identification if they did not appear for the competition. It is obvious that if the same model appeared on the air for two different fashion stores, the viewer might be confused (especially if she is a model who appears often), and memory recall of whose fashions were seen might be difficult.

Preparation of TV Copy.   When the merchandise has been pulled and the models fitted, the agency is called in to look over the pieces and write the copy. The fashion office may be called upon to provide the copywriter with a fact sheet on what the garment is, what department it is from, who is the designer, what is the fabric, what is its purpose, etc. Even with a fact sheet, which should also provide the writer with the correct and current fashion terminology, there will be questions.

"What do you call this kind of sleeve?"
"Would such an outfit be restricted to at-home wear, or would it be legitimate away from home?"
"What will you be calling this new color combination?"

Every new trend and every new commercial will bring new questions. The store's authority is the fashion office. The fashion director should make sure every member of her staff, even the newcomer, is kept up to date on the new answers.

Taping Time.   A representative of the fashion office should be on hand for the taping of fashion television spots or programing. It is good to have an advertising agency that can ride herd on all the details of televising, but fashion interpretation is the job of the fashion office.

As any good fashion magazine will testify, not a single model is photographed or makes the editorial pages of that publication without the presence and approval of the fashion editor in charge. She is on hand throughout the shooting sessions, making sure the photographer comes up with the accurate interpretation of the fashion and the accurate image or approach of the magazine. It is the same with the fashion director of a store. She and her staff are the editors of the fashion image of the store, the guardians of the fashion stories being photographed.

Every detail of how the costume comes across must be watched—the tilt of a hat, the tie of a scarf, the handling of a bag or umbrella, the drape of a gown. A mistaken approach can literally change the whole concept.

Also, if an economy of shots or takes is involved, the fashion director can give guidance on the most effective way to go. "Don't waste any time panning the waist and skirt; they're not new. But that shoulder and sleeve line is very new. If you are going to hit anything, hit that.''

The Television Fashion Show. If a portion of a show, a segment, or complete program is devoted to showing fashion, the pacing and movement must be well rehearsed and "on the button." Unlike a live fashion show, if a model is late, the commentator can ad-lib to fill the spot. On television this is deadly. One model must follow the other with marked precision. Even though most events would be done on tape where there is margin for error, studio taping time is expensive and the more retakes involved, the more changes or revisions, the more expensive the show becomes. A few ways to eliminate problems at the outset include:

1. Be sure there are enough models booked for the show to insure good pacing.
2. Book models who have had previous TV experience so not too much time is spent in explaining which camera is on, where and how to move.
3. Give the models sufficient time to rehearse. Advise them where they "hit their mark," and what kind of shots will be taken so they can relate their turns or movements to the gown and effect being sought.
4. Time the rehearsal so that no one is surprised when it is running short or running long. Rehearsal is the time to "fix" the pacing.
5. Remember that ten or fifteen seconds is a long time to hold on one model; that is plenty of time for the viewer to get the whole picture. If commentary requires a longer focus on a model, the costume should justify it.

Staging and Lighting. Television is a theatre. A cast of players provided with a good script and good direction must also have a good stage setting and good lighting. Staging on television has unlimited possibilities. One set can become many. A moving camera, another angle, a tight shot, a wide shot, a down shot, all magically transform a static set into a mobile unit.

Thanks to the flexibility of the camera, simple settings can go a long way. Especially when working with fashion, simplicity is most desirable. The intimacy of the camera and the concentrated area of the screen as the viewer sees it, should build up an immunity to overdoing. Fashion is most sensitive to competition in backgrounds. Simplicity permits the fashion item to come forth as the main focal point. The less distraction the better.

In addition to sets, the electronic miracles of special effects can create almost any desired atmosphere without the use of props or settings. For contemporary fashions a stylized type of background or lighting, surrounded with special effects in lens patterns, motifs, and movement, can create a contemporary mood that will be more memorable than a fully constructed set. Lighting, a complete art in itself in the television medium, is the best friend fashion can have. Without professional lighting, the most exciting, dramatic, and romantic effects might be missed. Colors and fabrics, too, require special attention. The fashion director, consulting with the television station's engineers, can help them understand what special effect or lighting is most compatible with a specific fashion look. If an advertising agency representative is available, such direction should be relayed through this channel—agency to TV director to engineers.

It is sufficient to say that a network of people and responsibilities take place to get a simple commercial on the air. What the viewer sees in a few fleeting seconds has taken many man-hours, a variety of talents, and no small number of advertising dollars to make it happen.

Afterview

The fashion office can be responsible for many of the pluses that come to a retail store through the medium of television.

Almost all cities have local television shows, which are emceed or hosted by a personality on a regular basis. Such a personality, in need of an extensive wardrobe, is usually an excellent source of fashion exposure for a store who is willing to furnish and dress said hostess in exchange for a credit line in the roll-ups each day. Sometimes, the personality is willing to mention her costume, describe it, and tell what department and store it came from in exchange for the generous service of a different ensemble every day.

Fitting and selecting fashions for such an arrangement would normally be the total responsibility of the fashion office. Management is usually delighted to cooperate. The personality is usually invited into the store, and a member of the fashion office escorts her around from department to

That
Great
American
know-how

department, helping her try on various looks, deciding what looks best on her, and what will make the best impression on the air. Eventually, the subject becomes so well known to the fashion office member responsible for handling the situation that she can select an entire week's wardrobe without any special fittings. Clothes can then be sent to the station a week at a time; clothes from the previous week can be picked up at the same time. Once the routine is established, it is quite painless.

Another television advantage is guest appearances on talk, interview, or variety shows on which store personalities from the fashion area can get free exposure—editorial exposure. Fashion directors or fashion commentators are excellent guests, very often appearing on a regular basis to reveal new aspects of fashion, present live fashion shows, and demonstrate new fashion ideas.

People such as visiting fashion designers and magazine editors are excellent guests for local TV talk shows. Pictured is an interview with the editor of *Vogue* in connection with the New York Collections show at Mass Brothers, Florida. (Courtesy of *Vogue* Magazine.)

Such arrangements can be made by the publicity director of the store or the advertising agency, but it is more likely to come about through the personal effectiveness of the fashion director herself. Her reputation, her personality, and her authority very often are invited to contribute to shows where personal impact develops viewers' interests. Members of a store's fashion office sometimes become famous as the community's authority on fashion, and television exposure is an ideal area for reaching people on a personal level unattainable to such a degree anywhere else.

If a beginner is preparing for a career in fashion, a general knowledge of the workings of radio and television is certainly helpful. Understanding

A fashion director, appearing on local TV, to be interviewed (below) or to present fashion shows (opposite) can increase her personal rapport with the viewer-customer.

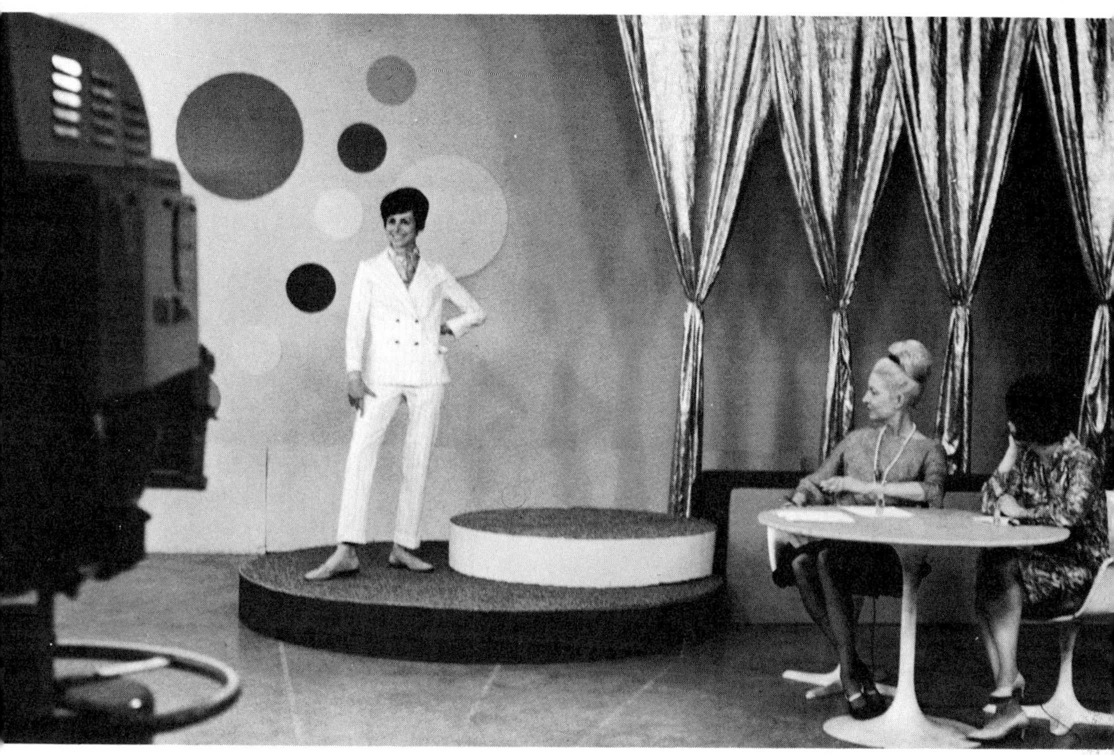

the "language" in itself is important in communicating with an advertising agency or the television station personnel. To know what is meant by "on camera" or "a dissolve shot" or "a pan" can make the entire experience more fun, if not more efficient.
Television is such an intricate part of our lives, anyway, that it behooves most of us to have enough curiosity to check out some of its mysteries, secrets, and potential.

❋ *Chapter 12*

❋ *Fashion Shows and Special Events*

In every type of live theatre, a play, a musical, the ballet, and certainly the greatest show on earth, the circus, there is an enchanting ingredient available to the audience, in addition to its obvious purpose of entertainment.

Moved to tears or laughter by the remarkable skill of a fine actor or held spellbound by the daring feats of a circus trapeze flyer, the audience can collectively enjoy the experience, but more important, people can individually dream a little and identify for a few make-believe moments with the brave and the beautiful, the gifted and the uninhibited. Identification and involvement are part of the thing that is nearest and dearest to the hearts of most everyone—the self.

Where the "self" is involved, the fashion show has much to offer. It has that irresistible ability to draw the audience into a personal relationship. Since what we wear or do not wear, enormously represents how we see ourselves or how we wish the world to see us, fashion, ego, and self are highly compatible. In fact, so much so, that it is not uncommon for a woman to walk away from a fashion show with a mood entirely different from the one with which she arrived. She can come away thoroughly delighted and inspired, or she might sulk out feeling totally abused, neglected, and even offended. So close, so fragile, and so intimate is the self involvement, that a woman with limited self confidence or understanding can be slightly shattered by a fashion review if she feels too threatened. To compete, to keep up, and to adjust are all challenges that confront the modern woman. Some meet such challenges with eagerness and excitement; some, whether they admit it or not, fear change, fear their ability to be elastic or versatile.

Fashion Show—the Educator.   A show is not a show without an audience. The better the audience, the better the show. Size is not all-important, but response and communication are. Admittedly, the word "communication" has become strongly overused. But, let's face it, without good communication, especially in the fashion business, nothing is going to happen. Customers need to relate. They need to understand. They also need to feel welcome and cherished. A good fashion show can, and must, do all of this. Although this is no small task, it is not too difficult if one understands the ground rules.

The customer is the first consideration. A good fashion office must carefully guard against becoming so sophisticated they forget that what is old hat to them may be new and mysterious to the customer. A good fashion show can teach, gently, cleverly, and uniquely, but always with a light touch. To talk down to an audience, or "instruct" is as deadly as no information at all. The subtle dropping of information is the trick.

Show and Tell.   The best fashion guidance in the well-coordinated fashion show is visual. At a glance, the viewer can learn:

How the fabric moves
How the lines of the garment fall and mold
How the ensemble is put together with head-to-toe accessories
How the model's makeup and hair fashion relates to the total look

Most of the fashion story is revealed in the "show," but some audiences require a commentator to "tell" what they have seen. They might like to know the name of the designer, fabric content, fabric performance, purpose of the garment, and perhaps price. Facts that are not obvious are usually welcomed by the audience.

To Comment or Not to Comment.   That, indeed, is the question. Some fashion offices would not consider the idea of eliminating a commentator. There are others, a bit more advanced and sophisticated, who avoid commentary wherever possible. Both approaches are right. Both have their place. Again, the audience is the deciding factor or at least the

The major fashion show—a highlight on the community calendar. The Symphony Fashion Gala, produced by Joseph Horne Co., a benefit for the Pittsburgh Symphony Orchestra, is a sellout year after year. (Courtesy of Joseph Horne Co.)

first consideration. In some communities, where the customer is not as well traveled or as involved with fashion, the descriptions and explanations of a pleasant commentator are expected. Even in communities where the customer is really into fashion, well informed, and well traveled, there are times, when all women enjoy a professional interpretation or clarification of what they have seen or heard regarding the future fashion. Such times might be at the outset of a coming season, the introduction of a revolutionary new trend, or a completely new approach to the use of fashion.

A great number of fashion shows, however, can live very well with a minimum of talk or none at all. For example, let us assume that a collection of knits are to be shown. The entire show is exclusively knits. It would be very simple for the fashion director or fashion show coordinator to greet the guests, make an enthusiastic and succinct introductory speech about the merits of these knits (their easy-care and versatility, their merits as the perfect packables, perfect travelers, and their general price range). If a printed program is provided, the customer can follow the models in the order of appearance and check those pieces she may like to try on later. In such a case, there is little need to ramble on about each individual piece when the facts are already established. A filler of good background music and a closing statement by the commentator could easily suffice.

Another example of when commentary can be eliminated is when a show is presented as the entertainment feature of a program, a glamorous benefit, or fashion extravaganza, complete with orchestra, choreography, and performers. The important thing in these cases is that the audience knows from which store the merchandise comes. If they have had a good time and go away with a warm feeling, it is very likely they will find their way to the store, even though they may not remember everything they saw in the show. All they need to recall is, "That was a great show . . . some really great looking clothes . . . I think I'll stop by tomorrow and take a look around."

Commentary Know-How.   Words can be wonderful things. They can also be a bore. A lovely fire that warms your hearth can also burn your hand. Careful. Handle with care. Words can be equally hazardous; they can draw the listener close or drive her away.

Fashion commentary can be a language of charm. It can be exotic, poetic, amusing, kicky, or bizarre. It can be whatever the traffic will bear. The terminology must be the newest, the most fitting. It must enhance the mood and the tempo of the fashion, or it does not belong.

The big taboo of commentary is to point out the obvious. "This red dress is contrasted with a white check jacket." If the audience cannot see the dress is red and the jacket is white, no need to pay expensive model fees. Black-and-white photographs would be enough. A commentator is justified in mentioning an obvious color, only when it is a point of fashion. "This new vibrant red is one of the leading brights of the coming season, as a strong ground for the new prints or as a unique combiner with other leading colors." The commentator this time has revealed a color story, one that will give the customer confidence when shopping.

Knowing what to say and how to say it are all extremely important in a fashion show. The more easily and skilfully it is done, the more professional is the tone of the show. Women can sense the sound of authority. That's why written commentary is less desirable than just notes. Better still, the ad-lib approach, which is even more authoritative if the commentator is capable. In order to do this, of course, the commentator must thoroughly know her merchandise and her fashion facts. An audience is much more responsive to being "talked" to than "read" to.

Type of Commentator. The sound of authority, expressed through effective words and delivery technique, can make a very ordinary show seem exciting. It will most certainly give it the professionalism that helps uphold the store's image as a fashion leader. This would naturally bring up the question of the beginner. A beginner is likely to sound like an amateur, but how does she begin? How does she learn?

It is to a fashion director's advantage to create opportunities for all members of her staff to exercise their talents, or potential talents, in all phases of assignments in the fashion office. Not the least of these is the job of fashion commentary. For one thing, the fashion director, as indicated in earlier chapters, wears many hats and covers many bases. Her travel schedule is usually heavy and in her absence, it is comforting to know that other members of her staff can take the microphone and hold the show together smoothly.

For the larger shows, in the fashion director's absence, the fashion show coordinator or her assistant can take over. For the smaller shows, area coordinators can and should step into those shoes. Branch coordinators, often required to handle all aspects of a show, also need to be trained to take on the microphone duties.

But the beginner, the new member of the fashion office, must first serve an apprenticeship in the area of fashion commentary to develop that sound of authority. An excellent place for the young beginner is in the area of children's shows. For starters, a young voice is ideal, and a young woman, (even a beginner) can substitute authority with charm. The audience, too, is less sophisticated and the show is less pretentious. The beginner can get the feel of handling the pacing, the models, the words, and the audience, all in an atmosphere of warmth and ease, the general climate surrounding most children's shows. No matter what the children do they are usually loved, and mistakes go easily unnoticed.

Shows for All Occasions.   A store need never be at a loss for a reason to hold a fashion show. The greatest problem is in holding the number down. The fashion show calendar, maintained by the fashion office, can be bulging at the seams at peak periods and lean at other times, or the steady flow of fashion show action can easily be maintained year round, week after week, day after day. Some stores believe very strongly in the fashion show approach, but some resist it strongly and do only a minimum of ''musts.''

In an operation which restricts its fashion show involvement to a ''must'' list, that list alone could be no small undertaking. For example, most stores feel they must do a benefit show or two when asked. They are likely to schedule seasonal shows, such as back-to-school and cruise and holiday. They might do special showings when a new fashion collection or new shop concept is being introduced. Also, they usually include bridal shows, about twice a year, on a must list. That same list could be extended to include fiber or fabric shows. Special individual showings of wool products, cotton, or man made fibers. And if one added to all the above, the shows offered in the pattern departments by pattern companies or import collections during special events (such as import fairs) the so-called minimum ''must'' list can grow quite long.

Whatever direction a store takes on the fashion show idea, it is plain to see that at some time, in some way, every fashion operation worthy of the name will become involved in fashion show business. It's inevitable.

It is entirely possible to build a fashion show around almost any new fashion idea or trend that comes along. An alert fashion office, whose store appreciates new and frequent applications of shows, will take special pride in developing a well organized and creative shop, in which all members who are "show biz" oriented can pitch in when needed.

The Purposes of Fashion Shows. Fashion shows provide many advantages. And right at the top of the list is selling. It is not an easy thing for a woman who is not closely associated with the fashion world to imagine how a new silhouette looks on the human form or how it should be put together. The live fashion show illustrates. A customer can easily overlook a dress seen on a hanger that might inspire her in a show. She needs and welcomes such help.

So it is with every type customer, the teen customer, the male customer, the half-size woman, the expectant mother, the debutante, the bride, the mother of the bride, and all customers with special interests. For them, the store has a specialized fashion show. The purpose, of course, is to sell, but in the process a special service is extended: a recognition of individual needs, one of the nicest ways to make friends.

Making friends is a big responsibility of the fashion office. That is why the benefit shows and private shows for women's clubs are so high on the list of the store's public relations projects.

Prestige is another sterling purpose of the fashion show, in the formal presentation of an important name designer's collection or through informal trunk showings of fashions. Other vehicles that carry big prestige insignias are the exclusive or community-wide, annual formal balls, such as St. Louis' Veiled Prophets Ball, Omaha's Aksarben Ball, mardi gras and cotillion balls everywhere.

For all the shows held outside the store to make friends, there are great numbers of shows held inside the store, in the auditorium, in the fashion departments, in the tea room, to build traffic. It all adds up to the same purpose—to sell.

How to Produce a Fashion Show

There are so many details to consider when planning a fashion show that the prospect may seem overwhelming. But, in truth, once a good routine is established, the whole project is relatively simple.

The Informal Show. To make the first step an easy one, the informal-type showing is a good place to begin. Under the heading of informal

Events with elegant pageantry open a social season and salute outstanding civic leaders. One of 32 royal attendants in coronation gowns. Court gowns are designed each year by a name designer.

The throne room of the annual Aksarben Coronation and Ball, Omaha, Nebraska, with the crowning of the Aksarben Queen, wearing a specially designed gown by Oscar de la Renta. (Courtesy of Donald Jack Photos and Aksarben.)

shows go the trunk shows, informal modeling in the store's restaurant areas, fashion departments, and throughout the store.

Trunk shows and informal modeling require no ramps, no staging, and no special props or lighting. All that is needed is the merchandise and the live models. Trunk shows (collections brought in for a limited special appearance) usually require a minimum of two or three good models.

The responsibility of the fashion office for the informal show might include:

1. Making sure that the trunk collection has been unpacked, pressed and delivered to the appropriate department in time for model fittings and the showings.

2. Booking the models. The Fashion Office will need to contact the buyer involved in advance to learn what size samples will be coming in. Since sizes 8, 10 or 12 are the usual requirements, it is wise to have a good file of these size models on hand. The type of model, of course, must be considered; she must be right for the clothes. She should also be personable. She will be in close contact with customers, very often involved in selling a garment if a salesperson or the designer is busy, and it is important that she has a thorough understanding of the fashion concept of the collection involved.

3. Scheduling the models. With informal modeling, models are usually paid by the hour or the day, rather than on the per-show basis. The model will need to be informed as to how many hours she will work, or if she will be working a staggered schedule with other models alternating. For example, a trunk showing schedule might read something like this:

MODEL	*DAY*	*HOURS*
Mary	Monday, Tuesday	11 A.M. to 4:30 P.M. French Room
Donna	Monday, Tuesday	11 A.M. to 4:30 P.M. French Room
Jackie	Monday	5 P.M. to 7 P.M. French Room
Suzanne	Monday, Tuesday	12 noon to 2 P.M. Tea Room
Corinne	Monday, Tuesday	12 noon to 2 P.M. Tea Room

All bases are covered. Two girls working the day hours in the French Room, one in the evening when the store is open, and two during the lunch hours. It is entirely possible for some models to double up on a schedule, such as working the day schedule and evening schedule, but that, of course, would depend on availabilities.

4. Accessorizing. Most pieces included in a trunk show (if modeled only in the department) require very little accessorizing, because the garment itself is the focal point, and changes are made repeatedly to allow customers to see several pieces. The important accessories, however, that would be required are the correct leg fashions—hose and shoes. Modeling in the Tea Room, however, might require more attention in the accessory

"Pulling" accessories for fashion shows requires signed memorandums of what was taken. Each item must be listed, then checked off when returned. (Courtesy of Bergdorf Goodman, New York.)

department. A coordinator from the fashion office would fit the models, decide who needs what accessory, and then go chase it down. For the beginner, anxious to learn the ropes, it would be a great idea for her to tag along, watching, and assisting the coordinator get the informal showing under way. It is a nice, easy-paced place for her to get her feet wet.

The Formal Show.   Now we get down to the real thing. The types, styles, and possibilities for formal, that is, ramp or stage fashion shows are astronomical. A good dividing line for instruction and learning how to put the formal show together, is the in-store show and the outside show. The in-store show usually represents specialized departmental showings, special fashion promotions, collections, and seasonal approaches. The other (the outside event) can become an entirely different experience. Benefits, entertainment programs for women's clubs, city-wide participations, all of these and more are by their very nature handled with a different approach than the show designed to bring traffic into the store. One is sell, the other public relations.

The In-Store Shows.   A show held in a special department, for a special customer, is the most effective in-store type. A teen show in the junior department, a show for men only in the men's shop or a bridal show, are good examples. Any show that is designed to attract only those customers who are truly interested, is likely to be a show that will sell. The following procedure of show production, with the variance of a few details, would be applicable to almost all in-store shows.

General Procedure.   Once the show is booked and cleared on the calendar, the first routine steps include:

1. Theme and title
2. Location of show
3. Facilities needed
4. Length of show (number of pieces)
5. Models (what type and how many needed)
6. Commentator (if one is required she must be committed as to date and time)

Using the above routine as a work procedure, let us plan one of the specialized in-store shows.

Miss Bergdorf Fur Boutique on Five
invites you to A Fur Affair
Thursday, September 17th, at 11:30 A.M
It's "Fall-in-love-with-fur-time"
all the time here, and we've just
the number to steal
your heart away.

BERGDORF GOODMAN
FIFTH AVENUE 57 TO 58TH STREETS • ON THE PLAZA • NEW YORK 10019 • PLAZA 3 7300
8-70

PARI

The Bridal Show.   This show (usually held twice a year) has something in it for every member of the fashion office, and when they get it off the ground they are likely to have learned lessons that will come in mighty handy next time out.

Filling in the answers on the general procedure list will be the framework for action:

1. Theme—Bridal, Title—"I Do"
2. Location of show—Store auditorium
3. Facilities Needed—Stage
   Bridal setting (see display department)
   Special rigging for lights (see display department)
   Live music
   Aisle-wide ramps (at least eight feet for bridal gowns)
   Microphone (for commentator)
   2 dressing rooms (1 for women, 1 for men)
   Flowers (see flower shop manager)
   Completely set wedding reception table with wedding cake, coffee, etc. (See food service department)
4. Length of show—45 minutes (40–45 pieces)
5. Models
   12 young women (brides and bridesmaids)
   3 mothers of the bride
   2 men (1 groom, 1 father)
   2 junior bridesmaids (8–10 years old)
   2 flower girls (5–6 years old)
   1 ring bearer (5–7 year old boy)
6. Commentator—yes—fashion director

Now the basics are squared away (on paper, that is) and the work begins.

Meeting of the Minds.   When a show of such proportion as a bridal show is in the offing, it is wise to have a meeting for all those people involved.

An in-department formal show of a boutique fur collection: the invitation; the window; the show (the window piece in the line-up). (Courtesy of Bergdorf Goodman, New York.)

The showing of a Givenchy collection in its own area. Givenchy Boutique. (Courtesy of Neiman-Marcus, Dallas.)

Fashion office
Display department
Advertising department
Bridal shop buyer
Divisional merchandise manager of women's fashion
Divisional merchandise manager of children's fashion
Divisional merchandise manager of men's fashion
Divisional merchandise manager of home furnishings.
Representative of the flower shop
Representative of the food service department
Representative from the bridal registry

All of the above are usually regarded as vital to the whole picture, but there are even others who might be included: the divisional merchandise manager of accessories and cosmetics, a representative from the photo department, a representative from the stationery department, and the home furnishings fashion coordinator.

Home furnishings figures strongly in the bridal show. Bridal services, too, for catering parties or the reception, and for renting everything from the punch bowl for the reception to formal wear for male attendants. This is the one big chance for the whole store to get together to court the bride for all her needs for the wedding and her new home, to reach everyone interested, from what to wear to the wedding to what gift to bring. The bridal show, therefore, deserves everyone's special attention.

At the bridal meeting, where everyone may hear the total plan, exchange ideas, and receive their own specific assignments, the bridal show plan is finalized. The food service needs to know how many people are expected, the flower shop needs to know how many bouquets, what kind, and what colors, the representative of the bridal registry needs to be informed as to when she will be introduced during the show, how long she can talk, and what is to be covered regarding the store's bridal services. One good meeting should do it.

Newspaper ad for the bridal show. (Courtesy of J. L. Brandeis, Omaha.)

The fashion office is now ready to get on with the show. In every city there is much competition for bridal business, so in order to attract big audiences and customers who will buy, the bridal effort must be an attractive one.

The Setting.   The bridal show is scheduled for the store's big auditorium. It may be a very ordinary room at other times, but for this event it must be turned into a breathtaking setting for one of the season's most beautiful shows.

If the setting was traditional last year, make it contemporary this year, whatever the fashion mood dictates. Never do the show exactly the same way. There is so little that can be changed in a bridal show, every possible change should be welcomed. True, the audiences change every year, but the word gets around. "That store does the most magnificent bridal shows. You are really missing something if you pass it up."

The display department can come up with some ingenious ideas for bridal show settings, but they do need fashion direction regarding the going thing. For example, one season the fashion director felt the usual organ music and traditional vocalist would be best replaced, for the sake of the fashion trend, with a guitarist and folk singer. The wedding setting was a garden, for the nature-child flavor. If the display director had not been tipped off by the fashion office as to the "feel" of the show, he could not have given her the compatible background.

Pacing.   Pacing is another important touch to make the bridal show more exciting. Even when scenes or groups are paraded in ceremonial fashion, and even if wedding marches are slow and precise, a fashion show with maybe a dozen weddings to show, can become a drag if the same here-comes-the-bride pace is maintained throughout. Take a little poetic license and keep the processions moving, smooth and easy, but moving.

Pacing can be improved, not only by the way the models move, but by breaking up the line-up. One can look at just so many bridal or bridesmaids gowns without getting somewhat confused if they are not divided into

A bridal show is a wonderful opportunity to turn an ordinary room: top, into a storybook castle; center, into a garden walk; bottom, into a beautiful hall. (Courtesy of J. L. Brandeis, Omaha.)

"theme" categories, color stories, or occasionally sparked with an unconventional bridal approach. One season, when evening pants became big, bridal pants were introduced. When the mini dress was at its height, mini wedding dresses were shown. When "hot pants" swung into the fashion scene, bridal shorts were made available, with or without overskirts. These novel, break-aways from tradition, are fun and make the show the last word.

Variety. Since an important part of a bridal trousseau includes lingerie, a segment of the show devoted to floating lovelies helps add considerable variety to a bridal show. Most stores have eliminated the travel clothes or going-away fashions in a bridal show, simply because ready-to-wear fashion shows are available throughout the year, and the bridal show is long enough without being overextended.

For a change of pace in a bridal or ready-to-wear show, include a scene or category of lingerie. In a glamorous setting it can be very effective. (Courtesy J. L. Brandeis, Omaha.)

The Door Prizes. Door prizes are always a delightful addition to such a show, especially if one of the prizes is a honeymoon trip for two, courtesy of some generous airline. If only registered brides are eligible for door prizes, then it is a gleeful experience to pass them out—lingerie for her honeymoon, a starter set of china, her veil, towel sets, a free wedding portrait, a free trip to the store's beauty salon for the full treatment on her wedding day. Awarding such gifts to the guests and sharing the delight of the surprises, gives everyone the feeling of attending a bridal party rather than a fashion show.

Gift for Everyone. A free give-away always delights an audience. It seems to have a special charm at a bridal show, especially if it is a gift of fragrance or cosmetics, or a gift from the home furnishing department, such as a spoon or some little token that makes everyone attending feel important and part of a "party." Lots of helpful booklets and pamphlets on things of special interest to brides are often available as free pass-outs. All these little additions make the show a special event.

The Reception. When the guests arrive, while the music is strumming, and before show time, invite the guests to a beautifully decorated reception table for wedding cake, coffee, nuts, and mints. They enjoy taking these refreshments to their seats and examining their gift bags while waiting for the show. Having young men, perhaps personnel from the store, dressed appropriately to serve as ushers and seat guests, gives the store an additional model or two of their men's formal fashions or rental service. It's a nice touch.

The home furnishings fashion coordinator usually arranges to have several beautifully designed table settings available for the guests to stroll past and examine, both before and after the show. These might be part of the lobby decor, part of the auditorium atmosphere, or the commentator might invite the guests to go to the china department to see the special table settings.

Throw the Bouquet. Squeals of delight result from the traditional throwing of the bouquet. Especially if the commentator has just given credit to the store's florist by eloquently describing a crescent bouquet of white orchids. Then to have the bride toss it suddenly into the audience (at the end of the show, of course) provides a fun finish. If fresh flowers are not used throughout the show, it might be wise to at least have one bridal bouquet made of fresh flowers for the "tossing," plus the center-piece of the reception table.

Even hard-nosed fashion show viewers get caught up in the charm of a bridal show if it is beautifully staged and executed. The audience is moved by the beauty and joy and fun of it all. It's a happy occasion.

That's the Idea.   Taking a clue from the bridal show, all in-store fashion events (or anywhere, for that matter) should send the audience away happy and satisfied. That's the whole idea. And that is why specialized shows, tailored to a special audience, have a greater chance for success. You are playing to their special interests, talking their language, and communicating with their feelings. It's a winner.

The Box Lunch Show.   Another show that has experienced considerable success in many department stores is the box-lunch show. Working girls, shopping on their lunch hour, or busy women trying to squeeze lunch and shopping into a short period before dashing home to drive in the car pool or prepare dinner, thoroughly appreciate the opportunity to see an exciting show, eat lunch, and dash off to other things. The whole thing can be done beautifully in one-half hour. If the doors open at noon and box lunches are sold for, say, one dollar, the customer can be seated with lunch on her lap and ready to see the show in only a few minutes. If the show starts promptly at 12:10 P.M. (for this kind of setup promptness is essential) and if only about eighteen to twenty-four outfits are shown, everyone can be out by 12:30 P.M. It's a delightful interlude for women of all ages.

The Out-of-the-Store Fashion Show

Under this category we do not refer to the off-the-premises show the store might itself create by simply holding the festivities at a hotel, music hall, or theatre. We refer here to the show that has resulted from an outside request made to the fashion office for a benefit, a program of entertainment, or a fund-raising project of some kind for a woman's club or civic group. For our example, we will use a benefit show. Here the ground rules are a bit different, the procedure very often different with every show of this kind.

Diplomacy.   The first rule is diplomacy. Since this is an undertaking more valuable as public relations than as a "sell" vehicle, charm and tact are the watchwords. The women who come to the fashion office to request a fashion show for their project are very grateful for the store's cooperation, though some chairmen or committee members, inexperienced in this area, may not know how to express it. Every member of the fashion office must be trained to bear in mind that they are not dealing with professionals, they are dealing with customers. A woman handling the arrangements of a fashion show for the first time is very unsure of which way to go and what is expected of her, and it is very likely that a charming show of patience and a courteous helping hand will not be forgotten.

General Procedure.   The general procedure, used by the fashion office to put a show together in-store or of their own creation, cannot apply here. The store may have little to say about the general procedure points listed earlier. All six points, in fact, the theme and title of the show, location, facilities needed, length of show, models, and commentator may be completely taken out of the hands of the fashion office. It is entirely possible that all that will be required of the store is to furnish the clothes, fit the models, plan the line-up, and work backstage to be sure the models get on and off properly.

Then again, all responsibilities for the show may be completely dumped into the fashion office's lap, leaving everything to the store's discretion. Most fashion directors would vote strongly for this approach. With this routine, the fashion office can move with freedom and in the way they know will bring the happiest results.

Meeting Time.   Unlike the meeting for the bridal show, very few in-store people need be invited to this meeting. It is wise, however, for the fashion director, members of her office, and the committee members of the women's club involved to get together to be sure everyone knows what the other fellow is thinking. The only other store member who might be included would be the display director, if the store is involved in handling the staging and settings. There are certain points that should be thoroughly covered at this meeting, and if a plan is worked out, the meeting time can be kept to a minimum.

1. Hear everything the women have in mind for the show. If what they are requesting is possible, then it's time to go on to step 2, but if it is not, this is the time to clear the air. For example, it is not unheard of for a

committee to ask for one hundred models and want a show that will last only forty-five minutes. It is obvious they have no idea about time and the gigantic undertaking of that number of models. A forty-five minute show can easily be handled by anywhere from five to eight professional models.

2. Get a thorough understanding of how many people are expected to attend, and get as much information as possible as regards the age level, special interests, and life style of the guests. It is also very important to learn, if the fashion office is not familiar with the group, the economic level of the expected audiences. The fashion director can tactfully discover this by asking what type and price range they would like shown. One does not show couture fashions to moderate or budget-priced customers.

Usually such events are played to a general audience, from granddaughter to grandmother. That's a tough one. A general audience can be the most difficult to please. There is always one age group or type who feels that not enough things were shown for them. The best way to get around this problem (and every fashion office in the world will testify that it is a problem) is to include as many "ageless" fashions in the show as possible, that is, the classic looks that most everyone can wear, and usually do, at one time or another. If a smaller number of young people are in attendance than the more mature, then perhaps a special category of their new fashion looks would suffice.

3. Discuss the models. This is another delicate area. Some committees insist that their own members or friends be used as models. When it comes to fitting guest models as against professional models there is absolutely no comparison. The professional model wears anything and everything she is told. If she is asked to change her hair, she changes her hair. If she is warned about handling the merchandise, reminded about wearing dress shields, she takes it in stride.

When a show is comprised of guest models, the situation changes. Guest models, even though asked by the committee to cooperate when being fitted, are highly sensitive to what fashions are assigned to them. Even the sweetest-natured woman, the best mannered, the most intelligent, can become terribly self-conconscious or upset about fashion when she becomes a model. Many a fashion coordinator has heard:

"Well, I will wear it if I have to, but I certainly wouldn't buy it."

"This is not *me*."
"Why does she get to wear a ball gown and I have to wear a tweed suit?"
"I'm glad my husband won't be there; he'd die if he saw me in this."
"I love this style, but do you have it in some other color?"

Amusing as it might sound, this is in no way intended to poke fun at the women who react this way in the dressing rooms when fitting for a show. When a woman is invited to serve as a guest model, she feels a strong responsibility. Also, she is being asked to do something for which she has no special training. Those two things make her less than comfortable, even though she is delighted about the whole thing. Down deep, she wants to be at her best, and anything which is shown to her that does not exactly fit her picture of herself at her best, is resisted. While the fashion office should not be called upon to assume the role of doormat, it can be generous and try to alleviate as much pain as possible on both sides.

Not all guest models are painful to fit, not in the least. Some are a delight, some are fun, some are such jewels you want to ask them back again and again, but because of the moments when the guest model-customer is unhappy, some stores make it a firm, blanket rule never to use guest models under any circumstances. Professionals, or no show.

Another strong reason for requiring only professional models for a show is the merchandise itself. It is difficult, because of size and types of guests, to get a balanced show together. Certain pieces that would make the show a stand-out might have to be completely eliminated because there were not enough models of that size or look.

Time, energy, and result are three reasons for resisting guest models. On the basis of all the foregoing, most fashion directors of leading stores throughout the country, stand pretty pat on the professional show.

4. Be sure and ask if the fashion show is the entire program or just part of it. Every once in a while, a fashion show has arrived to play a benefit or some such event, with a full-scale production, only to learn that they would be surrounded on the bill by a high school band, a church choir, a few dance numbers from a recent dance recital, and a vocalist with an armful of selections. It's a shock, to say the least. Not that one minds sharing the program, but if one knows this in advance, the show could be be scaled down accordingly.

5. Be sure and firm up the exact time the show is scheduled to go on.

Most models in the average community work very hard for a nominal fee, and usually get paid on a per-show basis rather than an hourly basis. Many models are young mothers who have to pay baby sitters. Therefore, it is only kind to check on the time the model should arrive and leave rather than make her sit and wait a long time unnecessarily. If it is a luncheon show, check the time of the luncheon and at what point they plan to start the show.

Transporting of Merchandise. All merchandise that leaves the store for a show must be itemized, checked into a hamper, locked, and sealed, for transporting to the scene of the show. After the show, all merchandise must be checked in again, locked, and sealed, before being returned to the store. The fashion office personnel is responsible for dispersing all show pieces back to the departments from which they came. Shortages is one of the big problems of retail stores, so all departments responsible for transporting merchandise in and out, such as the display department and the fashion department, must keep good records of their transfers and returns.

Keep a Diary. One of the smartest things a busy fashion office can do is keep a fashion show diary. Record on the fashion show calendar or in a special show diary everything pertinent about the show, after it has taken place.

1. Attendance promised—actual attendance.
2. Was the audience the right customer for the store's fashion department?
3. How it was received?
4. Were guest models or pros used?

A year later it would be impossible to remember such bits of information, but a year later, when the same group calls for another show, it is a lifesaver to have the facts at your finger tips. If a group promised an attendance of 500 and only 200 attended, it is entirely possible the fashion director would wish to pass the show up the next time around. Also, next year, there may be a new fashion show coordinator or secretary handling the fashion show calendar; such a diary answers a lot of questions and helps avoid making the same mistake twice.

How to Plan a Line-Up

We have reviewed the specifics as they apply to the informal show, the in-store specialized show (bridal), and the outside benefit or women's club show, but the one thing that must be developed for all shows, regardless of size (with the exception of informal modeling) is the procedure of appearance or line-up. Models need to know which of their costumes to wear in which order, whom they follow, if they model singly or in pairs or groups, and if and when there is to be a finale.

The Categories. The basis for the line-up is the categories. Just a parade of models in a hodgepodge of fashions, does not clearly relate a fashion story. But well-planned groups pulled into clear-cut categories, states better than anything a fashion commentator can say that here it is, this is the look, this is the way it goes together, and these are the examples.

The number of categories depends a great deal on these three factors:

1. Length of show
2. Type of show (specialized or general)
3. Current trends (some seasons are much more diversified than others)

For the average-length general show, lasting about thirty to forty-five minutes, five or six categories can be handled. And within those categories, five or six examples can be shown, maybe seven or eight, but a category that is short and sweet tells the story well without running it into the ground.

Categories or groups are based on leading fashion trends. If windows and ads are exploiting a certain trend it's smart business to have it represented in the show, at least in one category. A group should not be included unless the merchandise in that group represents the new way to go.

A general show line-up might look like this:

Group One—The Winter Brights
An unusual availability of bright, bright colors for winter in a variety of fashion looks, with all models on stage at once for a bright opening, gets the show off on a high note.

Group Two—The Cardigan Cousins
A new look of the cardigan, showing up in sweaters, jackets, dresses,

and coats, all kissin' cousins to other coordinated pieces. A great group to show in diversified modeling. Present some models singly, some in pairs to show companion pieces, and some in trios.

Group Three—New Pickin's in Pants

All the different lengths, combinations, daytime, or nighttime expressions. Avoid the old-hat tendency to show evening fashions only at the end of the show. There should be flourish and fun throughout the show.

Group Four—Applause for Plaids

New Plaids showing up in bright and beautiful expressions, not only in lovely wools, but in knits and tweeds, and even printed on velvet and chiffon. It's a pattern story.

Group Five—The Return of the Dress

With so many coordinated looks being shown, so many separates, an elegant category of the new dress silhouettes (the body dress, the jacket dress, the shirt dress, etc.) should be included for the woman who loves to "dress." Show her how to interpret the new lines, how to accessorize, and if individuality is the key here, show an outstanding example of each dress idea separately.

Group Six—The Three Little Bares

A new sophistication for the night side. Bare shoulders. Bare midriffs. Bare backs. The show began big and bright. Give it a little drama and glamor now with everything in black or, perhaps, black and white. A variety of fabrics, of silhouettes, of costumes. A knockout. Makes a great grand finale, too.

Number of Pieces.   To include six pieces in six categories provides a well-rounded average length show of thirty-six outfits. Naturally, for a smaller show, present fewer pieces in each group; for a larger show, fatten the groups accordingly. For a really big show, each category can be extended and more categories added. However, it is always a good idea to exercise economy in trying to show everything. Pick the top fashion trends, fabrics, colors, and patterns, and develop them in a strong fashion statement. Too much confuses the customer.

Economy should also be prevalent when selecting numbers of garments for an in-department show (sometimes called "on-the-floor" show) because traffic in the department is tied up and other buyers, not involved in the show, are sensitive about customers being kept away from their shopping. Eighteen to twenty-four pieces is enough to show "on the floor."

Organizing the Line-up.   Write it down, everything. For a small or average show, as each model is fitted, tag the outfit with the model's name and category. Then when all fittings are completed, arrange the garments under their specified category, in the order of appearance, and transfer the line-up onto a master order-of-appearance sheet.

This system is especially effective in a large fashion office. More than one show might be fitting at the same time, and the girl who was responsible for the fitting and tagging the merchandise is off doing something else when the secretary or other fashion office girl comes to transfer the information for the line-up.

With this order-of-appearance sheet clearly filled out, the line-up falls beautifully into place. When the line-up is typed up, it should include approximately the same information as the tag, plus entrance directions for the models, for example, stage right, stage left, or stage center. Also, if models are to appear together, this direction should be shown on the line-up, either by a bracket or note.

Some fashion show coordinators use a file card system when drawing up the line-up, especially for very large shows. A file card typed up at the same time the clothes are tagged, provides a complete file on the pieces and their sequence. After the line-up is typed from the cards, they can be punched and bound for the commentator's use.

How to Use the Line-up.   Make lots of copies! The line-up must be seen by everyone associated with the show.

1. Post plenty of copies in the dressing rooms and at all entrances and exits. The more models the more copies. Everyone must be able to get close enough to a line-up, on the wall, on the door, near the mirror, and wherever necessary, to check and recheck where they have to be, and when.

2. The starter is a very important person. She stands at the entrance (each entrance must have its own starter), with a line-up in her hand, checking the models about to appear and sometimes literally pushing them out on time.

3. The fashion director or commentator can use a copy of the line-up,

instead of cards, if she prefers and if it carries sufficient information about the merchandise being shown.

4. A line-up should be handed to the musicans if there is live music. Very often it can be used as a cue sheet for them on which they can make their notes during rehearsal. However, if it is a major production, with an

Show _______ The Bash _______
Model _______ Michaela Ancona _______
Scene _______ No. 3 _______
Category _______ Campus Coats _______
Item _______ Green suede with hood _______
Position _______ No. 7 _______
Note _______ Enter dancing with No. 8 _______

Tag each garment in a fashion show line-up with clear easy-to-read information from which a master line-up can be made.

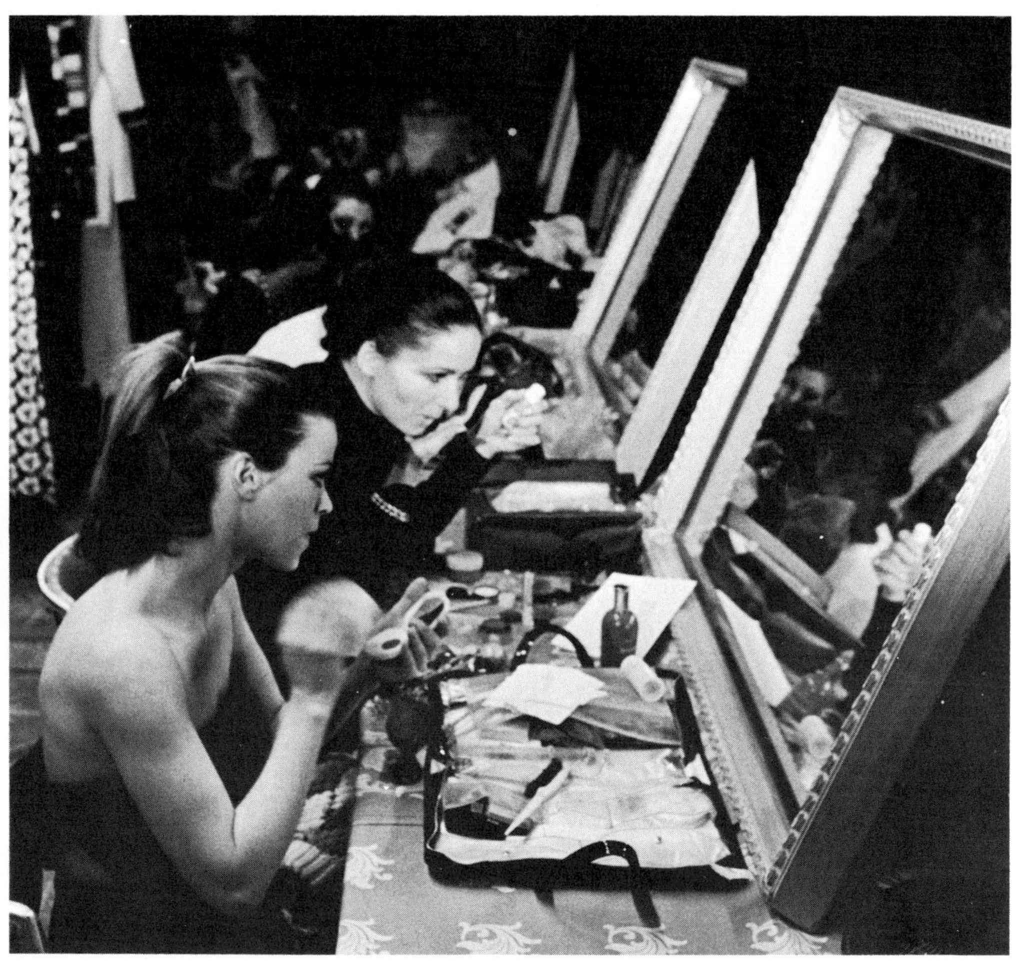

The model's dressing room. While getting ready for the show, a model studies the copy of the line-up. Several copies should be posted at all entrances and exits. (Courtesy of *Stores* Magazine.)

orchestra or group, a more comprehensive cue sheet for music will be necessary. Musicians accustomed to working fashion shows or with a particular store, can draw up their own cue sheet directly from the line-up.

5. The display people involved in the show, working lights, props, or any special effects (such as a media-mix of sound and film and slides),

must also have a complete rundown on the line-up. Everyone must know what is expected, and when.

The Rehearsal.   Not all shows need rehearsals. The small departmental show, where collections are shown on the fashion floor, are fitted, accessorized, lined up, and put on. The professional models know what is expected of them, the starter is on hand to keep the show moving, and the commentator does the rest. The average club or small benefit show, with professionals, can be handled as well without rehearsal. A short explanation to the models as to where they enter and exit, if the location is not familiar to them, usually covers it.

Rehearsals are a must for big shows. When several models appear at one time, or for the finale scene, rehearsal for placement and pace is important.

However, if it is a major production, an important benefit, or a large show with guest models, then by all means schedule one rehearsal or more, depending on how ambitious is the undertaking. Since professional models must be paid for rehearsals, most stores try to keep these extra trips to a minimum. Sometimes, asking the models to show up a little early, to check out some points in the staging, is enough to get the show smoothly on its way.

In the case of a major production with a large cast, it is important for the fashion office to have a check-in list posted at all stage door entrances. If the rehearsal call is 7 P.M., all participants must have checked in and reported to their assigned dressing rooms by that time. The routine is the same on the day or night of the performance. If the stage manager checks the list an hour before show time and names exist that have not yet been checked, it's time to call and find out what's holding up the missing cast members. The curtain cannot go up until all are present and accounted for.

How to Work with the Special Events Director

If the store has a special events director, he or she is responsible for all events of a special nature such as promotions, fairs, exhibits, and shows that do not necessarily relate to fashion. When a store-wide special event does relate to fashion, then the fashion office is involved and works with the special events director.

For example, an import fair may be in the offing for the store, and the special events director is responsible for pulling all the details together. If the fair is from Italy, England, France, Denmark, Spain, or Mexico, it is very likely that fashions from that country will have been selected by the buyers during a trip abroad, specifically to embellish the event. The special events director would ask the fashion director to plan on scheduling special shows of the imported couture or ready-to-wear fashions. He might even designate exactly where and when he would like the shows to take place; they will be part of an over-all plan of special events with personal appearances and exhibits brought in especially for the fair. It is his responsibility to balance the program and to have something exciting and attractive going on at special hours every day. The fashion shows will fit into the plan where action is needed. In such a case, the fashion director need not handle any of the details of advising advertising, for example, of what is going on. She will, instead, submit all information regarding the requested shows to the special events director, who will handle all publicity pertinent to the event.

The fashion show is an excellent vehicle for modeling other items besides ready-to-wear and accessories. Left, an afghan by Spinnerin Yarn Co. (Courtesy of the American Wool Council.) Below, Esteé Lauder make-up, dramatized with masks, is described by the commentator. (Courtesy of J. L. Brandeis, Omaha.)

Another "nonfashion" event that comes under the providence of the special events director but calls upon a contribution from the fashion director, is the opening of a new store or branch. Such an occasion might be hailed with all the markings of a grand opening, with store officials on hand to greet guests (the fashion director included), with music, cocktail party, and fashion show. The show might be formally staged, or it might be offered as informal modeling throughout the new fashion areas to add to the glamor of the opening event.

Afterview

The feeling that "there is no business like show business" is not entirely shared by everyone in the retail fashion business. In the big cities, where the giant retailers prevail, there is a resistance to fashion shows. Big cities, of course, have greater distractions and more sophisticated audiences, but even more than that, the big city retailer has big competition. His customer is being lured in many directions with quality, price, service, and selection. Merchandising, therefore, is the first consideration for this retailer. The big chains, too, prefer the fashion image of good quality at a price.

In many cosmopolitan cities, large segments of the population have been drowned in fashion shows, hounded to death to buy tickets to fashion show benefits, fund-raising affairs and club events of their friends. Retailers finding themselves in this climate must excel with every fashion show event. They have to dazzle, enchant, amaze, or shock every time out. Coming up with a new winner time after time can not only be energy and talent consuming, but highly expensive. Smashing shows are not produced on small budgets. This category of retailer resorts to doing fewer shows, but more spectacular ones. They have vowed no more church basements, no more bridge club programs. Only the ocassional star-studded production, in a grand ballroom of a hotel, in a theatre, in a music hall or art museum, or in the big auditorium of the store, would justify an all-out effort. In the process, these retailers with the big production approach are building very enviable reputations. They are famous in and out of the trade as great show people. Their shows are not to be missed. They make good press. Some even gain national attention and win awards. They are often imitated. When the word gets around, a good promotion idea or show technique sweeps through retail country like brush fire.

Retail fashion shows make extensive contributions to civic and charitable endeavors, as did the J. L. Hudson Company's Fashionscope Symphorama, on behalf of the Detroit Symphony Orchestra. Left, the 2-hour fashion and musical extravaganza began with ''Adam and Eve,'' to illustrate fashion ''from the skin out.'' Above, the stage of Ford Auditorium, Detroit, with guest star, Polly Bergen. (Courtesy of the J. L. Hudson Co.)

In the smaller communities of our nation (and there are more of these) fashion shows are much loved. It is a special event. In fact, women in very small towns, reading about a fashion show coming up in a nearby larger city, will make the trip specifically to see the show. This out of-town customer is very important. She is usually the most appreciative member of the audience.

It all adds up to an obvious truth—when fashion shows are well done, they are still big box office. The fashion show, with its multiple appeals is still the longest running show in the world. Its special merits cannot be lightly passed over. The fashion show is entertainment. It is public relations. It is a service. It not only serves as an educator, but also as a means of expressing the store's community spirit. Many people may not be aware that in the area of benefits and fund-raising projects, the department store gives its personnel, merchandise, and generous assistance free of charge, and that the money raised at the benefit goes directly to the charity involved.

Like all mediums of entertainment, the fashion show must continue to grow, improve, diversify, and change in order to deserve devoted audiences. That's show business.

❋ *Chapter 13*

❋ *How People, Places, and Things Affect Fashion*

Read the newspaper. Watch the stock market. Watch television. See a movie. See a Broadway or an off-Broadway show. View a new art collection. Walk through a bookstore, or just walk down the street. They are all clues as to why fashion is currently being expressed as it is, and clues as to what might be coming into fashion next. The clues come from people, from their interests, their needs, their behavior, the places they go, the things they do, and the things they create.

The citizens of the fashion community are governed by a multitude of high chiefs who are influenced by a multitude of extenuating circumstances which exist for a multitude of unpredictable reasons. It is a fuzzy thought, but that is the very texture of the fashion business. The fuzziness exists because these high chiefs may function within the fashion community or outside of it. For example, a designer may come forth with one fashion concept, but someone outside his fashion world (a celebrity with great public impact) may appear with a completely different fashion idea. If the public screams *"We want that!"*, the designer runs back to his drawing board.

301

To blur the picture even more, fashion is not controlled by any one central governing body—guided perhaps, but not controlled. It may seem to be so, because of a Paris which has reigned as the center of the fashion world for over 600 years. And rightfully so. But even Paris, and everyone who goes there, is subject to a higher power—the customer.

The fashion year of 1970 is remembered with pain by everyone, designers, manufacturers, retailers, and customers. Paris said it was time for a longer length. The short look, known as the mini and accepted with favor for nine years, was over. The longer length, reaching midcalf or above the ankle and called the midi or longuette by the press, was accepted by Parisian women but rejected violently by American women. "Absolutely no," they said. And their "no" was heard around the world. Their resistance to the longer lengths was a bloody battle; designers failed to exert their influence, manufacturers by the dozens closed their doors, customers stopped buying, and retail fashion figures took a big dip downward.

Haute couture, already showing signs of losing its power to dictate, bowed its head to the omnipotent command of the American customer. The following year, after the severe thumbs down on the longer length, the very designers who had proposed the fashion idea, came back with a complete reverse, short shorts for day or evening wear (hot pants), skating skirts (hot skirts) shorter than the mini had been. They also made a compromise on length, in the neighborhood of the knee, and many women were willing to agree that where daytime dresses and suits were concerned, it was not a bad neighborhood.

The fashion world is not a true dictatorship; it is strongly democratic. There is a two-party system existing in the ranks of the consumer, those who want to be individuals and those who want to emulate others (plus a radical fringe group or two who may wish to overthrow the entire system by creating antifashion). Therefore, it is very tough for the high moguls of fashion, wise and talented as they may be, to predict in any given fashion season, which way the customer will vote.

The Importance of Awareness.   Which fashion is likely to get the customer's vote, depends on how she lives, what she does, and where she goes. The perceptive fashion director soon learns that researching the market tells her what is available for sale and researching people tells her who will buy it. Although it may be impossible to avoid mistakes, through awareness it is entirely possible to avoid total disasters. One of the fashion director's most valuable assets is awareness.

This text has hammered away pretty hard in Chapters 5, 6 and 7, urging thoroughness and checking and rechecking of facts before suggesting that the store put its money down on the line for any new trend, color, fabric, or classification. Those earlier chapters deal with the available information and guidance *within* the fashion industry and its relative services. The awareness we speak of here deals mostly with the available information and guidance *outside* the industry in the world at large, from people, places, and things.

The People

To say that a man "looks like a Greek god" is to pay him the ultimate compliment. To say that a well-dressed woman "looks like a page out of *Vogue*" is a salute to her fashion excellence. Whatever the comparison, to "look like" something or someone highly admired, is a very desirable form of recognition. As far back as fashion records show, it has been as important to successfully "look like" someone as to be totally original. This inherent desire to imitate the celebrated, the rich, the powerful, the beautiful, and the revered, has been a basis for fashion trends and change throughout history.

Royalty. Fashion history has never been more magnificently embellished than in the days when fashion was led by royalty. Pre-Renaissance was a period of Spanish elegance. Many fashion firsts came out of that time—the corset, the hoop, silk stockings, and the ruff that encircled the neck holding it high and proud. During the Renaissance, when the cultural center of Europe switched to Rome, fashion, too, began taking direction from Italy. Opulent fabrics such as brocades, satins, and velvets encrusted with jewels, were the status of those of high rank. Law prohibited persons outside of royalty or high society from wearing such elegant fabrics. From this period, great new techniques for embroidery developed and the fashion for lace was introduced.

When fashion supremacy was taken over by the royalty of France, it was the beginning of a reign of dominance from then on. During the sixteenth century, Catherine de Medici of Florence became the queen of

France and brought with her the grandiose influence of Italian Renaissance. France became the new cultural center for Spain and Italy.

Throughout the long reign of Louis XIV and then Louis XV, the importance of fashion was elevated to a new height. Both of these brilliant courts were the criterion for all of European society. During the Louis XV period, names like Madame Du Barry and Madame de Pompadour took the fashion lead for the French court. Madame de Pampadour spread the taste for Chinese motifs. In 1780, the court of Marie Antoinette was influenced by Spanish fashions. During the eleven years that Napoleon was emperor of France, the Napoleonic influence on fashion and art was remarkably extensive. From his empire came the fashion word and look that remains today: empire, the high-rise bodice, the silhouette that is synonomous with Empress Josephine.

Hair fashions, too, were carefully copied from the royal courts of France. Wigs, for example, were out of fashion during the reign of Louis XIV, until he started to get bald. When he adopted the wig, his court followed.

The court of Napoleon III and Empress Eugenie provided the last of the royal innovations. The crinoline was created as a new kind of reinforcement for ball gowns, overlayed with several bouffant skirts. Through the patronage of Empress Eugenie, the House of Worth, the first couturier, gained recognition all over Europe. Other royal clients followed, and society women everywhere were clamoring to identify with the couturier who dressed the royal ladies.

With Napoleon III, the French court, that glamorous, romantic, plush, extravagant fashion showcase came to an end. Around 1871, when the Republic of France was established royalty's influence on fashion ended.

The Theatre.   New queens of fashion were destined to be born, not of royal blood, but equally as glamorous. The actress, that unique lady of the theatre, took the fashion lead. Celebrated, adored, and applauded, she was indeed a woman to copy. France had the divine Sarah Bernhardt, Italy had the inspiration of Eleonora Duse, and across the sea, America had the hour-glass fashion image of Lillian Russell, who dazzled the world with her magnificent costumes and hats.

Society and Early Couture.   Perhaps not everyone wanted to be an actress, but everyone wanted to be rich. To associate with the rich and powerful through imitation was perhaps the next best thing.

Before the turn of the century, many notable couture houses had opened in Paris, and their clientele, the socially prominent, were in a position to have gowns made exclusively for them. The designer received little publicity, but his client was observed in her original creation wherever she went. She was photographed for the new fashion magazines that were appearing about this time, and her fashion choice, admired and envied, was copied.

Designers Gain Stardom. Even though we are dealing here with influence on fashion from *outside* the industry, in the case of the name designer, an exception must be made. It is difficult to separate the celebrated designer from other celebrities influencing fashion. It was the same star quality, the same stimuli, that brought worshipers to their thrones. In other words, just as the masses of the consumer community chose an illustrious personality to imitate, the citizens of the fashion community chose to copy the celebrated designer.

Poiret, the First Trend Setter. After the turn of the century, a change took place with the couture, initiated by Paul Poiret. Instead of being guided by his clients, Poiret, an original thinker, preferred himself in the role of guide. His great distaste for heavily ornamental display in women's fashions started a trend for simplicity. As the first great trend setter, and perhaps the first fashion dictator, he spoke out boldly about his convictions.

In an article he wrote for *Harper's Bazaar* in the early 1900's he said, "I dined the other day in a fashionable restaurant. At the tables around me I noticed at least half a dozen women whose hair was dressed in exactly the same number of puffs and switches. All were dressed in equally expensive gowns, although I was not able to judge of the colors because they were all equally overloaded with beading, embroideries, gold, silver, or steel ornaments, with laces and fringes. . . . Instead of hiding their individuality, why did not each woman try to bring out her own personal type of beauty?"

The unconventional Poiret, who was determined to free women of rigidity in dressing and to stir their worship of taste, provoked a new fashion awareness among women. He also paved the way for a coming parade of celebrated fashion designers, who literally shaped the fashion destiny of women the world over.

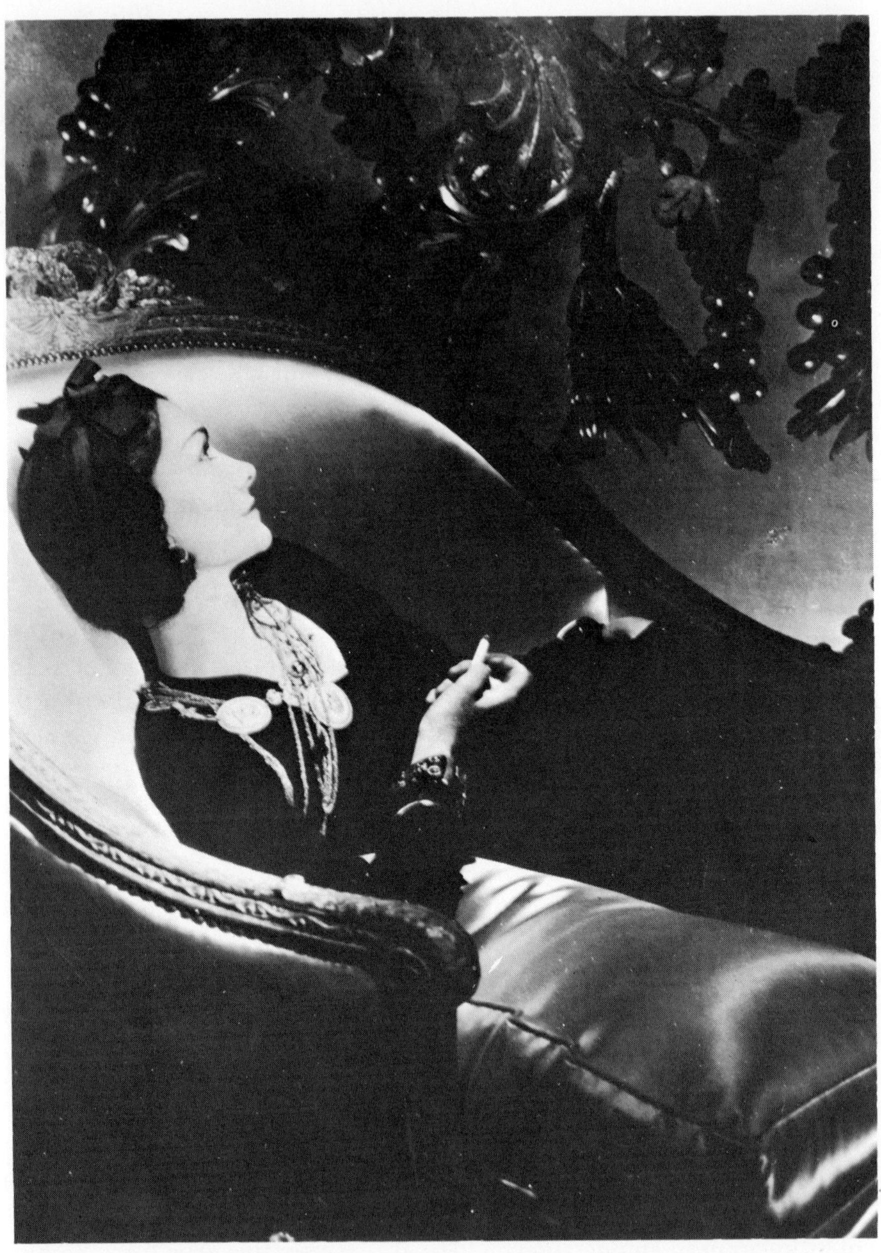

Mlle. Gabrielle Chanel, the great French couturiere, photographed in her salon in the late 1930's, the embodiment of her fashion credo of understated elegance and luxury. (Courtesy of Chanel, Inc.)

Chanel. Next came the incomparable Chanel, a provocative, enchanting rebel. Her longevity of fame in the fashion world was unprecedented. Her contributions are unforgettable. With Chanel's understated lines and simplified construction, the wholesale fashion business was born. The elaborate, complicated creations that preceded her prohibited mass production.

Chanel immortalized the fabric of jersey. She started the vogue of costume jewelry. She gave fashion the indestructible Chanel suit, the most copied idea of its kind. She was the first dressmaker to popularize a perfume under her name, the famous Chanel No. 5. Why No. 5 when it was the first? It was her lucky number.

Chanel, the designer who dominated Paris fashion in the nineteen-twenties, was preparing a new collection at the time of her death in 1970, at the age of eighty-seven. Her last collection, shown a couple of weeks after her passing, was hailed as "good Chanel," a splendid classic look, welcomed in a period that was returning to "civilized" fashion.

More Great Fashion Designers. Each great designer in the French couture was famous for special innovations. Each was imitated and copied with pride. Patou raised the waistline that Chanel had lowered. Recognizing the value of publicity, he was the first to offer a preview showing of his collection for the press. Vionnet contributed the bias cut. Schiaparelli ended the slouch look by bringing up the shoulders. Christian Dior made fashion front page news with his shocking new look in 1947. It was a turbulent change to return to small waistlines, full skirts, and longer lengths. Dior's look lived its nine lives until the crown was passed on to Saint Laurent after Dior's sudden death. Saint Laurent released the waistline and eased clothes into a relaxed simplicity. Another new trend began.

The sixties brought a star-studded era of European couture. Saint Laurent, Courreges, Cardin, Givenchy, Pucci, Valentino, and others became so illustrious that they were paid the kind of homage once enjoyed only by stars of the stage and screen. Instead of an autograph, their signature on a scarf of their design became a new status symbol. American designers, too, such as Norell, Beene, Brooks, Blass, and de la Renta were "signing" their accessories, or adding a fragrance line bearing their name. Adolfo signed his hats with bold script. Wearing the label on the "outside," so to speak, appealed to the affluent society that now could afford the "names" of high fashion, a privilege once confined to the fortunate few.

In the late sixties, the name designers branched out even more, to design and endorse in areas outside of their original efforts. Their names appeared as the creators of everything from shoes, jewelry, children's clothes, and men's fashions, to towels, sheets, and bedspreads. A store might have Saint Laurent or Cardin in the linen department, in accessories, in the cosmetic and fragrance department, in men's fashions, and in women's fashions as well. A woman might receive a silk-print-on-Florentine-leather checkbook cover designed by Emilio Pucci, for opening her accounts at a New York bank. A woman might buy Revlon lipstick or nail polich and find colors named after American designers Bill Blass and Norman Norell—Bill Blass Red or Norell Red. The merchandising of the big names was an undisputable testimony to their star quality. They were good box office; their names sold.

The great talents of the Haute Couture became illustrious stars. Above, Yves Saint Laurent. (Courtesy of Fieldcrest, Inc.) **Left, Marc Bohan.** (Courtesy of Christian Dior-New York.) **Far Left, Pierre Cardin.** (Courtesy of Fieldcrest, Inc.)

The Beauty Stars. The stars of fashion reached beyond the couture and ready-to-wear, toward the woman herself. Her hair and face, regarded as part of the "total look," had to change with the fashion trends, relate to the trends. To every potential Helen of Troy, the "bottles of hope" provided by the cosmetic industry held a promise of youth and beauty few women could resist.

Just as women loved to follow a "fashion authority" when selecting a wardrobe, she preferred "authority" for her hair and face, too. Because of this star system, the sixties developed authorities like Sassoon with his unique short haircut for women, Alexandre, Kenneth, and many others whose hair fashions were designed to relate to the whole fashion picture. The wig makers followed the hair fashion designers and provided replicas of the newest trend.

Face fashions had their own moments of glory. The sound of the name of the beauty leaders of the cosmetic industry was indeed the sound of authority. Helene Rubenstein ruled in her time like a queen. Elizabeth Arden considered the total woman so completely that she even had exclusive fashion collections designed to carry in her salons the world over. Max Factor's name was synonomous with the glamour of Hollywood. Esteé Lauder personally covered the Paris couture every season to be sure her beauty creations were fashionably compatible. Charles Revson (Revlon) personified the magnitude of fashion in beauty products. These fashion leaders, and others, were copied and imitated just as their couture counterparts.

New Faces. The couture, however, took the lead. The change in a fashion silhouette was motivation for a cosmetic change. Just as the point of focus on a woman's body shifts with the transposing of line in fashion, so does the focal point on the face.

In the forties (and revived in 1971), the bright red mouth was the important feature. In the sixties, the eyes had it. A rainbow of eye shadows and eyeliners, from romantic to sultry, were created to glorify the eyes. False eyelashes became the big accessory on every woman's dressing table.

The Creative Director. Fashion designers create clothes. Creative directors fashion faces. The creative director of a cosmetic house researches the fashion market to learn what the new colors, fabrics, and silhouettes will be. If a new fabric color is proposed as important, a congenial color in lipstick, for example, is in order.

One of the leading influences in eye makeup in the sixties was the son of an Italian count, Pablo Zappi-Manzoni, international creative director for Elizabeth Arden. Pablo was an innovator with false eyelashes for both the upper and lower lids. He is perhaps best known for the fantasy eyes he created for magazine and newspaper editorial photography. His magazine covers for *Vogue* were inspired creations of facial artistry. His unique eye designs might show up as zebra eyes, painted in bold, black-and-white stripes, an elegant jeweled eye, or an eye completely outlined with flower petals. In 1965, Pablo was the first makeup artist to receive the coveted Coty Fashion Award. Although Pablo's fantasy eyes were strictly to dramatize the spirit of the eye for the press, he, along with all other makeup

Great designers' names can be found in multiple fashion areas. Above, Saint Laurent bedroom for men. (Courtesy of Fieldcrest.) Left, Yves Saint Laurent fabric collection. (Window courtesy of Lazarus.)

The Sixties—the decade of hair—saw a reign of influential hair fashion designers, and popularity of wigs, falls, hairpieces. (Photo by Melvin Sokolsky. Courtesy of *Harper's Bazaar*.)

Stars whose cosmetic companies bear their name or are strongly identified with fashion and beauty are great attractions. Polly Bergen's personal appearance for her cosmetic line at Wanamaker's. (Courtesy of Polly Bergen.)

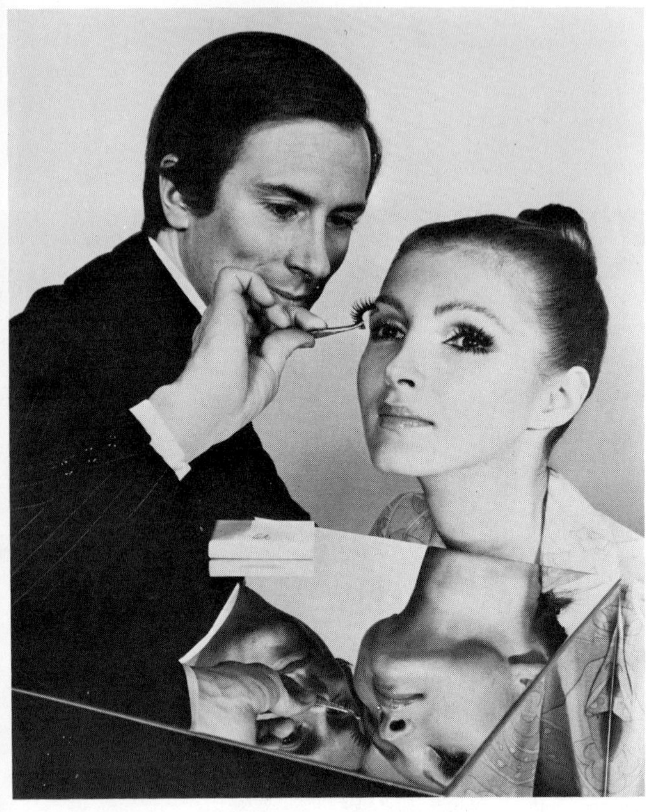

Pablo, one of the leading influences of eye makeup in the Sixties. (Courtesy of Elizabeth Arden.)

creative designers, stressed the natural, practical use of makeup, but in its new form.

The consumer was inspired. She wanted to know how those beautiful models in the magazines created those marvelous eyes. To help the average woman choose the correct products and to teach her the new techniques of application, the leading cosmetic companies conducted makeup clincs in department stores or sent trained consultants to demonstrate.

The adult customer had to forget old tricks and learn new ones, and the young customer, perhaps using makeup for the first time, needed instruction on proper use. Bonne Bell Cosmetics, for example, conducted makeup clinics in stores for the teen customer, training each store's Teen Board members to instruct and service the young customer.

Stardom for the Fashion Model.   At the outset, the fashion model was comparatively unknown as a personality. In the 1860's, Charles Frederick Worth, of the House of Worth, used his beautiful wife as a model. Poiret, also, used his wife as his model in the mid-1900's. The early fashion magazines used sketches of fashions, or photographed the celebrated in their own creations. It was much more chic to follow the prominent.

Through the innovation of previewing couture collections for the press, and the growth of the fashion magazines, the fashion models position grew in importance. She was selected as carefully by the designer as his fabric, and by the magazine as carefully as the photographer. *Harper's Bazaar* called Suzy Parker the model of the fifties. The sixties brought unprecedented fame to a very young English girl who came to be known

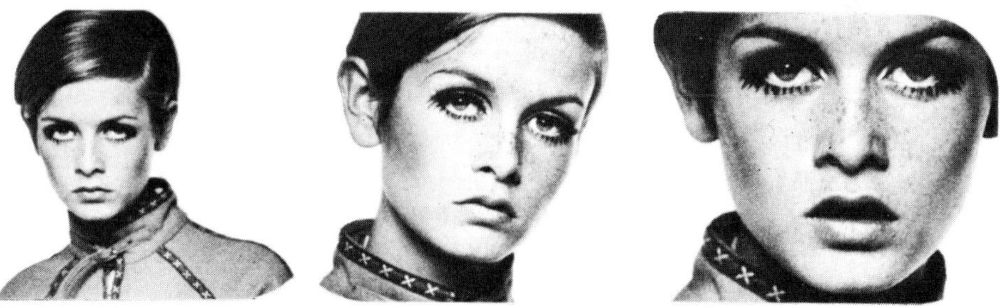

The fashion model "star": the sixties brought unprecedented fame to a very young English girl (Leslie Hornby) known the world over as Twiggy. (Courtesy of Yardley.)

the world over as Twiggy. A product of the Mary Quant generation (a time of skinny minis), Twiggy's very thin, long body personified the young look of the day. Equally famous were the Twiggy eyes, eyelashes drawn on the face, a new approach to eye makeup.

Fashions in models, of course, changed with fashion. Measurements, types, looks, and personalities flowed in and out with the tide of public acceptability, the reigning fashion ideal, and the dominating concept of designers.

Motion Pictures.   Of all the influences of fashion, perhaps the motion picture star enjoyed the longest and most powerful influence on the greatest number of people. In the twenties, from America's sweetheart, Mary Pickford, and the profound Helen Hayes, to the screen "vamps," every American woman could find a favorite to emulate. Theda Bera was the screen's sex symbol, and among the first to be toasted for their stirring pulchritude were Greta Garbo, Gloria Swanson, and Mae Murray. Even though much of what they wore was more suitable for reel people than real people, their "look" was enough to inspire adaptation.

The thirties brought another crop of celluloid queens, and their fashion impact is a matter of history. Shirley Temple was a merchandising dream, and the Shirley Temple doll became a household item. Mae West became an institution. Jean Harlow made blond hair a national craze, and the indisputable fashion powers of the screen, whose wardrobes were worth the price of admission alone to movie goers, included Katherine Hepburn, Bette Davis, Joan Crawford, Loretta Young, and Carol Lombard. Adrian, fashion designer for the screen, created such unforgettable looks as the padded "Joan Crawford shoulders." The Jean Harlow–Carol Lombard slinky look of the bias-cut and plunge backs and the Garbo slouch hat, all lived to be revived in the seventies. All these bright stars, plus Norma Shearer, Ginger Rogers, Hedy Lamarr, Claudette Colbert, and Irene Dunne, created an age of adoration from movie fans, the like of which was never quite known before and seldom achieved again.

From then on, an occasional great fashion force developed from the screen (Marlene Dietrich and Merle Oberon in the forties, or Audrey Hepburn and Grace Kelly in the fifties), but the heyday of motion picture influence was giving way to other outside powers.

Television. The impact on fashion via television did not occur in the same star-studded manner as it did through the motion picture. From the outset, television had its stars, but they were not innovators so much as models. Their names were household words, but their fashion image was forgotten almost as quickly as one series replaced another.

What really happened with fashion through the medium of television was unique. By the very nature of its continuity, television promoted fashion in four separate ways.

1. *Exposure.* A current fashion trend gained great momentum by the repeated exposure on the "tube." Personalities in contemporary situations (a drama, an interview, a variety show) dressed in the current fashion. Over and over again, the viewer saw the new trend, saw its various inter-

pretations by people of all types and sizes, and soon she knew exactly what she wanted for herself. Consciously or subconsciously, the viewer's fashion inspiration might come one time, for example, from Doris Day or Marlo Thomas and another time from Dinah Shore, long regarded as one of the best dressed women in television. In December 1971, Miss Shore was elected to the board of directors of the giant retail chain, The May Company.

The so-called "talk" shows were ideal showcases for fashion. The famous men and women who appeared as guests, provided a constant fashion show. From time to time, formal fashion shows were included as part of the format. These usually were parades of the way-out looks coming in, many of which became not-so-way-out after general acceptability.

Fashion's role in television specials is one of the big attractions. Throughout the award shows—the Oscar, the Emmy, the Grammy—the fashions that the celebrated wear to present or accept awards is as intriguing as who the winners are. The reviews of such shows almost always mention who the fashion stand-outs were. Days after the excitement of who the winners were has died down, women might still be talking about what Barbra Streisand or Elizabeth Taylor wore at the Academy Awards.

The women in the viewing audience may not wish to copy the fashion look of the stars (more often criticized than applauded for their choices), but it cannot be denied that such a parade of fashion dramatizes its ability to be provocative, stirring, glaring, and bold. Stars do not select their gowns for such occasions to win fashion awards; they select fashion to get talked about and make the press. At the same time, the viewing audience discovers that fashion can be exciting enough to steal the scene. And there are times when it should.

2. Merchandising. Because television personalities are such excellent models of fashion, and because they have such personal rapport with the consumer, opportunities for merchandising fashions as a tie-in with a TV star is a natural. Hence we have found that we can buy a Harry Belafonte shirt, a Glen Campbell wig, Jody and Buffy children's fashions, and Johnny Carson suits. The endorsement of these TV stars on a line of merchandise brings almost immediate acceptability. A personal appearance in a department store by such a star, brings unbelievable crowds.

In the case of John Whitaker (Jody of the TV series "Family Affair"), Jody made a personal appearance tour of department stores all over the country which were carrying Jody fashions. A fashion show of the Jody collection was presented along with the young star's appearance to record-breaking crowds. Young and old clamored to get a look at the Jody they had seen week after week on the air and to get an autographed picture when they visited the boys' fashion department.

Johnny Carson, star of the "Tonight Show," having demonstrated his excellence in taste and effectiveness with fashion, not to mention his unqualified acceptance with his viewing audience, was a top item for merchandising. At a time when men showed a growing interest in fashion, when they were ready to take lessons in color and fashion coordination from the men they respected and admired on the air, merchandising endorsements held promise. Every night of the show, Carson, and his musical director, Doc Severinsen, kicked around the merits of what they were wearing, (Johnny illustrating the contemporary, Doc the avant-garde). With the focus on their wardrobes, often as the springboard for Johnny's monologue, fashion importance was stimulated.

3. *Credits.* Many of the men and women on television are supplied with clothes by manufacturers, sometimes for cost, sometimes for credit. Since the fashions we choose are very indicative of our personalities, the actor in an episode or the cast of a drama, must be clothed in a manner in keeping with the tone of the character involved. It would be impossible for a performer to have a different change for every show, week after week, if he had to use clothes from his personal wardrobe.

Contemporary wardrobes might be furnished by a manufacturer in exchange for a credit noted in the roll-up at the end of the show. If the viewer admires the fashion look of the star on a particular show, he or she can learn from the credit line, "Miss Star's Wardrobe furnished by __________," where such fashions are available. Also, when a customer sees the manufacturer's label on a garment in the store, she is reminded that this is the label her favorite TV actress wears.

4. *Commercials.* Commercials can relate to fashion in two ways: (1) as wardrobe for the actor playing a role in the commercial or (2) as a direct fashion sell. The latter might be a commercial by a fiber company, fabric

mill, or a sewing machine company. Such an advertiser would present fashion illustrations in connection with their product.

The commercial selling a product unrelated to fashion is very often a fashion vehicle all the same. Whether the lady in the commercial is baking a cake, waxing a table, or playing bridge with a headache (until the headache remedy comes to the rescue), she is wearing fashion. If an automobile commercial includes people, their fashion look will relate to the style of car.

The combined stimuli absorbed by the viewer through television exposure, merchandising, credits, and commercials, afford fashion one of its most potent influences.

Public Figures. Public figures who become fashion influences, do so because they are intriguing and colorful in a way that is uniquely theirs.

A Tom Sawyer ''Jody'' wardrobe was inspired by the fame of ''Jody'' of TV's ''Family Affair'' show. (Courtesy of Elder Mfg. Co.)

Every night that Johnny Carson appeared on his ''Tonight Show'' on NBC, millions of viewers took note of what ''the king'' of television was wearing. (Courtesy of Johnny Carson Apparel, Inc.)

Of all the personalities to influence fashion trends, none was so effective as Jacqueline Kennedy. As the wife of President John F. Kennedy, she was the most photographed, most talked about woman of the decade. The sixties were aglow with the fashion leadership of Jacqueline Kennedy. Designers, such as Yves Saint Laurent, were elevated to greater success by her approval. The interest in the ''Jackie Kennedy look'' was enormous and, therefore, big business.

Weddings involving public figures have always influenced fashion trends. When Wally Simpson married the Duke of Windsor, the English king who abdicated his throne for ''the woman I love,'' the romantic public appointed the new Duchess of Windsor a fashion leader. What she selected for her trousseau, her wedding, and everything she chose in fashion for some time thereafter was news.

The wedding day is an important day, and who would be better to copy than someone very important? Even without a wedding in the offing, the general public is interested in the fashion story for the sake of fashion itself. When the younger daughter of President Nixon, Julie, was married, her fashion choices were reported by the press in detail. For Tricia Nixon's wedding to Edward Cox in 1971, her attendants wore long silk organdy gowns of mint green and lilac, with off-shoulder necklines and hand-kerchiefing surrounding the hemlines. It was expected by the industry that the public interest in this creation by Priscilla of Boston would be stimulated; copies of the fashion idea and the color scheme were inevitable.

These, of course, are not all of the people who influence fashion. The numbers are legion. They are, however, highly indicative of how people can promote a trend or create a new one. An awareness of who these

Jacqueline Kennedy, as First Lady, was the undisputed fashion leader of the sixties. (Portrait by Richard Avedon, courtesy of *Harper's Bazaar*.)

people might be, what they are wearing, and to what degree they are admired, is an important guide to which way general fashion acceptability might be going. This is the way, or at least one of the ways, a fashion director takes the public's pulse.

The Places

Even people who are not famous are capable of influencing fashion. Great fashion trends have come into being, for example, from fashion innovators at vacation resorts. Something contagious in fashion might sweep through the Riviera one season, another fashion idea might begin in the discotheques of Paris another season, in St. Tropez, at St. Moritz, or at Swiss Klosters. Other trends might be brought home from Corfu, the Greek island playground, or Greece's Mykonos, the favorite of the young international set, from Acapulco, Hawaii, or Palm Beach. Everywhere. At home or abroad, fashion-conscious travelers bring, exchange, and borrow fashion ideas from the natives or fellow travelers.

The Big Attractions.   Special events the world over bring fashion into the spotlight. During the Grand Prix de Monaco in Monte Carlo, race car fans from Europe and America can be observed day and night in an international fashion exhibit. From the Cannes Film Festival to renowned horse racing tracks such as the Royal Ascot in England where the sport of kings attracts the fashionably prominent, the new way to dress is extensively demonstrated. Every year the calendar is filled with special events that stimulate fashion awareness in those who come to participate or in the press who come to report on who was there and what was being worn.

Fashions Where the Socially-Conscious Gather.   The presence of the press at an inaugural ball, the dedication of a famous-name library or art center, or any occasion that merits the attendance of the rich and famous, will invariably provide fashion representation on a level of special interest to the reading public. Benefits and charities, too, of the $50 or $100 or $1000 per person vintage, bring photographers and reporters to translate the festivities of the event for their readers. What the guests wore to such important and exclusive events reveal the highest utilization of current fashion.

Important social events in all communities provide an influential showcase of what is being worn, plus excellent opportunity for merchandising. (Courtesy of L. S. Ayres & Co., Indianapolis.)

Fashions Where the Masses Gather.   There was a time when fashion filtered down from the top, from the choices of the rich and powerful. Everything thus far indicated in this chapter testifies to this system. However, beginning in the sixties, fashion made a complete reverse; it moved from the bottom all the way up to the couture. The street influence might have started in Greenwich Village of New York, Carnaby Street, Kings Road of London, or any street in any city in the world where young rebels of fashion explored new horizons of dress. They were their own designers, their own coordinators. What might have started out as a put-on, was picked up and developed as new fashion by fashion authorities in the industry.

Young designers, especially receptive to this new system of freedom in dress, glorified the out-of-the-attic, surplus store, granny's old clothes kind of looks. The followers became the leaders. For example, some resourceful, fashion-free thinkers in the Village tied knots in their white jeans, tossed them into some colored dye, and when they dried the patterns created by the knots were fascinating. The fad not only caught on with the young, but was picked up by designers and fabric mills and reinterpreted on luxury fabrics from velvet to chiffon. Tie-dyeing is an old art, revived in the sixties along with many other old crafts.

Be it a world premiere of a motion picture, a fund-raising dinner for a political candidate, a music festival, a visit to a fashionable restaurant, or a walk down any prominent street in a fashion-pioneering community (New York's Fifth Avenue, Bathesda Fountain in Central Park, Greenwich Village, the highly fashionable or highly rebellious San Francisco), anywhere, everywhere—fashion is happening.

The Things.   Fashion is reflected from and onto the things that surround us. Fashion changes the look of even the unchangeable. The unchangeable little girl pictured on the box of Morton Salt has changed through three generations with fashion.

As far as archaeological discoveries and the preservation of man's art forms can testify, fashion and art are inseparable. Mode of dress is revealed on pottery, vases, plates, reliefs, statues, frescoes, mosaics, stained glass windows, tapestries, drawings, and paintings. The artists of the world have recorded fashion for posterity, and from all these art forms, fashion artists have repeatedly revived and reinterpreted ideas to their own art form. From ancient Greek culture, for example, comes the Grecian drape, revisited again and again, indestructible in its grace and versatility.

There is unquestionably enough influence to be traced from the paintings of the old masters alone to fill another volume. When expressionistic or surrealist styles of art became popular, fashion picked up more inspiration. For example, Schiaparelli's "lobster dress" and a hat in the shape of a shoe with a shocking pink velvet heel, was inspired by surrealist Salvador Dali. Makeup created by Estée Lauder with a delicate Renoir touch was inspired by the paintings of Auguste Renoir. Every area of fashion calls upon art at one time or another to validate its motives.

Fashion design is electric with art inspiration. A color, a balance, a pattern, a rhythm, or a mood, originally captured on canvas by the artist, can reappear with an undeniable resemblance or "feel" on the designer's sketch pad. Artists themselves have had a kinship with fashion. Many have designed fabrics, jewelry, clothes, accessories, and even hairdos. Watteau (1684–1721), for example, designed a fashion look recorded in many of his paintings. The Watteau train, which falls from the back of the shoulders to the floor, is a look often seen in wedding gowns.

Cartoons and Fashion.   A fashion director's awareness of what's new in art will clue her onto what may be a new expression in fashion. A poster craze for old movie stars indicated a nostalgic interest in fashions of the thirties, forties, and fifties.

An art form that is as American as apple pie, the cartoon and comic strip characters, has been merchandised time and again, in one way or another. However, in 1971, cartoon art was picked up in fashion on all types of young ready-to-wear. It even became part of the home furnishings scene. Cartoon or comic strips reproductions were available in pillows,

A bedroom with comic strip bedspread and pillows, with matching drapes available. (Courtesy of Fieldcrest, Inc.)

Right, *Mademoiselle's* promotion, inspired by Paramount Pictures' musical ''Paint Your Wagon.'' Rit Dye and Butterick Patterns contributed to the ''sew-it-yourself-tie-dyed'' fashion ideas. (Courtesy of The Softness Group.)

Left, department stores involved their fashion boards and young customers in tie-dye ''Paint Your Wagon'' events when the movie came to town.

drapes, and bedspreads. The ageless charm of the animated characters seemed destined to continuous attention from the fashion world. A young boutique with walls papered with cartoon or comic strip reproductions, with an antique collection of comic books on display, and with a new collection of cartoon-inspired fashions, might be a suggestion the fashion director could make to her management.

Stage and Screen. In addition to the stars of stage and screen who influence fashion, the stage and screen themselves become a vehicle for merchandising fashion. The play or picture showcasing a costume or fashionably acceptable trend, might be susceptible to fashion exploitation. A manufacturer might tie in with the picture promoter to market a collection influenced by the costumes of the show.

When "Nicholas and Alexandra" became a film, fashion designers, the cosmetic industry and hair stylists merchandised the look. Barbra Streisand's "Funny Girl" was a good fashion tie-in. When "Oliver" hit the screen, a line of children's clothes was offered to stores for tie-in promotions. Revivals of musicals such as "No, No, Nanette" and "The Boy Friend" were excellent tie-in vehicles for the prevailing interest in nostalgia fashion. What happens is that the store that stocks the fashions related to the show, usually helps promote the production when it hits town. Windows, displays, ads, and fashion shows, all using the handle of the production, help stimulate interest in the fashion items.

The News. Earlier in the text, reference was made to Tobé's belief that "front page news makes front page fashion." This truth has been confirmed with every fashion change resulting from a war, a drastic stock market change, a new breakthrough in science, or a new comic strip character.

When very short skirts were being shown in spring-summer of 1971, often called skating skirts or hot skirts, some manufacturers tagged them as "Daisy Mae" skirts, the type the Al Capp character had been wearing for years in the comic strip. When the moon shot put men on the moon, outer-space fashions were improvised for that "last word" for the modern woman. When country music was enjoying a strong revival, bib overalls, country checks, and denims were big fashion news. The "depression sweater," a long-length cardigan, reappeared during the recession-inflation year of 1971. A national interest in ecology called for the promotion of "ecology colors—earthtones" in fabrics. The same campaign to "save the flowers, save the trees, save the animals" brought a sweep of "figuratives" of flowers, trees, birds, insects, animals, and fish in fabric prints, costume jewelry, and accessories. Almost immediately after President Nixon announced in the summer of 1971 that he planned to go to Peking, China, the fashion industry, always hungry for new inspiration, incorporated the

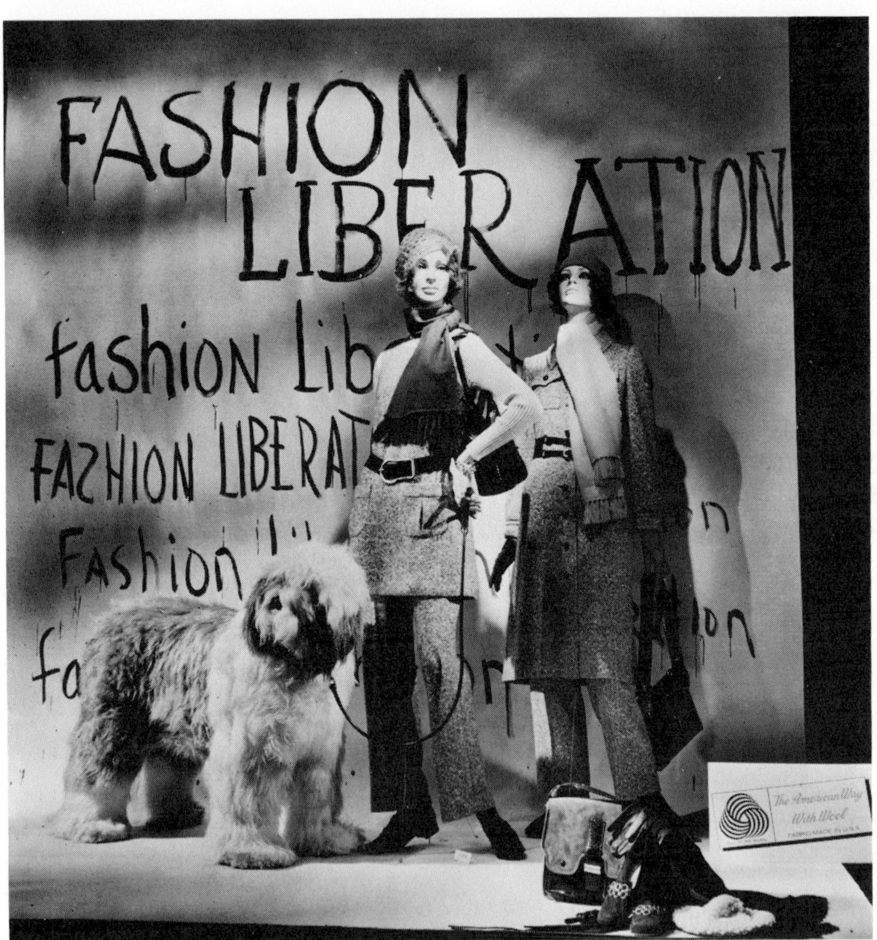

Influence of the news. The Women's Liberation Movement was picked up and used as a fashion handle. (Courtesy of Strawbridge Clothier, Philadelphia.)

Chinese influence in its fashion designs. Fashion, with eyes in the back of its head, is ever watchful, constantly reflecting.

News has always affected fashion, even way back when Columbus discovered America. The Spanish were awarded fashion leadership after the discovery of America. The prestige of their involvement in this great moment of history was enough to bring fashion followers to their door.

Afterview

All the people, places, and things that influence fashion are offshoots of life styles, what people earn, where they live, and what they do. But in addition to their external environment is their internal environment, their emotional needs, their dreams, their goals. All of this is reflected in the heros they choose, the standards they accept, the roles they play, and, ultimately, the fashions they select.

All aspects of fashion influences, the forewarnings of what might happen next, the sources on which we can count for guidance, must be tempered with an awareness of that on which we cannot count, namely, woman. Astrologists may attempt to predict the future, but fashion directors cannot predict fashion. Manufacturers and merchants take calculated risks, but neither they nor any magic power known to man, can predict fashion because it is impossible to predict woman. Today she wants something nobody else has. When she can get it, she will not have it until she is sure everybody else wants it. When everybody else is wearing it, she doesn't want it. The only reliable thing one can predict about woman is that she is unpredictable. She is not intentionally difficult; it is her nature.

This stumbling block has not been tossed in to confuse; it is a necessary truth to set the record straight about fashion experts. There is no such thing. There are, on the other hand, fashion professionals who work hard at accumulating facts to do the best possible job of giving the lady what she wants. The retailer who anticipates a woman's needs and fulfills them, comes closest to being an expert. Being expert in one's efforts is what it really takes to succeed in fashion. The rest is the tools toward that effort.

Chapter 14

Fashion Coordination Careers Related to Retailing

Fashion is everywhere. And as the old observation says about smoke and fire—where there's fashion there's fashion coordination.

Before fashion gets into the stores, there is an army of agencies and institutions working in many different ways to make fashion happen. Fashion directors, coordinators, stylists, and consultants guide the fashion expressions coming out of all those areas outside retailing.

A fashion office or fashion person can be found making a contribution in dozens of areas, from fashion manufacturing to home furnishings, to fiber producers and fabric companies, consultant firms, and buying offices. All these areas and more depend upon fashion direction from knowledgeable, fashion-tuned-in people. However, many of these areas are overlooked because many seeking fashion careers are not aware they exist.

A decision to seek a career in the field of fashion coordination, therefore, might also include a consideration of which job in which place seems more attractive and more suited to one's individual talents. A general inspection of each prominent area is a good way to begin.

Advertising Agencies

A great many women seeking careers in fashion are totally unaware of the opportunities available to them in the advertising agency business.

Advertising agencies, especially those with fashion accounts, are greatly in need of a fashion director and/or a fashion department. The size of the agency's fashion department is determined by the type of accounts in the house. Textile, retail, and cosmetic accounts, for example, all require considerable fashion attention. To provide this kind of fashion service, Grey Advertising, Inc., New York, has maintained a fashion department of eleven people, and J. Walter Thompson's New York office has operated with eight. Both of these fashion staffs, headed by a fashion director, are considered extensive. There are other agencies that specialize in fashion accounts, servicing such accounts as garment, shoe, lingerie, jewelry, and fabric. It must be understood that agency jobs are primarily big city jobs. Agencies tend to headquarter (although they have many branches) in the big cities, where clients, facilities, talent, and contacts are more readily available.

The Agency Fashion Director. The fashion director, supervising the fashion staff of a large advertising agency, is usually assisted by a secretary and sometimes an associate fashion director. The balance of her staff consists of stylists, assistant stylists, and coordinators.

Like her counterparts in retailing, the agency fashion director must be well informed on current and upcoming fashion trends. She needs to be equally ahead of the consumer; by the time the ad comes out, or by the time the commercial has run many weeks or months on the TV screen, the fashion recorded there must be ahead enough to remain current or it will kill the effectiveness of the ad before its time.

Fashion directors of ad agencies research the fashion market and the fabric market at home and abroad. Each season, they view the collections in advance, and make personal contacts among designers in anticipation of fashion needs for upcoming ads. In addition to awareness of contemporary

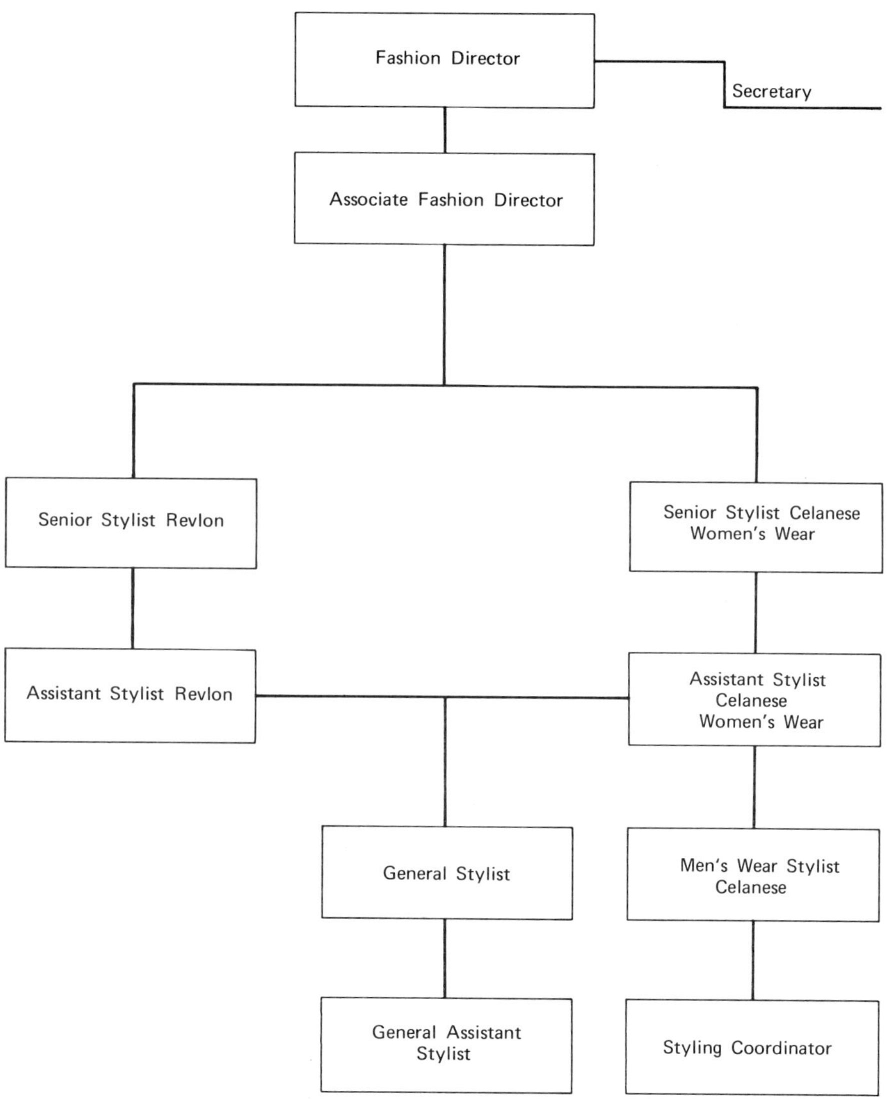

Fashion office of the Grey Advertising Agency, New York.

fashion, the agency fashion director often finds herself digging through the archives of a fashion magazine or newspaper or through the library's collection on costume books to come up with authenticity for period costumes that are needed from time to time in ads and commercials. Besides supervising the fashion department's personnel, controlling its budget, and "dressing" print ads and television commercials, the fashion director provides a fashion environment for the agency and fashion guidance for its accounts.

Fashion Guidance.   In the area of fashion guidance, the fashion director helps a client get involved with fashion ideas. She might develop a new idea for a fashion show—schedule a show of a client's fashions in a new discotheque, shopping center, or museum that would relate to or enhance the fashion message. She might stimulate a fashion approach to an otherwise nonfashion account, perhaps putting an automobile account in touch with a name fashion designer.

Some of the most exciting uses of fashion by the advertising agency have involved nonfashion accounts. For example, Joan Glynn, former vice president of Doyle Dane Bernbach agency, before becoming a vice president of Bloomingdale's department store, New York, styled the uniforms of stewardesses of American Airlines. Mary Wells, while associated with Jack Tinker and Partners agency, not only restyled uniforms for all Braniff personnel, but the Braniff planes as well. She reaped such fame and success from this effort that she was able to start her own agency, Wells, Rich, Greene, Inc., with Braniff Airlines as a client—and subsequently married Braniff's president. At this writing, Mary Wells is the most highly paid agency president in the business.

The agency fashion director may extend a further fashion service by submitting a semiannual color forecast from her findings in the market. Such a color report could be used by one client to help decide the color interior for automobiles, by another as a guide in buying fabrics, or still another for designing sunglasses. The color forecast might be helpful to the members of her own shop as well, the stylists in the fashion department and the art director or set designer of the agency.

Working with Magazines.   Fashion directors of ad agencies work with fashion magazines like their retail sisters, but with different departments. In the case of the agency, the magazine's promotion department is mostly

Mary Wells (Lawrence), who personified the effective use of fashion for a nonfashion account (Braniff), pictured with Peter Godfrey, president of Menley & James. Together they developed Love Cosmetics for the young contemporary woman. (Courtesy of Menley & James.)

involved. The retail fashion director works with the merchandising department of the magazine.

The agency fashion director would be concerned with preparing a merchandising kit on the client's products "as seen in Town & Country," or whatever the case may be. She would also work with the merchandising division of the magazine when a client wants help in projecting his message to retail stores. Also, the agency fashion director works with the magazine's fashion editors, to learn what they are planning for future issues and what their fashion thinking is.

Other Assignments. Sometimes the assignments are unique and apply

Advertising agency crew on location for fashion ad shooting. Location: A farm in New Jersey. Client: Celanese. Theme: Folk knits. Right, fashion director overseeing models arranged for a "take." Below, the ad as it finally appeared in *Glamour* Magazine. (Courtesy of Grey Advertising, N.Y.)

only under special conditions for a client. Gayle Carlisle, fashion director for J. Walter Thompson, helped Eastman Kodak Company develop a new camera carrying case with a fashion look that would be more appealing to ladies.

Market research is sometimes conducted for a foreign fashion account. For a blue jean manufacturer in Brazil, the agency would research the American market, talk to retail stores, and review manufacturer's lines for their best colors and styles. A similar service would be provided for a fiber company in Australia. The agency fashion director would assemble a fashion presentation applicable to that company's needs, based on research of the American market.

The agency fashion director can make an enormous contribution to the agency's clients by writing reports and analysis not only on fashion trends, but also on future and changing life styles. Such information helps the client uncover the new application of a product, needed change of a product, or to find a product to be marketed a different way. In other words, good, advanced, far-seeing trend information helps the client relate his product to the future consumer market.

The Agency Stylist.   Whether the product of an agency's client is advertised primarily through print (magazines, newspapers, billboards) or through television, fashion coordination is needed. Having learned a client's needs and special likes and dislikes, some agencies feel it is more efficient to assign the same stylist to the same client for all fashion work done on that account.

Another agency might operate the fashion department differently. The stylists might work on a general assignment basis; one time working with one account, next time with another. Of course, only in the very large agencies is the special-assignment stylist possible (see chart). An agency with few fashion accounts might operate with only one or two stylists who do everything. A small agency might have one stylist who wears another hat or two depending on what accounts are in the shop.

What the Agency Stylist Does.   The agency stylist selects, fits, coordinates, and supervises the use of fashion by actors or models in print ads or television commercials. In making her decisions about what clothes to select, several points are automatically taken into consideration.

1. What is the client's message?
   Elegance or economy?
   Glamor or comfort?
   Performance?
   Service?
2. Will the ad be in black and white or in color?
3. Will the photography be stills or action shots?
4. How many fashion changes will be required?
5. What is the location for the shooting?
6. What are the details of the set, motif, pattern, colors, etc.?
7. What is the budget?
8. Is the ad a one-time shot or part of a series in a campaign with established theme?

The answers to these and other questions are obtained by the fashion department through consultation with other staff members working on the account.

Staff Consultation. The account executive relates the client's message to the agency. He spells out exactly what should be told through print or television, or both. The budget is established. The creative staff of the agency takes it from there. The writer, art director, and producer (the art director for print, the producer for television) create all aspects of exactly what will happen on the printed page or the television screen.

The Writer. The fashion director or one of her stylists talk over specifics with the writer and art director to learn how the ad will be "dressed." The writer may say, "the message is for real people doing real things. Keep all sophistication out of it." Or, the case may be to "tempt with glamor." Or, the message might have a gay, lighthearted, young approach, "the look must be the last word in young fashion." The fashion department, knowing the facts, knows what to select.

The Art Director. Perhaps next will come a separate conference with the art director or set designer. How is he expressing the writer's language into the physical atmosphere? Will it be an outdoor location? Will it be a specially designed set? Will it be shot in someone's fascinating apartment?

What happens in the background is highly pertinent to what clothes the actors or models will wear. If the wall is going to be red, a red costume would be lost. If the background is extremely "busy" in pattern or decor, a strong pattern in the fabric of the costume might be deadly. Coordination, all the way, gets it all together.

The Producer.   Where TV commercials are involved, the producer pulls the whole production together. How will he interpret the message? Lots of movement? Will the story come across quiet and soothing? Will it be jump-up-and-cheer stuff? A storyboard is drawn up as a guide, from which the producer will instruct as to which way to go with the fashions. Covering the ground thoroughly at the outset will help avoid gross errors in costume choices.

The Casting Director.   A casting director will be responsible for bringing in the appropriate models or auditioning actors for the television commercial. Based on the type, mood, character, personality of the message, the casting director brings in cast members to be approved by the producer and/or client. If they relate accurately to the texture of the client's message, the stylist gets the go-ahead to start work on wardrobe.

When casting a print ad, the fashion department may book the models, or sometimes the art director or the photographer books the models. When the model is highly identifying with the product's image, the choice may be reviewed by the client on a "go-see," (see Glossary) photograph, or "name" basis. The mere mention of the name of a well-known model may be sufficient.

When the personalities or models have been booked for a TV commercial, the fashion department finds it more efficient to check out sizes, heights, measurements, etc., directly with the talent, rather than through

The two following pages illustrate the agency stylist and TV commercials. Produced for the Singer Company for the Burt Bachrach Special, with Singer Fashion Director Francine Coffey as hostess.

Left page: Top, Pre-production meeting where all aspects of the commercial are discussed (story board in the foreground). Stylist gets her directions. Lower left, fitting in the fashion department, with stylist and art director. Lower right, Francine Coffey, Singer Fashion Director (left) and agency stylist select models' garments.

Right page: The "As Produced" script and the commercial (frame of on-the-air spot). (Courtesy of The J. Walter Thompson Company, Advertising Agency, N.Y.)

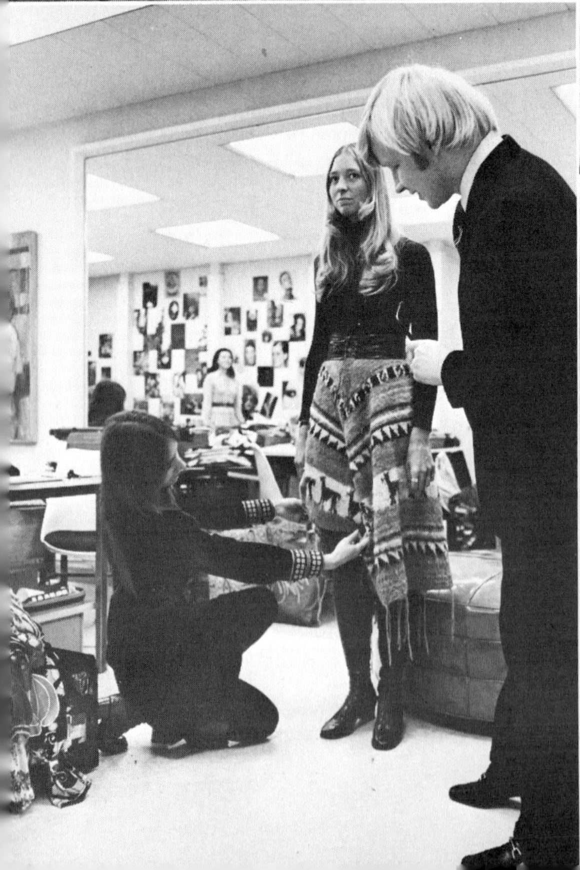

TV COPY

ACCOUNT THE SINGER COMPANY

DATE   AS PRODUCED FEBRUARY 26, 1971

STATION

VIDEO

AUDIO "SINGER PRESENTS BURT BACHARACH" SPECIAL
60-SECOND COMMERCIAL
"STRETCH FASHIONS"

1. OPEN ON FRANCINE WITH ASSISTANT WORKING IN SECTION OF SINGER CENTER...

FRANCINE: (DIRECT, OPEN MIKE SOUND) Knits come in such fabulous colors.

ASSISTANT: (UNDER) It'll be the best show ever.

2. CUT TO FRANCINE WORKING BACKSTAGE FITTING MODELS.

(CONVERSATIONAL SOUNDS UNDER AS FRANCINE DISCUSSES OTHER CHOICES

ANNCR: (VO) As fashion director, Francine Coffey plans many fashion shows for Singer.

FRANCINE: I think so too, and especially working with knits (UNDER) We can't possibly fail.

3. CUT TO MODELS DRESSING. FRANCINE IS SUPERVISING.

ANNCR: (VO) Here she's choosing Singer fabrics for a show of knit fashions ... And Singer has them... in everything from....

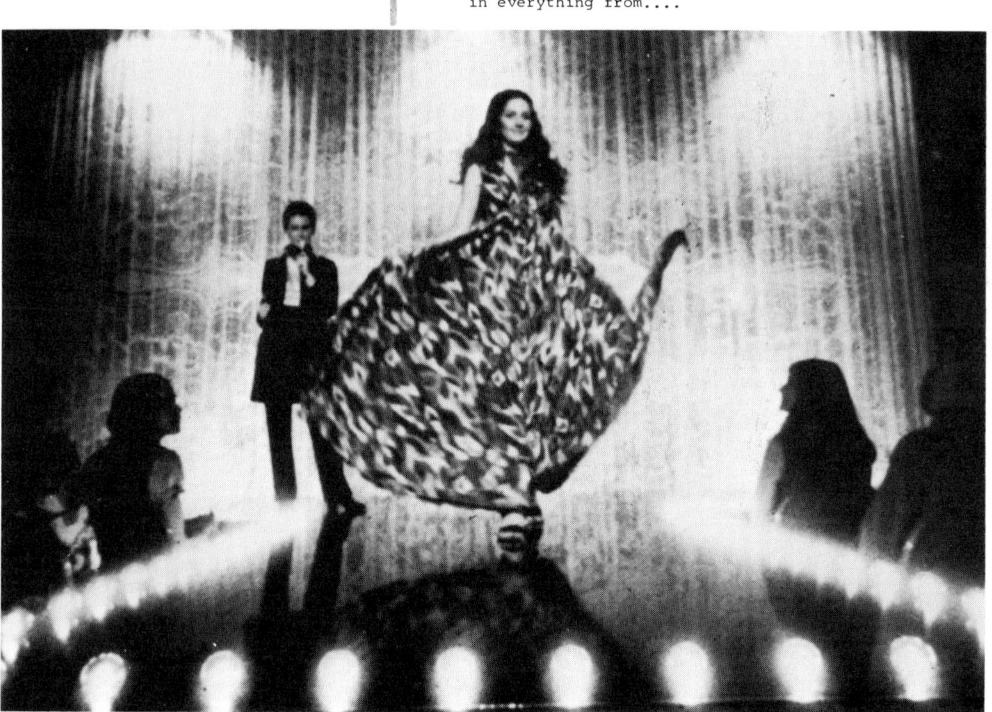

9. DISS TO MODELS GOING UPSTAIRS TO SHOW FRANCINE. (MUSIC COMES UP)

FRANCINE: (DIRECT, NATURAL SOUND) OK, girls, hurry now, just three minutes to show time, hurry now.

10. DISS TO FASHION SHOW SCENE. FRANCINE AS NARRATOR. SERIES OF CUTS FROM MODELS IN FASHIONS FRANCINE COMMENTS ON... TO AUDIENCE REACTION... BACK TO MODELS AND FRANCINE. END WITH MODEL IN STRETCH TERRY OUTFIT.

FRANCINE: (VO) Good afternoon! Welcome to the Singer Company featuring a brand-new collection of polyester double knits...

the casting director. For print ads the procedure may differ. When models have been booked by the photographer, for example, his studio would send to the agency's fashion department, composite photographs (comps), which all professional models have, with their sizes for dress, shoes, hat, etc., plus height, figure measurements, and other necessary information. With all these details established, the fashion director or stylist is ready to shop.

Shopping Time.   If the agency is in New York or California, it is very likely the agency stylist will shop the wholesale apparel market as well as the manufacturers of fashion accessories. It is also very likely that she will shop I. Magnin or Bullock's of California, or Bloomingdale's, Ohrbach's,

Storyboard of 30-second national television commercial. (Courtesy of Yardley of London.)

YOUNG & RUBICAM	CLIENT:	YARDLEY OF LONDON
PRODUCT: YARDLEY	TITLE	COMML. NO.: Y-5-30-67R1

1. (MUSIC) WOMAN: When I was little, . . .

2. everyone used to say Jeanie Shrimpton's got the shiniest hair in the whole countryside.

3. But you grow up and you to lose that wonderful shine,

4. so Yardley created Londonderry Hair Shampoo, (MUSIC) it does something perfectly smashing.

5. It puts the shine back in your hair. (MUSIC) Londonderry Hair Shampoo.

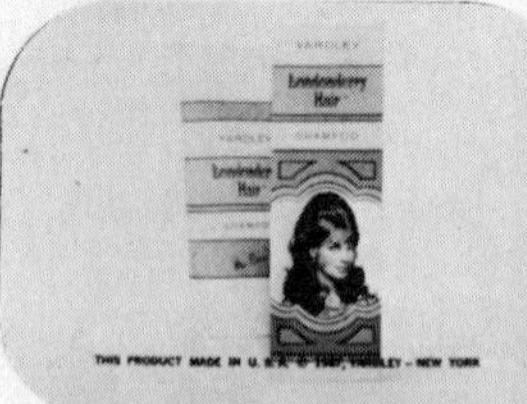

6. It makes your hair shine li when you were little.

or Saks, New York, and pick something right out of stock. And, maybe, she will select something right out of stock from the Salvation Army.

The fashion requirement might be such, however, that something more exclusive is in order. In such a case, the stylist might contact a name designer, such as Oscar de la Renta, to have something special made. She might even have special fabrics designed and printed. Another occasion might prompt the stylist to approach a theatrical costume designer to create something original. Or, she might make a trip to a costume house to rent the clothes. This would be especially true when period fashions are in order.

There are still other sources for costume selection. It is very possible that the agency might maintain a wardrobe, accumulated from other ads or commercials, still current and suitable for reuse as is, or adaptable to a new look with the help of a seamstress. A wardrobe of shoes, for example, can be reused while still in fashion by dyeing or covering with fabric to relate to the costume.

Occasionally, the agency is responsible for having fashions made from scratch. For example, fashions for the Singer Company's ads and television commercials are especially made up for that client's product exposure. Also, all pattern companies have garments made up especially for ads from their patterns.

When budgets are a contention, the actors are sometimes asked to wear something of their own, especially when the roles they will play are to depict a realistic flavor of real people in everyday situations.

If something out of the ordinary is needed and is difficult to find (and it is amazing with all the resources available that "that certain something" can be difficult to find) the stylist herself might take the initiative to rig something with loving hands at home. She might even ask one of the secretaries in the office who is extremely talented in knitting, for example, to go to work on something that provides that certain look, maybe in the colors or motif of the client's packaging which is not for sale anywhere.

In other words, the fashion department uses every ounce of ingenuity at its disposal to accumulate the best possible wardrobe for the required theme of the ad, even if the fashion director has to cut up some drapes or a bedspread (makes a great evening coat) to do it.

Fitting Time.   As soon as the wardrobes are accumulated, fitting times are set up for the models or actors. A national print ad or national television

For a print ad, the agency stylist checks all details on fashion, hair and makeup. Above, stylist and agency executive pin model's dress. Right, the Esteé Lauder magazine ad as it appeared. (Courtesy of AC&R Advertising Agency, N.Y.)

commercial consumes a great deal of the client's advertising budget, so all fashion details are carefully executed.

For a display print ad, the fashion department handles all aspects of the fittings, maybe calling the art director in if there are any serious questions. To consult on a TV fitting, it is possible that the producer or art director will be present, along with the fashion department personnel. Here is the place to take a final check and reacquaint everyone with the possibilities before the actual shooting. Since there are deadlines to meet and everyone is more or less working against time to meet shooting schedules, fittings should be thoroughly prepared. If any changes or adjustments are to be made, the fitting session is the end of the line.

It should be noted, however, that models' clothes are sometimes deliberately fitted too loosely for easier movement as instructed by the photographer, art director, or producer. The clothes are then pinned to fit properly, according to the required action or pose, right on set.

The return to real makeup
calls for the richness of
Estée Lauder's Tender Lip Tints
in rare new shades of Summer Wine.

Estée Lauder gives your lips new depths of color, new
dimensions in intensity to enrich the richest mood fashion has
ever been in. New Summer Wine shades of Tender Lip Tints
are: Claret Pink, Rum Swizzle, Mulberry Punch and Sherry Fizz.

Estée Lauder

As to accessories, the agency stylist often borrows from manufacturers, and, therefore, they are not available much before the day of shooting. The agency stylist usually brings several possible choices for each costume change. She may review her selection with the photographer and art director, giving them a choice, or she may try a variety of ideas with each outfit and decide herself on the best way to go.

Hair and Makeup. The head must fit the body. A good stylist, well versed on the newest trends, will carefully instruct the models on the required hair fashion for the specific shooting, as well as type of makeup. If the fashion is bizarre or extremely high fashion, a hair fashion expert or makeup artist may be called in to design something special.

What Fashion Can Do. How often we have picked up a magazine and seen a beautiful model in an ad, draped on a magnificent couch, dressed in an opulent gown, so uniquely elegant and so ultrafeminine that it completely dazzled the imagination of a pampered life of luxury. The ad was not selling couches or gowns, but perfume. The stirring association of the beautiful woman with the product did the job—a fragrance that could make you "feel" like this. That is, in part, what good fashion selection can contribute to the ad and to the client's product.

In a television commercial, another wonderful thing can happen with fashion. Movement of flowing chiffon, swirling wool or crepe, or crisp lines of linen can help underscore the mood of an automobile, a diet food, a laundry product, or the fabric itself. Whatever the case, the presence of effective fashion unmistakably enhances the story.

The Unforgettable Focus.   To help identify an ad, or create a memorable focal point, a single accessory or fashion item might be called into play. For the close-up of a hair-color or shampoo ad, a devastating earring. A hand lotion or nail enamel ad might be glorified with a totally unique ring (maybe borrowed from Tiffany's). A bath product may be dramatized with a bath towel bearing the same special design and colors of the packaging. If it caught on, the makers of the bath product could tie in with a towel manufacturer to market the item in a new collection. Stranger things have happened, and all through the inspiration of an effective fashion presentation.

Shooting Time.   All is in readiness. Whether the shooting is on location (anywhere in the United States and sometimes Europe), in the photographer's studio, or in the television studio, along with the agency production crew comes the stylist from the fashion department. If the commercial or ad is a simple one, with only one or two people involved and only one change, the agency stylist may not be required to remain on the set for the shooting. She may just see that the wardrobe is pressed and delivered to the shooting site and see that it is returned when the job is finished. However, for more complicated productions—sometimes there are twenty-five to thirty changes of wardrobe—her presence and supervision is a must.

The stylist makes sure every ensemble and every change is checked out as planned. It is her responsibility to see that everything is laced up correctly, fitted properly, draped effectively, according to plan. The preferred tilt of a hat, drape of a wrap, closing of a jacket, handling of an accessory, all of these are in her province. The agency's stylist works closely with the photographer and his stylist, if he has one, to help "transmit" lighting, movement, and mood, as regards fashion.

Who Gets Jobs in Agency Fashion Departments.   Fashion department staffs are selected by most agencies on the basis of the accounts they service. An examination of the personnel working in the fashion department of agencies revealed that many have a retail background, anywhere from a post on a store's training squad, to an assistant buyer, assistant fashion coordinator, or divisional fashion coordinator. Some had worked in publicity or advertising jobs, some as fashion directors of fiber or fabric companies. Still others had been studio stylists for photographers. Girls with experience on fashion magazines, *Women's Wear Daily*, or pattern companies have also invaded the advertising agency fashion jobs.

But in addition to those who came with some kind of fashion experience, many who were fresh out of college or graduates from professional schools specializing in fashion education, were acceptable for on-the-job training because of their fashion preparation.

Photographers' Stylists

While some photographers' stylists move along to the advertising agency fashion departments, some stylists from the agencies transfer to the photographer as studio stylists. The studio stylist (an absolute must for the commercial photographer) is finding more opportunities in this area than ever before. Even when an advertising agency stylist is on hand for the shooting, the photographer's stylist also needs to be present. Small agencies, unable to maintain their own fashion departments or having only an occasional need for a stylist, depend entirely upon the photographer and his studio stylist to interpret the client's message.

Requirements of the Studio Stylist.   Most photographers will testify that taste is a prime requirement, good taste and an alert awareness of what is happening in fashion. Next, the photographer must have a stylist who can accurately interpret his directions. Without this, nothing happens. Naturally, a rapport with any employer is important, but in the case of the photographer with his stylist, it is the incomparable combination that produces the best results.

The studio stylist keeps close tabs on fashion trends by checking the wholesale market, the stores, and the fashion magazines. She must anticipate what is coming in strong, what is going out. As stated earlier, ads become quickly outdated if the fashion image is not plucked from advanced trends.

Responsibilities of the Studio Stylist.   Like the agency stylist, the studio stylist sometimes buys fashions for models or actors and sometimes borrows them. Her personal contacts are helpful. Also, there are places that specialize in renting clothes and props of various types to photographers' studios. Knowing who these people are and what they have, saves the stylist a great deal of time and shoe leather.

The studio stylist is not only responsible for the production's wardrobe but the props as well. She works with the photographer and client on what kind of setting and props will be used before she goes out to look for them. Very often, all the details that contribute to a setting, the props, furnishings, accessories, and sometimes even the set, are chased down and assembled under the supervision of the studio stylist.

At the shooting session, the watchful eye and assistance of the stylist is imperative. She helps interpret, organize, and arrange the props and the fashions she has selected for a job. It is also her responsibility, with the aid of messengers, to be sure that everything borrowed is returned when the job is finished.

When an agency stylist has done the fashion coordinating, she has all the outfits and accessories sent over to the set, where the photographer's stylist takes over. The agency stylist may be on hand, as noted earlier, but the photographer's stylist knows how to slip onto the set to make adjustments exactly when it should be done and when it will not interrupt the photographer.

The stylists with some photography studios also book models. They keep in touch with the agencies, reviewing their needs and supplying them with composites for model selection or for the agency's fashion department's information regarding types, fittings, etc.

Free-Lance Studio Stylist.   Many smaller photographers' studios prefer free-lance stylists because their shooting schedules do not always require the help of such fashion guidance. Or, the load of a photographer with one or two stylists already on his staff becomes so heavy that it is necessary to call in an additional free-lance stylist or two to help, perhaps one to collect props and wardrobe and one to work on shootings. Some stylists work completely on a free-lance basis, establishing contacts with photographers and serving them as their work load permits.

Fiber Industry—Fabric Industry

The fiber industry can create miracle fibers and yarns for converters and mills to turn into yards of cloth for apparel and home furnishings, but it takes a fashion director to help turn a piece of fabric into fashion. Yarns, blends, textures, weights, and performance are all very impressive and important terms, but without a fashion message the consumer would turn a deaf ear. In a season when fashion looks are expressed with soft lines, soft fabrics make it happen. In fabrics, therefore, fashion comes first.

The day is gone when people buy fabric or clothes that will wear forever. Nobody wants clothes that will wear forever. If they did, they would buy bulky, stiff, rugged clothes and the fashion be damned. Not so. They may insist that the fabric holds its shape and be wrinkle-resistant, but chances are they will by-pass a durable fabric if durability is all it has to offer. A beautiful fabric, one acceptable to the current fashion picture, is more likely to get the nod. After fashion, there would be more interest in easy care. Is it washable? That question would come up long before how does it wear? The translation of fibers and fabrics into fashion is one of fashion directors' giant contributions to the apparel industry.

The Textile Fashion People.   At the place where fashion begins (with the fabric), fashion research is as intense, or more so, as it is on the designer or retail level. At this place, working much further ahead than any other phase of the fashion industry (with the exception of the leather people), the stuff that garments for men, women, and children are made of, must be available (and available in desirable textures, weights, colors, and patterns) early enough to be utilized by those who would turn them into finished products. Since designers and manufacturers are guided strongly by the fabrics available, the fabric designers are something of a power behind the throne of fashion.

The Fashion Director in the Fiber Industry.   Before the garment comes the fabric, and before the fabric comes the fiber. Therefore, working far ahead of the garment and fabric makers, would be the fiber company's fashion director. If she learns through her research that a forthcoming season will be expressed with filmy, draped, or constructed silhouettes, she will work with the mills, to develop that type of fabric with her company's fibers.

An Example.   The program that Ruth Sublette, fashion director of

Celanese, instigated to assure maximum use of Celanese fibers, is a good example of the contribution the fiber company needs from its fashion director. Her three-step plan included:

1. Working with fabric mills a year or more in advance to develop fabrics (using Celanese fibers) which will be desirable for the type of clothes that cutters will be making for a particular season.

2. Providing sketches, illustrating how the fabrics can be styled. These then become the subject of a slide and film presentation shown by appointment at the Celanese offices in a specially-designed little theater, to designers looking for fabrics.

3. Revamping the slide and film presentation (after the designers have made their fabric selections and incorporated them into their designs) to show visiting retailers what specific styles they can buy which are made of the specific fabrics.

Color Coordination. The fiber fashion director must research the color story for each season. If her company sells colored yarns for fabrics, like woven plaids or space-dyed knits, (as against fibers that are made into fabric and then printed and dyed), she must advise her company on the exact tint as well as the right color to dye the fibers. For example, if she decides red is important but recommends an orange red instead of the preferred blue red, all is lost. Yarn dyed the wrong color or wrong shade won't sell.

The Fabric Library. Most fiber houses maintain a fabric library or fabric room, as a visual file of everything that is new and important in fashion fabrics containing their fibers. It is an available reference for the company's merchandising staff, a display of the range of fabrics available to designers and manufacturers. It is a fashion information center on fabrics for buying offices, the press, and retail fashion directors and buyers. Completely changed each season, the library is visited (by appointment) by many people in different areas of the fashion industry who take away fabric swatches as samples and information on which mill made the fabric in question and the price of that fabric.

Fashion Presentations. From this up-to-date fabric library, the fiber fashion director creates fabric presentations on men's and women's wear to be sent to designers, manufacturers, buying offices, fashion magazines, chains, and other retailers. Communication with retailers is another aspect of her job. For the retailer she performs a most comprehensive service (see Chapter 7), supplying color and fabric forecasts, fashion forecasts, and reports on European fabric and apparel collections.

Fashion Shows in the Fiber Industry. Very often, fashion shows of a manufacturer's line or a designer's special collection will be shown at the facilities of the fiber company for members of the press, buying office representatives, and retailers. These collections, of course, would be made of fabrics using the company's own fibers.

Also, fiber companies often schedule special events to launch a new fiber or show new uses of an existing one. The fashion director might work with a name designer to create garments illustrating what can be done with the fabrics incorporating her company's fibers. These are usually one-of-a-kind collections (such as a Qiana Paris designer collection created by Du Pont) launched at a prestigious show for the press, designers, and manufacturers, and then they are sometimes made available for special showings or benefits sponsored by retailers throughout the country. Sometimes, through such efforts, new and exciting fashion ideas are inaugurated and fashion history is made. For example, Du Pont commissioned Sylvia DeGay to create a special group of shirts and blouses in fabrics of Du Pont fibers. As part of this group, she designed the body shirt, a look that revolutionized the shirt and blouse industry. The body shirt became a trend and helped make shirts an important fashion item once again.

The Fiber Fashion Director and Imports. Through her travels in Europe, the Orient, and anywhere and everywhere in the world where new things are happening and new inspiration is available, the fiber fashion director might seek out and bring back collections for a special gala fashion show for the trade or for display to special segments of the fabric and apparel trades. Knitting mills, for example, might be invited to view some European knits, to examine their construction and technique, and to discuss how they might be interpreted in the American market, using the fiber company's products.

The Fashion Director in the Fabric Industry. Nearly all converters and mills have coordinators, usually called fashion directors, to research the trends and advise the colorists and print stylists on all fashion decisions relating to their fabric production. This is a tremendous responsibility because of the huge investment in setting up a warp for a new weave. A fifty-thousand yard warp may cost $25,000 or more. Naturally, the converter must be sure that the colors dyed and the prints created are fashionably accurate and salable.

Color Coordination.   The colorists and print stylists rely on the fashion director to help them translate the company's color choices into the exact shadings and the right print looks for a forthcoming season. In this connection, the fashion director works with the dyer and finisher on the colors. There is usually a man at the converter's who handles all matters with the dye plant. She works through him. Hand dips are made first with a few yards to perfect a color, and to see how it looks in a certain weave. "No, that's too light . . . too dark . . . has too much yellow in it . . ." she might say, until it comes out right. Color accuracy is established before big dye lots are put in.

The colors that have been incorporated for a coming season or a coming year, are organized into a fashion presentation and color card. The fashion director usually designs the color presentation, names the colors, and writes the copy. A sample line of the fabrics and color cards are available for customers in the showrooms of the mills or converters. Also, a capsule version is designed as forecast fashion information, complete with fabric swatches and color chips, for buying offices, manufacturers, chains, and department stores (see Chapter 7).

More Bases Covered by the Fabric Fashion Director.   The fabric fashion director sees designers, manufacturers, and buying offices for a mutual exchange of ideas and to learn "what is in the air."

She will review the lines of manufacturers, who have sampled their fabrics to see which fabrics were actually used (not all fabrics sampled are used) and to get the style numbers made with her company's fabrics. Ultimately, she will use this information in various forms of publicity, to advise retailers, for example, what resources and what numbers are available in their fabrics.

The fabric fashion director works ahead of the fashion magazines (as does the fiber fashion director). When her new fabrications are ready, she shows the fabric samples, colors, and prints to magazine editors. She will also provide the editors with the names of cutters who have sampled the fabrics since an editor may be interested in certain numbers created by the manufacturers named.

In addition to providing fashion information for consumers, the press, and retailers, the fabric fashion director must also assume the role of educator within her company as well. In a manner similar to the retail fashion director, the fabric fashion director is responsible for the fashion training of the company's personnel. In her case, the sales staff is of prime importance.

Trend Shows.   To make the salesman's job easier and more efficient and to help establish the mill's fashion image to the consumer, the fashion director presents trend shows, perhaps in a multi-media form, of film, slides, sound, and music. After the salesmen and internal personnel have seen the production, it is available for showings to designers, manufacturers, buying offices, and retail executives. Also, school groups studying textiles and fashion, benefit from such a presentation, because it teaches how fashion happens.

Import Shows.   Textile fashion directors research the foreign fashion markets, just as their retail counterparts, but their function goes a step forward. The textile fashion director not only writes and distributes a report on her findings on fabrics and fashions abroad, but she also buys samples of merchandise, men's women's and children's, for import shows at home. Such a show helps American designers to think more about what is being done fashionwise around the world, and it helps them translate what they see into suitable adaptations for mass production here.

General Shows.   The textile industry, through its fashion departments, is a source of all types of exciting fashion presentations. Their live fashion shows might be held at a hotel for a benefit luncheon, at the offices of the company for buying office representatives or retail buyers, or on the deck of a ship for the press. Such shows are excellent for exhibiting fashions created by important designers using the fabrics of a particular mill. For these shows, the fashion office staff coordinates, accessorizes, and lines up the models in much the same way as the staff in a retail fashion office (see Chapter 12).

The In-Store Fabric Show.   In a previous chapter we examined the

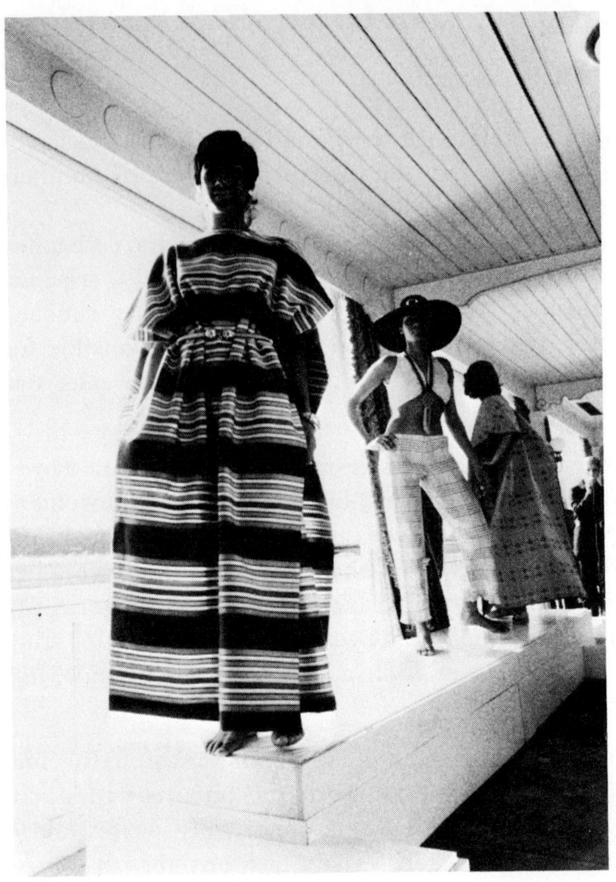

Fashion show on the deck of the Ile de France. (Courtesy of Galey & Lord.)

in-store fashion show provided by an outside source, from the vantage point of the retail fashion director. Now we will take a look at it from the other side.

Most of the big fabric companies who sell to fabric departments of stores, have fashion coordinators who handle all details of fashion shows held in retail stores. Because of the big upswing in the sewing trend, most mills and converters tie in with a pattern company and are available for fabric shows. Sometimes it is the stylist of the pattern company who puts the show together and travels with it, or, the pattern company and the fabric company will divide the cities, presenting the show separately in different areas.

Tied to the fashion fabric department, the show is offered to the store or requested by the fabric buyer. The fabric coordinator does all the advanced work on the show before making her personal appearance. She has put together a collection of sew-at-home fashions which illustrate the merits of her company's fabrics. These show pieces usually arrive ahead of the coordinator (from the last city in which she appeared) and are directed to the store's alteration department or fashion office for pressing.

When the fabric coordinator arrives at the store, it is her responsibility to fit, accessorize, and line up the models. Sometimes she brings her own accessories that are special for the wardrobe she shows city after city, or she may use accessories out of stock from the store, mentioning in her commentary what departments they are from. The models and backstage dressers are supplied by the store's fashion office. To represent the fabric company to the consumer, the fabric coordinator usually serves as commentator for the show. The fabric coordinator also supplies a printed program for audience distribution. This program is especially essential for fabric and pattern shows; customers can check the pattern numbers and note their fabric choices as models appear.

The Regional Coordinator. A fiber or fabric company may have what they call regional coordinators working in the field. Their duties cover regions of the country in which they concentrate to service retailers, offering and setting up promotions, handling all television and radio publicity on those promotions, plus whatever it takes in public relations to gain recognition for their company's products.

The regional coordinator may handle one part of the fashion story or everything in which her company is involved, such as women's wear, men's wear and home furnishings. In this connection, she will be responsible for educating sales personnel and the consumer on what her company's fibers or fabrics have to offer. The sales personnel may be exposed to the merits of her product during a training breakfast. The consumer may be invited, as a guest of the store, to a demonstration clinic on interior decorating, sewing with new fabrics, or new ways to use and care for new fabrics.

The presentation of new fashion trends, prepared by the company's fashion director, may be channeled to the retailer through the regional coordinator. Some companies have found that this is the most efficient way to get the material to the right people in each store and perhaps on a more personal basis.

Traveling frequently in her territory, the regional coordinator develops a strong sense of what is selling and what is catching on, and she feeds this information back to her headquarters. A communications network of this kind all over the country would obviously provide the company with valuable information and fashion direction.

Advertising.   Fiber firms and fabric companies are among the biggest national advertisers in the fashion business. In telling their fashion story, certainly a yard of cloth or a cone of polyester fiber would do absolutely nothing for the company's fashion image. But a show-stopping garment from a designer's collection made with the company's fiber or fabric product, certainly could do the job.

The fashion directors, therefore, of both fiber and fabric companies, are called upon to select exciting fashions from collections or even to have something special made up for advertising purposes.

Naturally, all fashion directors, as so often indicated throughout this text, work differently. This holds true in many ways in the area of fibers and fabrics. The essence, however, is that they all must do research to arrive at the decisions upon which they base their highly influential recommendations. They must interpret the fashion picture for their company and their company's customers. All of this they must do far enough in advance to keep one step ahead of the speeding treadmill of changing fashion.

Linens and Domestics Industry

From the moment white sheets and white towels fell from favor and were gloriously upstaged by color and then by a windfall of never-before-heard-of-patterns for bed and bath, the linen and domestic industry became a fashion market.

The fashion director came into being in some cases as an offshoot of the office of publicity director. White sheets needed no fashion direction nor did unimaginative blankets, bedspreads, and rugs, but when fashion colors, stripes, florals and, patterns were employed to bring interior-design type of high fashion into this area, fashion direction was definitely in order.

The Fashion Director for Linens and Domestics.   Linen departments with a lot of fashion to sell, welcome the people best equipped to give help on how to sell that fashion. To meet this need, the linen company's fashion director travels throughout the country, visiting the company's major accounts, appearing on radio and television to relate the fashion story, meeting with the press, and training the store's personnel.

At her home office she prepares fashion releases for mailings to stores and press, keeps informed on home furnishings trends and new life styles. She spends a great deal of time in her company's showroom, showing the line to magazine editors, to retail fashion directors, and to the press. She is also involved in planning press parties and showings, as well as doubling as hostess.

Fashion Guidance for Personnel.   In almost all businesses where a fashion director is required, the fashion information for personnel, as well as for the customer, is a top priority assignment of the fashion office.

The linens and domestics fashion director works with her company's designers, sharing with them all she has learned about relative fashion trends. She will undoubtedly make fashion presentations at her company's seasonal sales meetings and interpret the new collections in fashion terms. She will acquaint the staff with the importance of new name designers whom she herself may have recommended or engaged to design for the line. On the retail level, she might travel to the major accounts and, perhaps at a training breakfast, present the new fashion story. Salespeople are more likely to push a product they understand, one they are excited about, and one with whose representatives they have a warm rapport. The living, breathing, personal touch of an effective fashion director can do wonders.

In-Store Fashion Promotions.   Bringing the fashion story to the fore helps sell the product; it is as true in the linen department as in the ready-to-wear department.

When a linen company is fashion oriented and uses the services of a fashion director toward this end, fashion approaches can be instituted more effectively. Relating to the store on the local scene, for one thing, offers many pluses. Everyone in the department is aware of the special attention directed to the product. The fashion event contributes to the store's fashion image and helps build traffic, all very dear to the heart of the retailer. However, most buyers and their stores are more interested in getting involved in an ambitious undertaking if the linen company provides someone to oversee and expedite the special chores.

How to Handle an In-Store Promotion. Proposal for an in-store fashion promotion for the linen department would undoubtedly be made to the buyer of the department and the merchandising manager. Once it has been accepted, committed, and scheduled, the linen company's director takes over most of the details.

Since most people relate fashion to apparel, the linen fashion director may have advised her management that such a fashion approach would be ideal to rub a little of that image onto linens. Therefore, a fashion show, with all show pieces made out of the linen company's products would be an attention-getting, in-store event. This is accomplished by the linen company's fashion director. She enlists the talents of well-known fashion designers (big names give the collection more authority), and provides them with linens, blankets, bedspreads, towels, etc., to be transformed into ready-to-wear.

It is not every day that the linen department can come up with a fashion show. The buyer may decide she would rather have the show in the department instead of in the store's auditorium. She sees it as a great opportunity to build traffic.

Date, place, and event all set, the linen company's fashion director takes steps to make her show as painless for the store as possible. Advance contacts must be made with the store's department heads who would have a part in getting the show on the road.

1. Special events director—schedule the date, assist in coordinating props, have pictures taken of the event, give in-store assistance
2. Advertising director—offer material and ideas for ad layouts
3. Fashion director—arrange for models, fittings, accessories, music, props, runway, microphone, and backstage dressers
4. Publicity director—local newspaper, radio, and television coverage of the event

The groundwork has been laid. The real work begins when she arrives on the scene, usually the day before the show. The wardrobe, too, has arrived the day before the show. The store's fashion office has unpacked, pressed, and hung everything in readiness for the guest fashion director's arrival. She will tactfully check with the store's fashion director as to how she would like the show line-up handled (every store is not the same) and how she would like the costumes accessorized, even though she might have brought some accessories along with her.

It is customary that the guest fashion director will represent the company to the public by doing the show's commentary. She may also hold a press interview and appear on television while in the city to promote the event. She will extend her company's hospitality while visiting the store, by holding breakfast meetings, luncheons, or dinners for store executives. She might even hold home furnishings clinics for that division's personnel if time and management are in accord.

The process is repeated in each city. From every city she accumulates documentation of the results of the event, pictures, tear sheets, invitations, and press clippings, to help with her report on what took place. The fashion director in the linen and domestics industry finds that her responsibilities change annually. A new fashion happening creates a new fashion approach. Next year, instead of a fashion show, the promotion may be tied to interior design.

Fashion Manufacturing

Another area and another completely different use of the fashion director is in the world of manufacturing, however, here she is more often called a stylist. As in retailing, it is certain that no two firms use their fashion specialist in exactly the same way. Markets are different, juniors, coats, sportswear, and dresses all have different needs, different approaches to fashion projection. But in spite of these differences, their objectives are similar enough for a stylist to train with one manufacturer and be qualified to serve another.

The Manufacturer's Stylist. From the manufacturer's point of view, perhaps the most important service she fulfills is making fashion presentations for the sale force. Four or five times a year, or whenever a new line has been produced, the stylist organizes shows for all personnel involved in selling fashion.

The stylist books the models, supervises the fittings, accessorizes and coordinates the pieces. Bearing in mind that salesmen are not fashion experts, she writes descriptions of the fashions, making sure they are carefully informed about all the new terminology, new combinations, and new purposes. In her commentary during the show, she points out the various possibilities of mixing pieces in a group with parts of another group. This is very important if the manufacturer has a sales force on the road. The salesmen, in turn, can instruct the retailers on whom they call. The stylist's guidance on how to accessorize the collection is also important. Many a storekeeper depends upon the salesman to aid him with display ideas and windows. Also, the salesman may be called upon to conduct a fashion show for a store and he must know how it all goes together, what is worn with what.

Still in the area of training, the stylist might be called upon to produce films and slides for training sessions, for staff use in the national office, or for those in the field throughout the country.

To the retailer, the manufacturer's stylist is someone who arranges for fashion shows or trunk showings in the store. If it is a full-fledged fashion show, she sometimes does the commentary, sometimes helps with the accessorizing, but in most cases works directly with the store's fashion office.

The Stylist's Other Hat. The manufacturer's stylist sometimes wears another hat—or two. She may work in the showroom, reviewing the line piece by piece for retail buyers. She may have the job of working as liaison with the fashion magazines, putting editors in touch with designers, sending over fashion pieces the editor may have selected for editorial exposure, or having something designed especially for the magazine.

She may cover the fabric market in advance of the season to spot trends and bring back fabric suggestions to her management. She sometimes works out the firm's color story, based on her research with fabric people and color specialists. She shops the stores to check out what is being displayed and sold. She may find design ideas she considers worth her company's attention. Therefore, she would very likely buy a fashion garment and take it back to her firm's designer to examine for cut and construction.

The manufacturer's stylist might also be involved in creating mailing pieces to be sent to customers or distributed by her company's salesmen. The piece may be an itemized report on the manufacturer's fashion story for the season, suitable for reference or for reorders of numbers in the line when the salesman is not around.

Pattern Companies

A great deal of fashion happens in this industry, and women the world over are sewing more than ever. All of these women want their fashion to be up to date, just as the woman who buys ready-to-wear, so the pattern companies must create patterns that are indeed the last word in fashion. These might include designs from their own design department or from name designers who create especially for the pattern books.

Fashion Research.   Fashion inspiration for what goes into the pattern line and catalog is not unlike every other fashion area that must look ahead and anticipate what will be happening in fashion next season, next year. Fashion trips abroad, are made perhaps four to eight times a year, to visit couture showrooms, inspect the boutiques in Italy, Spain, England, France, or wherever important fashion is happening. Such research also includes a survey of the best of American fashion, and the composite of all the findings is what influences the design department to create patterns that will go into the book. A hot trend can be crash programed and inserted in the book in a few weeks. The fashion people of pattern companies, like the retail fashion office, carefully scrutinize fashion information as it comes into focus. To be sure that the sketches or photographs in the pattern books are properly accessorized and that the hair fashions and makeup of the models are the correct ones for the clothes, members of the fashion staff shop the accessory market, gathering the last-word information on shoes, gloves, bags, belts, jewelry, and scarves, plus trends in hair and makeup fashions.

The Fabric Library.   The silhouette is only part of the fashion for home sewers. The fabric is the other part. Pattern companies, therefore, maintain remarkable fabric libraries, complete with every new and important fabric, the newest colors, textures, and patterns, to inspire the designers further and to help with the illustrations for the book. The library is also available to editors and to retail store executives who wish to come and look.

In conjunction with the fabric library, which might include over-the-counter fabrics from 200 resources or more, the fashion staff of the pattern company supplies a comprehensive report for spring and fall with swatches of fabric trends for subscribers to their pattern catalogs. They also publish fashion magazines that illustrate the newest fashion looks with photographs or sketches to report on new trends.

The Pattern Fashion Show.   Almost everything that happens in conjunction with the fabric in-store fashion show also takes place with the pattern show. The pattern company's fashion representative brings her own show pieces, (models of patterns in the current book), and handles all details of the show, fittings, accessorizing, and commentary.

This is an area that could be of special interest to the beginner interested in a career in fashion. Many large pattern companies (such as Simplicity and Butterick) maintain a staff of traveling stylists. They are often girls right out of school and often home economics majors.

The pattern companies' stylists not only travel throughout the country most of the year with their shows, but also report back to their companies on any fashion trends they spot during their travels, such as fabrics and patterns that are selling, what people are wearing, and the type of merchandise the stores are carrying. Also, they are often interviewed on radio and television and by local newspapers to publicize their shows.

Next to retailing, the pattern company stylist is one of the best jobs for the beginner. Many have gone on to become fashion coordinators in other areas, especially for fabric or fiber companies.

Cosmetics and Fragrance Industry

Few of the titles of the fashion people found in other areas are evident in the cosmetics and fragrance industry. Titles like creative director or publicity director are more frequently used. Fashion direction is administered in one or both of these offices. The creative director researches the fashion world to find guidance for fashion decisions in cosmetics. The season's new colors and trends will need to show up in "face fashions." Face designers, therefore, will create new trends in cosmetics as readily as the fashion designer does in the couture and ready-to-wear (see Chapter 13).

Promotions.   In the cosmetic business the greatest impact with a new fashion story comes from personal appearances. Celebrities, makeup artists, and stars whose cosmetic companies bear their name, are the most dependable attention-getters for launching a new line or a new cosmetic concept. An illustrious personality, strongly identified with fashion or beauty, is most effective in this area which depends upon personal appeal.

Cosmetic Fashion Forecasts.   The cosmetic buyer, the merchandise manager, and the store's fashion director are kept well informed about what the cosmetic world is planning for a coming season through releases issued by their publicity director (see Chapter 7). These might also include trend interpretations of the apparel market, especially as it relates to makeup trends. Fashion authority is very important in this field. The endorsement of a famous beauty, fashion designer, or celebrated "face designer" provides the product with the impact it needs to be recognized as a bearer of miracle gifts of beauty and fashion excellence.

Fragrance and Fashion.   Fragrance is always in fashion. What makes it appeal to the consumer, however, is the level of her fashion and her emotional needs. Copy in ads and fashion environment in ads, sell fragrance. Image sells fragrance. To accomplish all this and relate it to the fashion world, fragrance companies often tie in with fashion shows in stores where the fashion image is compatible with their own. Gifts of fragrance to the audience in exchange for a few words from the commentator or credit in the program, help keep the name and the product before the consumer.

Other Important Areas for Coordinators

Grouping the following together under this heading does not mean that they are less important than those areas highlighted separately in this chapter. In fact, some of the following are bigger and present even greater opportunities for the coordinator. However, to cover in detail the functions of the buying offices, for example, would be unnecessary repetition because they have already been covered earlier in the text (see Chapter 6 and 7). Also, the consultant firms, their service and the duties of their coordinators, were included in Chapter 7. The buying offices and consultant firms, both very close to the fashion scene and both keeping their members or subscribers informed on what is happening and what it means to their store specifically, have places for retail-trained fashion people.

The Shoe Industry.   The fashion director of a shoe company works far ahead with the tanners to make leather selections for coming seasons. The colors and textures selected are to be expressed in designs of footwear suitable for the forthcoming fashion apparel season. The fashion director of a shoe company researches those areas that influence fashion decisions, the apparel market (usually abroad, because they work far ahead of the domestic market), the fabric market, and the magazines.

The classics or staples come up with a fresh look, and the very new or high-fashion models are carefully designed to win friends as quickly as possible. It is expected that some looks will be slow getting off the ground, but a trend that is expected to be around for a while requires patience. The fashion director helps relate the fashion story in this area in much the same way as it is done in other fashion areas. She trains the selling staff of her company as well as the sales people of the store whose shoe salons carry her shoes. For the store's sales staff, she might arrive at the store early, go to the ready-to-wear departments, select appropriate samples for her illustrations, and show which shoes are meant for which looks.

She also helps get her fashion story to the consumer through the fashion magazines. If an editorial on shoes appears in an issue, or some footwear worn by models on an editorial page of ready-to-wear, it is very likely that the shoes have shown up (with a credit line for identification) through the efforts of that shoe company's fashion director.

Publicists.   The publicists' fashion office is in a way related to the mechanics of the advertising agency's fashion department or the photographer's stylist, yet a completely different breed. The fashion people working for publicists are concerned with selling the client or his product (sometimes both) through good publicity instead of advertising. For example, press pictures must be beautifully done. Only good pictures, exciting, and creative, get picked up by the press. Since getting as much good press space as possible for fashion clients is a prime responsibility of the publicist, this area is very important.

The publicists are also promotion-merchandising people. For example, to promote prints in fashion, the Bell & Stanton public relations agency, on behalf of their client, the Printed Fabrics Council, conducted a design contest among new young talent. This kind of effort makes the news and publicizes prints. The Softness Group, publicists for Rit (dyes), made an outstanding contribution to promoting tie-dying. In connection with *Mademoiselle's* Paint Your Wagon promotion and other efforts, they made personal appearance demonstrations and involved retail teen boards and young customers in "tie-dye parties."

The creation and development of the Coty Award in 1942, by publicist Eleanor Lambert is a fashion legend. The contribution to the fashion industry through the coveted Coty Fashion Award is a matter of record (see Chapter 7).

The Fashion Magazines. Fashion magazines do not have fashion directors. They have fashion editors. However, it cannot be passed over as being entirely unrelated. The editorial pages are created by the fashion editors and the merchandise is selected, coordinated, and photographed under their watchful eye and direction. In researching the fashion market, one editor may cover the coat and suit market, one the dress market, another the accessory market, and so on down the line. Each brings back her findings, and they are utilized as they relate to the concept of the magazine. The merchandising department of the magazine develops all the promotions and fashion tie-ins with retailers, working closely with the store's fashion director and merchandisers (see Chapter 7). Because of their close association with retailers, almost all of the national fashion magazines have on their pay rolls (especially in the merchandising division) young women whose background includes fashion experience in retailing.

The Similarities of Fashion Coordination Jobs

Touching on a diversified list of industries where careers in fashion coordination are available, one very prevalent fact shows up: the requirements and responsibilities are similar enough to permit a crossing of boundaries from one area to another. In other words, training in one fashion job is good preparation for another, even though the industry and the product may be different. Advertising agencies, photographic studios, and public relations companies can easily interchange fashion personnel, and any of these can move back and forth from fabric or fiber companies or magazines.

For every area mentioned in this chapter (those fashion careers outside of retailing but closely related) retailing is the great training ground. Consider the similarities:

1. All are involved in researching the fashion market for future trends.
2. Most are responsible for fashion presentations and/or training of personnel.
3. Most are involved in fashion shows, promotions, and public relations activities related to the consumer.

These points alone more than substantiate the relationship of the entire profession of fashion directors, embracing all areas of the fashion business.

Miscellaneous Contributions from the Fashion Industry

The public relations or promotional efforts of fashion departments in any or all of the fields included in this chapter, have made unique and valuable contributions to the fashion industry and to the nation as a whole. Through the ingenuity of a fashion department with vision, seeing a need and filling it, careers for young beginners have been launched, consumers have been aided, and retailers have been benefited. Some efforts contributed to public morale and well-being. Some benefited the underprivileged. Scholarships, contests, competitions, sponsored by all phases of the fashion industry to discover and encourage new talent, have started many a promising career on its way. The worthy efforts are legion, and new ones are being instituted every day by perceptive fashion directors everywhere. The few examples noted here are highly indicative of the meritorious work being done.

An interesting example of fashion design competition, spearheaded by Burlington Industries, Inc., started the winner on a successful career in fashion design and made a large fashion contribution to the national community. Until 1968, the United States parade uniforms at the Olympic games were hit-and-miss selections, sometimes just some left over fashions off the pipes of the manufacturer's back room. It took some time before it was generally noticed that the U.S. Olympic teams were the worst dressed among the nations represented. Something had to be done. The executive director and members of the Olympic Committee came to Burlington Mills for help. From this meeting which included Florence K. Lentz, fashion promotion director of Burlington Industries, came the idea to have the young design for the young. The United States Olympic Apparel Committee was formed to coordinate the design, the manufacture, and the fit of clothing worn by United States athletes at the Olympic games. Several hundred entries were submitted by colleges and professional schools participating in the United States Olympic Apparel Committee's national competition to have American youth create the designs to be worn by the young champions who make up our Olympic team. To coordinate with the winning designs, fashion accessory manufacturers contributed the necessary accessories. At last, for the 1968 winter and summer games, United States Olympic athletes paraded in fashions that demonstrated American apparel know-how and presented the team as a shining example of well-dressed young Americans. The 1972 Olympic parade uniforms were executed under the direction of Sears Roebuck and Company. The fashion director of Sears had several groups of fashion ideas specially designed and submitted to the United States Olympic Apparel Committee for final selections.

From the creative director of Elizabeth Arden, Pablo, came a special makeup approach for the woman recovering from plastic surgery. Greater numbers of women were taking advantage of cosmetic surgery than ever before. The weeks of healing following surgery were presenting some restless moments for many women. Sensing a growing need, Pablo lectured to plastic surgeons at a medical convention and presented a slide presentation to illustrate how to use makeup to aid the psychological recovery of patients during the postoperative healing period.

Under the heading of public service, Bonne Bell Cosmetics initiated a special beauty clinic for blind teenage girls, conducted on a national scale in department stores, to teach the sightless how to "Make a Pretty Face." Blind girls were invited by the local store to be their guests for a makeup session, for lunch, and perhaps some music by local talent. Learning that blind girls want to "feel pretty," the program included kits written in braille, a record with step-by-step instructions on skin care and makeup, and a makeup kit complete with all the products necessary. The clinic itself was conducted by Bonne Bell representatives and the store's fashion director. Each blind girl was aided by a sighted teenager, usually a member of the store's teen fashion board, trained in advance for the event.

The "before" fashion look of the U.S. Olympic Team and "after" the fashion industry came forth to help. (Courtesy of Burlington Industries, Inc.)

Above, the 1952 U.S. Girls Track and Field Olympic Team taken in Helsinki, Finland.

Below, Judges review sketches submitted by college and professional school apparel design students.

Above, the winning sketches that changed the look of the U.S. Olympic Team. Right, parade uniforms, a winning design by Karen Denise Saloomey a senior at the Rhode Island School of Design, for the U.S. Olympic Team, Winter Games, Grenoble, France.

Fashion's purpose is to make life more pleasant. Certainly it would follow that the fashion industry in all areas would feel a responsibility and, by its very nature, be sensitive to the needs for beautification.

Afterview

With all the choices available in the field of fashion coordination, finding the right place presents an interesting challenge. A good starting point would be to relate to the area or kind of product that interests you most. The shoe industry? Ready-to-wear fashion houses? The advertising agency or public relations world? The photographer's studio? The fiber or fabric business? The retail field?

Of course, a great deal depends on where you live, what is available, and where you are willing to go. New York or Chicago may be a good place for a top advertising agency, but Boston or St. Louis may be better for the shoe industry. New York or California may be the wisest choices for good fashion houses, but department stores all over the country provide the kind of training ground that will equip the beginner with the experience she needs.

The records are filled with case histories of fashion coordinators who have left retailing to go to fashion magazines, to fiber companies, to fashion consultant firms, or to advertising agencies, and then back to the retail business for high level responsibilities. As indicated earlier, whether it is used as a springboard to other fashion associations or as a permanent career, retailing has much to offer.

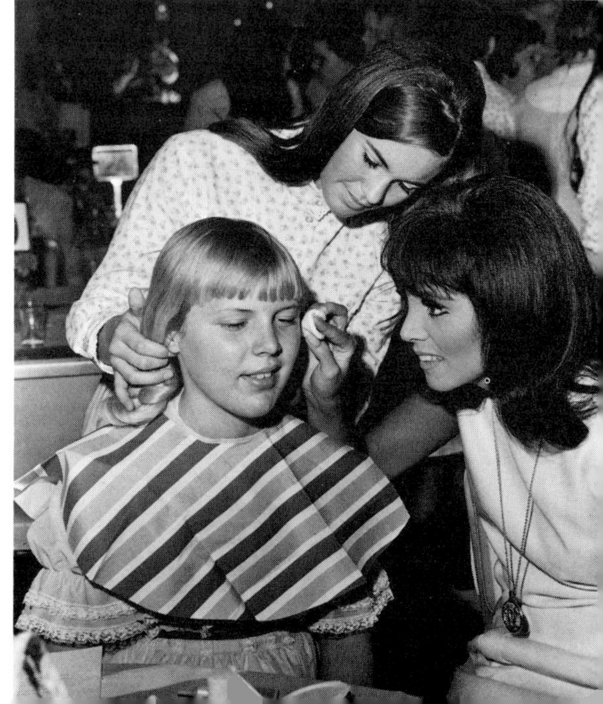

Above, ''Make a Pretty Face''
event for blind teenage girls at
the May Co., Los Angeles.
Right, actress Marlo
Thomas came to participate in a
makeup clinic for blind girls at
the May Co., Los Angeles.
(Courtesy of Bonne Bell
Cosmetics.)

 *Chapter 15*

* One More Thing...

The moment has come. It is time to place all the facts face up, end to end, for a final review. It is time to ask for a realistic total of the rewards and the demands, the advantages and disadvantages, the blessings and privations of a career in the field of fashion.

On the basis of aptitude and interest, one could conceivably give the area of fashion coordination a try, take a flyer and see what develops, but no one can or should give the full measure of devotion required by the fashion business without having a pretty good idea of how well or to what degree it pays off. Economy is important, of course, but the kind of money one can make in this field is only one of the many reasons for pursuing such a career. Money or no money, if the pros do not outweigh the cons, the joys of satisfaction will be sadly lacking.

The Advantages

Every career has its share of advantages, but the character of those found in fashion coordination make up a very attractive list.

Action. There is lots of it. Every scratch on the calendar represents a whirl of activity; up and down escalators to

373

visit fashion departments, stockrooms, buyers, merchandisers, display, advertising, publicity, special events, store executives; in and out of meetings, dressings rooms, ballrooms; in and out of airports, hotel rooms, conference rooms, fabric rooms, showrooms.

Action, always running in high gear in the fashion business, can be classified as an advantage only by those who thrive on such an atmosphere. If one is fortified with boundless energy, the constant flow of action will be met head on and, in most cases, thoroughly enjoyed. Without a good flow of top-level energy, the surge of activity could be too overwhelming.

The versatility of the action, however, is in itself a stimulant. Heavy action of one kind might be harder to handle, but a busy schedule, bursting at the seams with all kinds of different activity, different assignments, different challenges, and different people, provides renewed stimuli. This is the kind of action that is considered by those involved in fashion co-ordination as a true advantage.

Personality Asset: ENERGY

Creativity.   Creative people need to create. If one does not possess enough excellence to pursue a career in the world of visual or living arts, but is possessed, all the same, with the temperament of a creative person, a home can be found in fashion coordination. Here is a chance to create with ideas, with showmanship, and with innovations for the merchandising of fashion.

Paralleling the physical action of the job is the mental action. With all the guide lines provided in this text, there is still latitude for bringing to the job what the individual, and only the individual, can provide. Because the product with which we work, fashion, is never static and always changing, so must be the relative occupations dealing with it, especially fashion coordination. The changes are felt more readily in this area than perhaps others. They do, however, make possible the elastic creative opportunities.

To make things happen, to properly use those creative instincts, the person most likely to succeed in fashion coordination creates unselfishly, not only to please herself, but especially to please the customer and the store. That is a big order. It can only be filled by a big person.

Also, creativity in this field cannot be hemmed in by tradition. There will be those who will say "We have never done it this way before." It will take strength to reply, "it is time that we did." Live dangerously now and then.

Personality Asset: COURAGE

People. People can be the biggest advantage or the biggest disadvantage; it all depends on viewpoint. In an accounting firm, for example, many of the people would be of a typical nature, similar in temperament, similar in educational preparation. This is not so in fashion. Personalities are extremely different—running the gamut from the very gentle to the very tough, from the quiet and easy-going to the very vocal and uptight types. Prima donnas in fashion can easily tie with those found among opera stars or the acting profession. Giants of strength, pillars of accomplishment, stand tall and firm at the heads of fashion institutions, and those on top, plus those on the way up, come from all walks of life, all kinds of backgrounds, bringing to the industry the wealth of their combined experiences.

Whether the man at the top inherited his throne or pulled himself up by his own bootstraps, his style of dedication and contributions to the industry have often been pace setters of imitation by those following him. Their message has been a very clear one. Halfway measures in fashion don't work—not for the president, not for the fashion director.

Surrounded by people, therefore, who demand such a great deal of themselves, it can well be expected that they will demand a great deal of everyone else as well. If kept in proportion, such demands can urge the best performance to come forth, and can carry one to heights that otherwise might not have been attained. Whatever brings out the best in us is undeniably an advantage.

The melting pot of personalities found in the fashion Industry, contributes largely to its special charm. The composite of influences, and the blending of ambitions and goals, ignite a bombardment of happenings that make the industry an explosive powder keg most of the time. Even though the fireworks are not going off all the time, one is aware of their presence, especially in the area of retailing. If every day is not the Fourth of July, some inventive merchant will find a way to make it so. The feeling arises that in the world of fashion, even though some days could be very ordinary, no one in the fashion community would want it to stay that way for very long.

The citizens of the fashion community are colorful, hard working, aggressive, unique, spoiled, ambitious, temperamental, hungry. Such qualifications might be death in other professions, but in fashion they are splendid. They make things happen—remarkable things. To work with such people can be totally enchanting or completely unnerving. The effect is entirely dependent on one's viewpoint, love them for what they are, or at least accept them for what they are. It must be remembered that they, too, will need to love you for what you are or just accept you for the same reason. An interplay of respect and sympathy for others efforts (very important) will help make a fashion director the people-person she needs to be.

Personality Asset: PATIENCE

Travel.   This can be, if one is endowed with a sense of adventure, one of the best advantages on the list. A fashion director travels considerably. Her travels not only take her to the market places, from New York to California, but to many stops in between. She oftens finds herself on a plane to new cities to check out other fashion stores, to examine branches of her own company if it is a chain operation or conglomerate, or to attend special meetings in cities near and far.

In addition to the above, she might be taking off on a junket as a guest of a fiber company to examine their mill operation. She might be the guest for a holiday in Hawaii, Mexico, or Puerto Rico, sponsored by a manufacturer. Not the least of all this packing and unpacking are the fashion trips to Europe, to the Orient, to the Middle East, to all the fashion capitals of the world, those known and some trying to be known.

The beginner in the fashion office might eagerly await word as to when she might get in on some of this travel-is-broadening education. It is entirely possible that a fashion director will take her assistant along on some market trips, her area coordinators, her teen coordinator, or anyone else on her staff if the trip is relative to their function. These instances usually are for meetings or showings in the United States. To go abroad, get promoted.

The art of getting the most out of travel is very important to fashion coordination. To look and not see is something of a tragedy for one seeking fashion knowledge. From the time she boards the plane, she watches what her fellow passengers wear, she checks into her hotel and notices travelers in the lobby, out to dinner, at the theater, at the meetings, everywhere.

Combining her people-watching with what she learns from the industry, she comes home inspired, refreshed, and informed. A meeting inside a room in any city can provide her with only that which goes on inside that room. But what she sees outside that room, on the street, in the restaurants, in the stores, in the homes, is what makes a visit from one city to another important.

Personality Asset: CURIOSITY

Economy. In exactly the same proportion that one gets out of a job what one puts into it (there are some who testify this does not always follow), so are the economic rewards in proportion to the service. The world is certainly not without injustice, but most injustices suffered on the pay scale are vulnerable to change. Good fashion jobs in the fashion office might range anywhere from $6,000 to $50,000. In some cases, even higher. In addition to the pay check itself, fashion people enjoy the privilege of house discounts on all merchandise, and sometimes special arrangements are made for contributions to their wardrobes. These side benefits usually apply only to those in retailing areas.

Perhaps in very few fields are there more opportunities for good paying jobs, faster promotion, better chance for growth than in the fashion world. Even if one is merely using the fashion office as a stepping stone to other things, it is a splendid training ground for related careers with bigger pay checks. It all depends on one's individual needs, one's drive and scope of ambition, what the traffic will bear, what heights may be reached.

Personality Asset: HUNGER

Fringe Benefits. There are many fringe benefits that pop up for those in the fashion office. They are sometimes small and intriguing, sometimes large and enviable. For example, free samples of a new product. Sometimes these come under the heading of small and intriguing, not significant but fun—a new lipstick, a new lotion, a new fragrance. Or, they can come under the banner of being significant—an unlimited supply of new hosiery fashions, sunglasses, lingerie, cosmetics, wigs, cameras, or miscellaneous accessories. One should never expect these things because their appearance is spasmodic and sometimes nonexistent, but when they do appear it is delightful.

Freedom of movement, too, is a decided advantage, the kind of fringe benefit that some might consider of top importance. For the temperament that resists being tied close to a desk on regular nine to five schedules, the freedom of the fashion office has much to offer. There are days when some members of the staff do not even set foot into the office; they are off fitting a show, executing a production, visiting the branches. The versatility of the activity pointed out earlier in this chapter, permits this freedom of movement.

Contacts are not the least of the fringe benefits. The freedom of movement places fashion office personnel in contact with every level of professional in the fashion business, from the stock boy to the top executive. Outside her own organization, she will meet salesmen, promotion people, designers, manufacturers, magazine editors and publishers, members of the press, celebrities, company presidents, civic leaders, and political officials, to name a few. Where these contacts lead can have very interesting results, a way to make friends for the store, to make personal friends, to make points for another career. The constant flow of personalities in itself guarantees sparkle to the life of the fashion director.

The unique exposure to a wide variety of people, the experiences of travel and the education one can reap from it, the experiments with creativity, the constant need to explore and dig and uncover, to discover, invent and direct, to set one's pace as fast or as easy as the job will allow, to taste the joys of being a self-starter, self-explorer, to gamble and lose, and gamble and win (expecting both, enduring both), to take a stand, stick the proverbial neck out, live dangerously, all add up to remarkable advantages. It is all there. Few careers offer so wide a sweep of involvement. And for the beginner, hidden between the folds of all this experience comes the most rewarding part of all, the chance for personal growth.

The Disadvantages

So that we do not overglorify the merits of a career in fashion coordination, an honest appraisal of the disadvantages must go on the record. There is no doubt that some of the points listed as advantages could also be noted under disadvantages. Take travel, for example, for the woman who hates to leave home, hates to pack, is afraid to fly, dislikes strange places, this would certainly be a big problem. What is needed here is an individual evaluation.

Pressures. Now here is a point that would immediately seem only acceptable for listing under disadvantages. Not necessarily. There are those who thrive under pressure, and everybody needs some. But we deal here with the excessive pressure that can realistically appear in the life of the fashion director or coordinator. For example, a fashion director serves so many lieutenants it is entirely conceivable that they might start pulling from different directions, all at the same time, and often they do.

Even the most organized fashion office will find that projects will pop up unexpectedly, situations beyond the fashion department's control will demand immediate and special attention. Shows will be back to back; business trips and fashion presentations requiring lots of preparation, will run neck and neck; meetings, interviews, fittings, shooting schedules, and personal appearances, will take place almost simultaneously. All busy offices are busy, naturally, so why the big fuss about pressure? For one thing, the expected and the planned can usually be handled without too much pressure, no matter how busy. It is the unexpected and the un- planned lunging out of nowhere that puts the pressure on high. It is part of the nature of the retail business, however, it is also a basic truth in fashion.

Another thing, the different types of hats the fashion director wears, requiring a different set of personality traits or approaches, add consider- ably to the kind of personal demands on energies and feelings that regulate the pressure gauge. A pressure even more basic where the fashion office is concerned is the pleasing of a multitude of personalities, please the customer, please the boss, please the press, please the buyer, please the audience. This routine can provide an undercurrent of pressure, ever pres- ent and unrelenting.

Whatever the pressures, they are not pointed up here as unendurable. Thousands of fashion office people endure them very well, indeed, even enjoy them. But the so-called fools who rush in where angels fear to tread should be tipped off to all the ramifications. In other words, if pressures are expected, they can be more of a challenge, less devastating.

"We never know what might be coming up when we unlock the fashion office door in the morning or pick up the phone," one fashion director said, "but that is what makes us go."
Personality Asset: SENSE OF ADVENTURE

The Hours. Oh, the hours. There are plenty of them. Tabulating all the fashion directors queried in the country, this is very likely to appear at the top of the list of disadvantages. The hours—often long, often irregular— disqualify many people who have other strong demands on their time, home, marriage, family, recreation. All of these will feel the pinch of the demanding hours. Sometimes only during peak periods, sometimes only during a special promotion, but it is wise to have a realistic awareness that consuming hours come on strong very often. The bigger the responsibility, the bigger the clock.

Clock-watching, per se, is a no-no. Not that anyone is keeping tabs or clocking in or out, but just as the pace may be slowing down to a healthy jog, along comes another one of those "unexpecteds." Clock-watching is just not practical, even though the freedom of movement permits an ease of coming and going. Flexibility helps considerably. The calendar, not the clock, dictates the time for coming and the time for going.

Personality Asset: ENDURANCE

Dedication.   Whether or not this factor can be considered a disadvantage depends, of course, on the extent of dedication or the reason for it. The fashion business is a very jealous lord demanding total devotion, no other false gods, total commitment. For some, this may be asking too much. Some cannot give it. Others may pledge total devotion but do so with resentment. Unthinkable. Unworkable.

Dedication given because of one's eagerness to get the most out of what they are giving makes a plus out of a minus. Dedication because the challenge itself becomes totally consuming pays off better. For those who dream of a spot at the top in the field of fashion coordination, dedication will become unavoidable.

Personality Asset: SURRENDER

Special Preparation

Even though fashion office personnel comes from many directions (from the ranks of models, teen boards, secretaries, buyers, merchandisers, publicity and advertising areas, to name a few), a good educational background will help you arrive better prepared and in a position to command a better salary.

A college degree need not be restricted only to the areas of fashion and merchandising, although this is, naturally, most desirable. A couple of the biggest fashion coordination jobs around are held by women who majored in political science. However, it must be noted that a career in fashion was not yet their goal while in school, nor was specialized fashion training available.

For the young woman who knows what she wants, who looks to fashion coordination as her goal, the sooner she gets into the swim with specialized education, the better. Competition has become keener, requirements set higher. The retail fashion business has become more specialized, and specialized people are more in demand.

Fashion Design. Fashion design is excellent background for fashion coordination. There is no better place to learn a respect for the intricacies of fashion creation. A solid knowledge of construction, detail, balance, and manipulation of fabric, is a perfect background for the professional fashion director.

The workmanship, the special finishes, the trims of a garment, all contribute to its cost, all in proportion to the degree of excellence and skill. Without an exposure to such details, the novice will be a longer time catching up on facts that will prove highly valuable. Such a tiny detail, for example, as understanding that color-coordinated pearl or bone buttons perfectly matched to the fabric increase the cost of the garment. Such understanding helps the fashion director appreciate the manufacturer's efforts and the buyer's choices. Yes, and even the customer's preferences.

Home Economics. The fashion business is alive with home economics graduates, especially in the textile area of fashion. Many of the relative fashion courses offered in some universities and most junior colleges who are anxious to update their programs, come under the department of home economics. These are good places to start the program of fashion, together with on-the-job training in a retail store that cooperates with the school.

Merchandising Schools. In addition to merchandising divisions of universities, there are excellent professional schools that specialize in merchandising and fashion training. They offer highly comprehensive programs for careers in fashion, taught by staff members who have been formerly active or are currently active in the field of fashion.

These institutions are famous for their alert approach to the current methods of merchandising fashion, with a continuous updating to meet the personnel demands of retailers, manufacturers, agencies, and mills who are likely prospects to draw from their student body for new talent. In other words, they keep a constant finger on the pulse of the industry to develop accurately trained fashion people to fulfill realistic needs.

The Professional Fashion Director and Schools. Specialists in the fashion industry are often invited to serve as instructors or as guest speakers. The retail fashion director, or the fashion director of a fabric company, fiber producer, linens and domestics company, fashion design house, or advertising agency, is often invited to universities, professional schools or local colleges to speak on their industry and fashion experience. Also, teaching aids for home economics teachers or instructors of specialized fashion schools are often provided for classroom use by the industry. And it is usually the fashion director who compiles the material.

For Women Only?

Is the field of fashion coordination, the career of the fashion director, strictly a woman's world? Not really. This text has been directed to the female student or reader, because over ninety percent of the fashion directors are women. However, in the places where men have assumed the duties of fashion director, their records have been impressive and indicate that there is a place for creative men, depending upon the responsibility structure and types of assignments in a given store or company.

In the realm of retailing, male fashion coordinators or directors have been more in demand in home furnishings divisions and in the men's and boys' ready-to-wear divisions. There have been a few men (enough to prove it can be done) who have distinguished themselves as corporate or divisional fashion directors for women's ready-to-wear. For example, Rich's in Atlanta, Wanamaker's in Philadephia, and the Franklin Simon stores, employ men fashion directors. In the fiber industry, Monsanto enlisted the services of a male fashion director.

Afterview

The very existence of so many ways to go in fashion coordination, inside and outside retailing, is an immediate testimonial to the importance and scope of the area. The population of the world continues to grow. The fashion industry continues to grow. The field of fashion coordination, spanning a wide range of possibilities and choices, also continues to grow in proportion. The surface has barely been scratched.

With fashion growing more complicated, bigger changes, faster changes, and fashion institutions expanding and spreading, one great cushion against "future shock" is the well-equipped fashion director who can pull the entire fashion picture together for her management.

The ever-present needs to meet competition, to make a profit, exploit a new product, create a new market, uphold an image, keep in personal touch with the consumer, require dependable fashion know-how. The well-trained fashion director, coordinator, stylist, or administrator, whatever her title, intellectually and emotionally equipped to direct fashion with a here-I-come-world initiative, can be the most exciting and most profitable thing that can happen to her firm.

One more Personality Asset: A SENSE OF HUMOR

Bring it along.

The industry needs she who has one, and she who has one is blessed.

❀ *Glossary*

❀ *Fashion Industry Terms*

Accessories   All articles, ranging from intimate apparel to hosiery, shoes, bags, gloves, scarves, hats, etc., worn to enhance or complete an outfit of apparel.

Accessorizing   The process of adding accessory items to relate to apparel for purposes of display or for models in fashion shows, or for customer's clothes upon request.

Apparel   The all-embracing term applied to men's, women's, and children's clothing. Wearing apparel.

Blowup   An illustration or other material that has been enlarged, perhaps several sizes, from the original.

Boutique   A shop or area within a retail store, devoted to specialized merchandise for a special-interest customer. Usually includes new and unique apparel and/or accessories or other items not found elsewhere in the store. (See Specialty Shop)

Branch   In retailing, a suburban extension of the downtown or flagship store, operated under the same ownership and usually carrying most of the same merchandise.

Camera-ready   (advertising term) Art work and ad copy pasted up and ready to be photographed.

385

Chain   Retail store group, centrally owned and operated, with policies regulated and most merchandise selected and bought by a regional or national office.

Classic   Fashion trend or style that has enjoyed longevity of acceptance. A staple or basic item.

Classification   Dividing merchandise into classes or groups, according to fashion looks. In fashion fabrics departments, classifications would be according to fabric content.

Collection   A manufacturer's or designer's group of fashion creations for a specific season. The season's total number of fashion pieces, accumulated for presentation to buyers, comprises a collection.

Confined   When a line or label is sold to one retailer in a city on an exclusive basis.

Converter   (textile term) A concern handling gray goods (unfinished goods) as they come from the loom. The converter gives the goods its finish—print, color, and any other treatment. The process of converting textiles into fashion fabrics.

Copy   In advertising, the words or phrases used to describe the item(s) to be advertised, to be set in type, and to be reproduced in printed form.

Cost price   Price at which goods are sold to a store.

Couturier   French term for (male) proprietor or designer of a couture house. Couturiere (female).

Crop   In advertising, to cut off or trim parts of an illustration which are not to be included in the finished printing.

Cutter   Apparel manufacturer. One who cuts and sews the fabric into a garment.

Department store   A sizeable retail operation, selling men's, women's, and childrens' apparel and accessories, other soft goods, and merchandise for the home (hard lines).

Design   An original or individual manipulation of fabric, color, and line to create a style concept.

Designer   One who creates in his own manner an interpretation or concept of a style in apparel, fabrics, accessories, etc.

Distribution center   Centralized depot that receives all merchandise for the retail organization, marks, processes, and distributes the merchandise to the various branches.

Divisional merchandise manager (DMM)   Retail executive who supervises a specific division of a store (i.e. women's ready-to-wear division) and directs the merchandising activities of the buyers within his division.

Dominant sell   Item or items dominating a big share of a department's sales. Also known as volume sellers.

Dominant store   In retail, the store that dominates in a given area.

Double truck   (Advertising term) Double-page spread. Two full pages of newspaper advertising in an adjacent position.

Editorial credits   Publicity extended by consumer magazines at no charge to retailers (on-page credits or back-of-the-book credits), in order to advise the reader where items featured editorially are available, in which city, and at which store.

Fad   A fashion trend that comes in and goes out quickly. Short lived fashion.

Fashion   Term awarded to styles or trends during a reigning period of strong consumer acceptability. That which is no longer widely accepted is no longer fashion.

Fashion look   Design, style, or silhouette of wearing apparel.

Fashion press   Reporters who specialize in covering fashion news for magazines, newspapers, and broadcast media.

First cost   Wholesale price quoted by vendor abroad to export buyer. (see Landed Cost)

Format   In advertising, the theme, size, shape, general makeup of an ad. Repeated or consistent layout or appearance of ads, often used by retailers to establish continuity or easily identifiable ads in print (and for television commercials).

General merchandise manager (GMM)   Retail executive to whom all divisional merchandise managers report, and through whom the GMM supervises the merchandising activities of the divisional's buyers.

Go-see   Term used in the advertising agency business when a client (i.e.) goes to see and approve the use of a model for an ad.

Haute couture.   The leading dressmaking houses of Paris. Important designers of custom-made clothes.

Hard goods   In retail, it is a term classifying merchandise other than ready-to-wear—such as appliances, housewares, etc. (see hard lines)

Hard lines   Term describing certain classifications in the home division of a retail establishment. Hard lines usually include appliances, hardware, housewares, small electrics, paints, garden shops. (see home division)

High fashion   Fashion that has limited acceptability. Fashion that is more unique, advanced, and individual as against trend fashion.

Highly promotional   A classification of store that concentrates on volume. Promotes price rather than fashion.

Home division   Area of a retail establishment devoted to merchandise for the home. Fashion departments of the home division would include furniture, draperies, linens, carpets, pictures and lamps, china and silver. (for other classifications in the home division see hard lines)

Image   Impression or understanding the consumer has of a retail store's position on fashion leadership, quality, service, selection, price level, and general personality.

Knock-off   A copy of a higher priced garment.

Landed cost   Retailer's actual cost on imported merchandise. First Cost, duty, transportation, insurance, handling, and commissions must be added to establish Landed Cost. Where applicable, inland freight must be added, plus a discount load, depending on the store's policy.

Layout   (advertising term) The arrangement of art and copy, based on material given to layout artist who designs the ad.

Line   As regards apparel, the contour of a silhouette, design, or style.

Line (collection)   The all-embracing term for a manufacturer's collection of styles in a given season (i.e. spring line, fall line, etc.).

NRMA   National Retail Merchants Association. Trade association of leading American retailers.

Openings   The showings of new collections by fashion producers and designers at the beginning of a season. Term used most frequently in connection with the European fashion market. (see showings)

Open-to-buy   The amount of money a buyer has to spend monthly for merchandise.

Paste-up   Copy and art for an ad, pasted into position, in preparation for camera reproduction. (see camera-ready)

Pret-a-porter   French term describing ready-to-wear apparel.

Proof   Copy of an ad or advertising piece, with art and copy assembled exactly as it will appear when printed, offered for corrections before publication.

Pull   An expression used by the fashion office or display department, in connection with selecting (pulling) merchandise from stock for temporary use in a fashion show or store display. In advertising, to "pull" an ad is to eliminate or cancel it from running.

Ramp   Elevated stage-like platform, usually available in separate units that can be used alone or assembled for a variety of lengths, widths, or shapes. Used mainly for fashion show modeling. (see runway)

Resource   The retailer's term for supplier of wholesale merchandise (manufacturer). (see vendor)

Retail price   Price at which goods are sold to the consumer by the retailer.

Runway   Area or aisle (on the floor or elevated for visability) for fashion show modeling. Audience space is usually provided on either side or surrounding runway area.

Showings   The presentation of new lines or collections at the beginning of a season by manufacturers and designers. (see openings)

Signing   Retail display term for identifying merchandise in interiors and windows with signs.

Silhouette   Term for fashion look or style.

Sleeper   An item or trend that received a small amount of attention from the retailer, but became important because of consumer demand.

Soft goods   In retail circles, the term used to classify all ready-to-wear merchandise. Also a term applied to textile fabrics.

Special event   A retail effort to attract "traffic" (customers) to the store. Usually presented as an exhibit, show, demonstration, or fair. A special attraction or unique merchandising presentation offering entertainment or special information.

Specialty shop   A retail outlet, usually a free-standing establishment or separate shop within a shopping center, that carries special classifications of merchandise for a special customer, (i.e. a specialty shop for women's apparel only, for children's only, for men's, home furnishings, etc.). Also, sometimes called a boutique.

Specialty store   Usually a fashion store, devoted to wearing apparel and accessories only, excluding budget areas and home furnishings departments, such as furniture, large appliances, or hard lines found in the complete department store.

Style number   An identification number given to a design or style by the manufacturer. The retailer uses the number when ordering or re-ordering the item and for stock identification.

Tear sheets   An advertising term for printed pages "torn" from a publication, to be used as file copies or as documentation and proof (for vendors, for example) of what was printed.

Texture   The look and feel of all fabrics.

To write   To order. The writing or placement of orders for merchandise by the retail buyer.

Trend   Fashion trend. A fashion concept that is enjoying acceptability. The direction in which fashion is moving.

Trunk show   A designer's collection of samples, brought into a store for a limited time to show customers the selection (not stocked by the store) from which customers can order style numbers in their size or color for later delivery.

Twig   A retail operation offering merchandise in limited portions of certain classifications, (i.e.) cosmetics and ready-to-wear accessories and/or some ready-to-wear fashions. Usually a small shop, away from and independent of the parent store.

Vendor   One who sells. To the retailer, vendor is another term for resource or supplier of wholesale goods.

Vignette   In a retail store, a special display area devoted to the presentation of merchandise in a dramatized manner.

Volume   Amount of gross sales annually done by a retail store.

Warp   (textile term) Yarns which run vertically or lengthwise in woven goods.

Glossary

Television Industry Terms

Ad-lib Action or speech that is impromptu, not written into a script.

Audio The sound portion of a telecast.

Boom Television equipment. A cranelike device for suspending a microphone or camera in the air.

Bridge Music or sound, film or slide, used to link one scene or sequence of a show with another.

Closed circuit Telecast that does not go over the air, but is shown from camera to monitor only, (i.e. closed circuit television usually used for private viewing, not broadcast for public viewing).

Close-up (CU) Camera shot of an object or person seen close-up.

Cue A signal (by sight or sound) to indicate start of action.

Cue sheet A list indicating cues for a show or production.

Cut In television, an order (usually given by the director) to stop action.

Cuts Portions of a script or program to be eliminated.

Dead mike Microphone which is not connected or not working.

Dissolve A television technique for overlapping (fade-out) of one picture and the bringing up (fade-in) of another picture.

Dolly   A moveable platform or truck carrying a camera, to be wheeled around for advantageous shooting positions during a production.

Down-and-under   Instruction given to sound effects or music to bring volume down to a soft level so that the voice of announcer, actor, or singer can be heard.

Dry Run   Rehearsals prior to actual performance.

Dub   Recording of a sound track on a film. Also, a copy of a sound recording.

Edit   Electronic technique for adding one portion of taped TV program to another portion.

Feedback   Squeal or howl from improper mike hookup.

F.C.C. (Federal Communications Commission)   Guardians of broadcast practices and station licensing.

Fluff   A mistake in speech or action.

Key   To key in a camera shot. Superimpose one image over another. A process through which an object or person can be made to look miniature or giant in contrast to surroundings.

Key lighting   Strong light directly on the object or person, eliminating background.

Mock-up   Facsimile of products.

On camera   Talent or announcer seen on the air. As opposed to off camera, when the announcer is heard but not seen.

Open cold   To start a show without theme or musical introduction, usually without titles.

Open end   A show or film with the commercial parts blank, to be filled in at the time of broadcast.

Pan   Moving the camera from one object to another or across a set to view other parts of the scene or items.

Participating program   A television program sponsored by more than one advertiser.

Script   The complete written material for a television show or commercial.

Simulcast   The broadcasting of a show or program on television and radio at the same time.

Special effects   Electronic technique for audio and/or video treatment, to create special animation, lighting, movement, or any other effect not created by the camera or microphone alone.

Stand by   A cue or alert that a television program is about to go on the air.

Station break   Intervals during broadcast time designated for station identification.

Story board   A set of illustrations showing the sequence of action or pictures (video) as related to sound (audio). A planning board for the television production of a commercial.

Telecast   The broadcast of a television program.

Video   The picture or visual portion of a telecast.

Voice over   The commentary or narration of a film or show, usually filmed or taped without sound, with sound or "voice" added later.

❋ *Bibliography*

Ballard, Bettina. *In My Fashion*. New York: McKay, 1960.

Brockman, Helen L. *The Theory of Fashion Design*. New York: John Wiley & Sons, Inc., 1965.

Cahill, Jane. *The Backbone of Retailing*. New York: Fairchild, 1960.

Chase, Edna Woolman, and Ilka Chase. *Always in Vogue*. New York: Doubleday, 1954.

Corinth, Kay. *Fashion Showmanship*. New York: John Wiley & Sons, Inc., 1970.

Dior, Christian. *Christian Dior and I*. New York: Dutton, 1957.

Epstein, Beryl. *Young Faces in Fashion*. Philadelphia: Lippincott, 1956.

Ferry, J. W. *A History of the Department Store*. New York: The MacMillan Co., 1960.

Harper's Bazaar (edited by Jane Trahey). *100 Years of the American Female from Harper's Bazaar*. New York: Random House, 1967.

Jarnow, Jeanette A., and Beatrice Judelle. *Inside the Fashion Business*. New York: John Wiley & Sons, Inc., 1965.

Patter, M. David, and Bernard P. Corbman. *Textiles: Fiber to Fabric*, 4th ed. New York: Gregg Division/McGraw-Hill Book Co., Inc., 1967.

Pistolese, Rosana, and Ruth Horsting. *History of Fashions*. New York: John Wiley & Sons, Inc., 1970.

Poiret, Paul. *King of Fashion*. Philadelphia: Lippincott, 1931.

Readings in Modern Retailing. New York: Merchandising Division/National Retail Merchants Association, 1969.

Saunders, Edith. *The Age of Worth*. New York: Longmans, Green & Co., 1954.

Snow, Carmel. *The World of Carmel Snow*. New York: McGraw-Hill Book Co., Inc., 1962.

Troxell, Mary D., and Beatrice Judelle. *Fashion Merchandising*. New York: Gregg Division/McGraw-Hill Book Co., Inc., 1971.

Warwick, Edward, Henry C. Pitz, and Alexander Wyckoff. *Early American Dress*. New York: Banjamin Blom, Inc., 1965.

Wilcox, R. Turner. *Five Centuries of American Costume*. New York: Charles Scribner's Sons, 1963.

Wilinsky, Harriet. *Careers and Opportunities in Retailing*. New York: E. P. Dutton & Co., Inc., 1970.

Young, Agnes Brooke. *Recurring Cycles of Fashion, 1760–1937*. New York: Harper & Brothers, 1937.

❋ *Index*

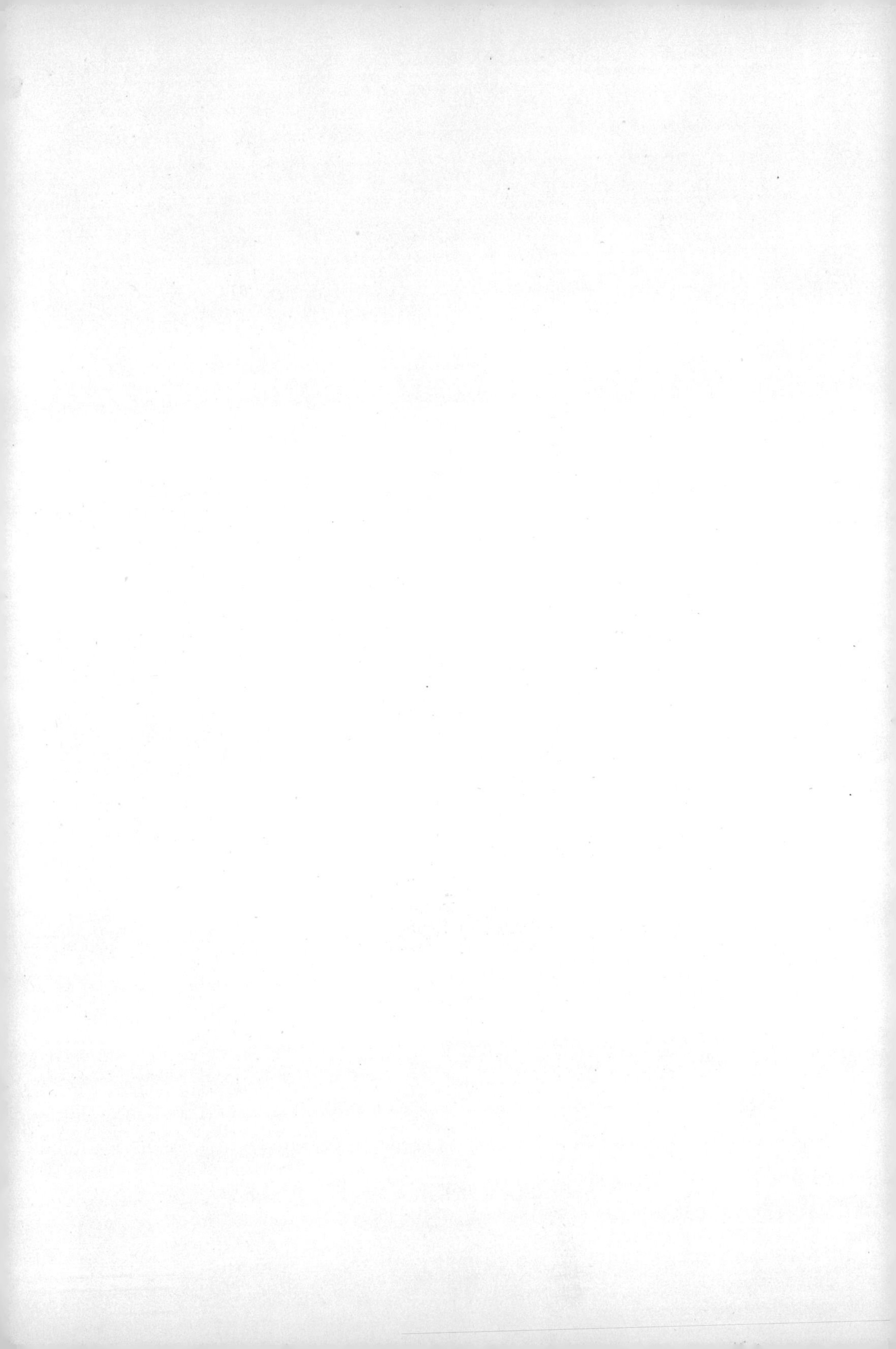